Organizational Learning from Performance Feedback

A Behavioral Perspective on Innovation and Change

Revisiting Cyert and March's classic 1963 *Behavioral Theory of the Firm*, Henrich Greve offers an intriguing analysis of how firms evolve in response to feedback about their own performance. Based on ideas from organizational theory, social psychology, and economics, he explains how managers set goals, evaluate performance, and determine strategic changes. Drawing on a range of recent studies, including the author's own analysis of the Japanese shipbuilding industry, he reports on how theory fits current evidence on organizational change of risk taking, research and development expenses, innovativeness, investment in assets, and market strategy. The findings suggest that high-performing organizations quickly reduce their rates of change, but low-performing organizations only slowly increase those rates. Analysis of performance feedback is an important new direction for research and this book provides valuable insights in how organizational learning interacts with other influences on organizational behaviour such as competitive rivalry and institutional influences.

HENRICH R. GREVE is Professor of Strategy at the Norwegian School of Management BI, Norway.

Organizational Learning from Performance Feedback

A Behavioral Perspective on Innovation and Change

Henrich R. Greve

CAMBRIDGE
UNIVERSITY PRESS

PUBLISHED BY THE PRESS SYNDICATE OF THE UNIVERSITY OF CAMBRIDGE
The Pitt Building, Trumpington Street, Cambridge CB2 1RP, United Kingdom

CAMBRIDGE UNIVERSITY PRESS
The Edinburgh Building, Cambridge, CB2 2RU, UK
40 West 20th Street, New York, NY 10011–4211, USA
477 Williamstown Road, Port Melbourne, VIC 3207, Australia
Ruiz de Alarcón 13, 28014 Madrid, Spain
Dock House, The Waterfront, Cape Town 8001, South Africa

http://www.cambridge.org

First published 2003

Printed in the United Kingdom at the University Press, Cambridge

Typeface Plantin 10/12 pt.   *System* LaTeX 2$_\varepsilon$ [TB]

A catalogue record for this book is available from the British Library

ISBN 0 521 81831 1 hardback
ISBN 0 521 53491 7 paperback

Contents

Figures

Tables

Acknowledgments

As a reader of books I always thought the acknowledgment section was a polite gesture to friends and loved ones. Now I know that in the course of writing a book, one accumulates numerous debts that should be acknowledged here. I have also found that two seemingly symbolic phrases found in acknowledgment sections are completely true: Many have helped me, but the remaining flaws are mine only. I can only mention those who have helped directly by reading and commenting on the manuscript, which means that the intellectual debts to researchers whose ideas I have used are not mentioned here. The reference list gives some indication of how much I have gained from the work of other researchers.

The book owes its existence to James G. March, who sent me an email saying it was time to write a book reporting the findings on aspiration-level learning that others and I have made. He also supervised the research on diffusion that started my career, and supplied the idea and funding for collecting the data on market shares that formed the basis of my first paper on aspiration-level learning.

Several careful readers have helped me improve the book. Pino Audia, Phil Bromiley, Hitoshi Mitsuhashi, Martin Schulz, Zur Shapira, and the referees for Cambridge University Press made challenging and developmental comments on draft chapters. Some of their comments could not be taken care of in this book, but are a valuable cache of ideas for future work. My first paper on aspiration-level decision making appeared in *Administrative Science Quarterly*, and I am grateful to the editor Christine Oliver and three anonymous reviewers for helping sharpen the arguments and noting issues that needed further work. Also at *ASQ*, Linda Johansen's editing and advice on style in that and other papers has greatly improved my writing. My work on performance feedback in the shipbuilding industry has benefited from the comments of Chris Ahmadjian, Giovanni Dosi, Raghu Garud, Don Hambrick, Paul Ingram, Theresa Lant, Steve Mezias, Reinhardt Selten, and anonymous reviewers. Chris Harrison at Cambridge University Press provided valuable editorial advice.

As all authors do, I owe a great deal of gratitude to my supportive family, especially my wife Takako, but also my children Jan and Ryo. Still, I want to dispel the myth that book writing unavoidably means a temporary absence of normal family life. I recently asked Jan whether he knew that papa had written a book, and he said no. It is possible to do such work within nearly normal work hours with some discipline and a supportive school.

The data collection has been helped by a string of extremely capable research assistants. At Stanford University, David Barba coded the radio ratings data, and other radio data were coded by Joe, Mary, and Mireyah. At the University of Tsukuba, Shunsuke Iriguchi, Toshinobu Iriguchi, Masanori Osame, and Lisa Shimizu coded the shipbuilding data.

The data collection on radio stations was supported by a grant to me from the Stanford Center of Organizational Research and a grant to James G. March from the Spencer Foundation. The data collection on shipbuilding was supported by a grant from Japan's Ministry of Education (administered by the Japan Research Foundation).

1 Introduction

This book is about how organizations react to performance feedback. It presents a theory of organizations learning from their experience by collecting performance measures, creating aspiration levels based on their own past performance or that of other organizations, and changing organizational activities if the performance is lower than the aspiration level. The mechanism is one of simple self-regulation by attempting to reach a goal not currently met but not seeking, in the short run at least, to go further than the level that just achieves it. Organizations with performance below the aspiration level of their managers have higher rates of strategic change, R&D expenditure, innovation, and investment. These activities influence the performance and risk of the organization, but otherwise they have little in common. All are affected by the organizational performance because managers are willing to try a wide range of strategic actions to solve a problem of low performance.

We can see this reaction to performance feedback reflected in the behavior of individual firms. After the Japanese car makers had great successes in the 1980s US auto market, General Motors was still the world's largest auto maker and the dominant firm in the USA. It was doing less well than it had in the past, however, with its domestic market share in cars falling from 49% in 1980 to below 40% in 1987.[1] During this period, General Motors implemented a remarkable series of projects to make up for the perceived shortfall. It continued a massive investment program in its factories that had been announced in 1979 and aimed to make GM's manufacturing more automatized than that of any other car maker. This program would eventually cost $40 billion, making it perhaps the largest non-government investment program in history. GM started collaborative manufacturing with Toyota in the now-famous NUMMI plant, and took equity positions in foreign car makers such as Suzuki, Isuzu, Nissan, and Daewoo. GM supported this push into Asia by building a

---

[1] This paragraph is based on information in three Harvard Business School cases (Badaracco 1988; Green 1993; Keller 1994).

Japanese-style supply network complete with equity positions in key suppliers and a supplier association, departing from its usual practice of obtaining supplies internally or from competitive bidding. It made the new car brand Saturn, which was managed by a subsidiary that incorporated several innovative design, manufacturing, and marketing practices, and was located in Tennessee, outside GM's Midwest manufacturing belt. The facility investment program was initiated before the falling market share had become a palpable problem, but was continued unwaveringly after the reduced sales might have suggested that it would lead to excess capacity. The other change activities were initiated after the fall of market share had become a problem, and seemed to be ways of searching for solutions to it. In particular, both Saturn and the Asian alliances focused on the small car market, where General Motor's market share decline was particularly pronounced.

General Motors is an extremely large organization, so the scale and scope of its change activities would be difficult for others to match. The basic pattern of changing in response to disappointing performance is well known across many industries and organizational sizes, however, so it is clearly not special for GM. Intel shifted its market strategy from computer memories to microprocessors after finding itself losing the battle over market share, and thus economies of scale, in each successive generation of computer memory (Burgelman 1994). In 1988, the small Japanese company Nichia Chemical started research on blue LEDs (light-emitting diodes), a technology that had frustrated the development efforts of much larger firms, after having entered successive markets with semiconductor products and found itself beaten by established competitors every time (Johnstone 1999). It would eventually become the first company to commercialize a blue LED, and its success in developing this technology is as remarkable as the fact that such a small company attempted a research project with so high risk and expense in the first place.

The routine of searching when the organization is doing poorly but not when it is doing well is a central part of managerial lore. When the search for solutions succeeds it is called a "turnaround," and it is a milestone event in the career of the responsible manager (Dumaine 1990). When the firm fails after searching for solutions but not finding any that work, the search may be referred to as "floundering" and, with the benefit of hindsight, seen as misdirected or futile (Saporito 1998). These post hoc judgments based on the outcomes obscure the similarity of the behavior: troubled firms seek to change (Bowman 1982), and since the result of strategic changes is nearly always uncertain, large gains or losses are both possible. Turnaround and floundering are different post hoc evaluations, but they start the same way.

Searching for solutions when doing poorly is one side of the coin; the obverse side is the failure of successful organizations to search for ways to improve. This is called the "competence trap" (Levitt and March 1988) or "paradox of success" (Audia, Locke, and Smith 2000), and a good indicator of its prevalence is all the talk about the importance of continuous improvement in the managerial literature. Rigid adherence to a high-price, low-volume strategy with no licensing of the operating system proved to be Apple's bane in the late 1980s (Carlton 1997), but the immediate profits of this strategy were so large that management did not consider its long-term consequences. The strategy conceded so much market share that Intel and Microsoft gained strong footing for launching their Wintel challenge, leaving Apple with a long uphill battle for higher market share which, as one might expect, it started after the performance fell. Such lack of foresight is not a sign of unusual managerial ineptness, but seems common in firms that are doing well. A well-known symptom of competence traps is the late and tepid response of successful firms to new technologies that threaten their market (Christensen and Bower 1996; Cooper and Schendel 1976; Tushman and Anderson 1986).

While the cases suggest a general pattern of changing in response to low performance, they leave many important details open to question. The first issue is what exactly is meant by low performance. The feeling of crisis in General Motors was triggered by a fall in market share, but GM was still the largest automaker in the US and the world by a wide margin. This was not good enough for GM's managers, however, as the experience of being the world's dominant automaker since the 1920s (Carroll and Hannan 1995a) had left them expecting a higher market share than their competitors. Similarly, GM's profits were still high at the time that many of its change efforts started, but not as high as they had been. It turns out that there is no clear delineation of high and low performance on the measures that managers use to evaluate their organizations, only rough rules of thumb. Managers set their own standards for what level of performance is desired. Such standards, which will be called aspiration levels here, are influenced by the organization's history and its competitors' performance. The mechanisms for adjusting aspiration levels are an important part of research on performance feedback in organizations.

The second issue is whether organizational responses to low performance are as strong as they should be. There is ample evidence of organizations failing to change even when their performance is low (Lorenz 1994; Meyer and Zucker 1989; Starbuck and Hedberg 1977), contrary to the suggestion that adversity spurs change (Ocasio 1995). Indeed, General Motors was criticized for passivity in spite of all the changes it made in response to the fall in market share (Green 1993). Such criticism sometimes seems unfair, but it raises an important point. Organizations may change in response to low performance, but still not change *enough* to solve the problem. Whether organizations make enough changes or not is a question of the functional form of the relation from performance to organizational change. The critique that organizations make insufficient changes in response to low performance does not mean that they do nothing, but rather means that organizational failure spurs change less effectively than organizational success reduces change. As will become clear later in the book, improved performance will often cause the rate of organizational change to drop by a considerable amount, but a deterioration of performance of the same size results in a barely perceptible increase in the rate of change. This asymmetry in the response to success and failure suggests that organizations react conservatively to negative performance feedback: managers seem willing to believe that all is well until they have been presented with strong proof to the contrary. Organizations and individuals have powerful defenses against radical changes (Hannan and Freeman 1977; Kuran 1988), and these make it possible for organizations to change without changing enough.

Third, one may wonder whether it makes sense for successful organizations to be inert. Should managers "leave good enough alone" and only fix the organization when it is broken? The case for recommending changes in successful firms is usually built on environmental changes, such as changes in markets and technologies. Environmental changes can cause the competitive strength of a successful firm to erode if it does not adapt. This argument is true, but it is limited to highly dynamic environments. A more general case for changing successful firms can also be made. Managers of successful firms may have ideas for how to press their advantage so that the firm can become even more successful. The ideas may be untried and risky, but so are changes done in unsuccessful firms. Why are such ideas often rejected in successful organizations? The answer is that the same amount of risk is less appealing to managers of successful firms than managers of unsuccessful firms. Later I will show that this risk aversion in successful firms makes sense in some competitive environments, but not in others.

Finally, there is a question of how general the pattern of changing in response to low performance is. Case studies are suggestive, but do not prove that performance feedback is a mechanism of change. There are so many organizations in the world that it would probably be possible to find cases supporting any theory of why organizations change, including weird theories like sunspot cycles.[2] To present a strong case for performance

---

[2] There *is* a theory of sunspot cycles and economic activity. It does not suggest that sunspot cycles directly cause economic cycles, but rather that beliefs in economic cycles that follow sunspot cycles can cause them to happen through behaviors that cause the expectations to be self-confirming.

feedback as a regulator of organizational change, it is necessary to analyze the behavior of broad samples of firms under a variety of conditions.
One of the aims of this book is to present systematic evidence on how
search and risk taking is guided by performance feedback. The evidence
gets depth from covering the behavior of individuals, organizational subunits, and whole organizations, and it gets width from covering multiple nations, industries, and change behaviors. Performance feedback
effects on risk taking, research and development expenses, innovations,
and market niche changes have been studied extensively. All are potentially important for the performance of organizations, so it is reasonable
to expect that managers will change them in response to performance
feedback.

The mechanism of initiating search and change activities when the organizational performance falls below the aspiration level is very simple
and intuitive. The simplicity is part of the appeal of this theory, but it is
not its sole basis. The second appeal of the theory is that it appears to
be true: it has been tested repeatedly with highly supportive results. The
third is that it is general: performance feedback affects many behaviors
of many different organizations and environments. The final and perhaps
decisive appeal of the theory is that it is important. The behaviors that are
affected by performance feedback are uncertain and consequential strategic choices; they rank among the most important decisions a manager can
make.

Performance feedback theory has direct precursors in both the organizational and the psychological literature, and thus integrates ideas that
have been pursued by a diverse set of researchers. Performance feedback
has been on the agenda of organizational researchers since the behavioral
theory of the firm (Cyert and March 1963). Psychologists have been
interested in performance feedback effects on risk taking and other adaptive behaviors (Kahneman and Tversky 1979; Locke 1978), and have
investigated how individuals seek to evaluate themselves by creating aspiration levels from available information (Lewin et al. 1944). Economists
have examined how performance feedback affects the economic adaptation of individuals (Crawford 1995). This deep rooting in different
research traditions also makes performance feedback theory noteworthy.
Researchers interested in how organizations behave should be reassured
by seeing that so many theoretical assumptions are supported at the level
of individual decision making. Researchers interested in how individuals
behave should be gratified by seeing experimental findings confirmed by
research on high-stakes decisions made by professional managers. Most
importantly, the convergence of findings from research done by many
different methods and in many different contexts offers additional assur-
ance that this is a good model of how organizations behave.

The work presented here has been motivated by curiosity about how individuals and organizations react to success and adversity. Many puzzles in human behavior have caused researchers to wonder what kinds of thinking processes cause them and why these differ from some of our normative ideas of how rational persons should react. Similar puzzles in organizational behavior have made us speculate about the mechanisms that can cause an apparent need to change a given organization and the actual change to become so loosely coupled. Though driven by curiosity about how individuals and organizations function rather than a specific desire to repair them, the research has clear implications for how organizations should collect and interpret measures of performance. It turns out that the responses to performance feedback predicted by this theory have a form that can give organizations adaptive results such as a high chance of survival and high performance. The basic behavioral rules are not defective. They can be fine-tuned, however, and how these rules are applied can make an important difference to an organization's life span and performance. This gives the theory considerable practical value for those who design and manage organizations.

Although performance feedback theory can offer useful advice, it also points out some organizational dilemmas. Managers face some decision-making problems where uncertainty about future conditions leaves them with no options that are clearly best, only a tradeoff between different forms of risk. The tradeoff is remarkably similar to the tradeoff between type I and type II errors in scientific research: the error of overlooking something (type I) and the error of falsely detecting something (type II). It is seen in the choices of how often to evaluate the performance of the organization and how to react to small deviations from the aspiration level. Frequent evaluation and reaction to small deviations would create hair-trigger management with changes in response to small performance signals. Managers would be very quick to discover actual deterioration of performance, but would also be prone to implement changes in response to low performance caused by incorrect measurement or singular events in the environment. They would rarely overlook problems, but would often react to problems that do not exist. Conversely, managers can evaluate performance in ways that cause them to react only when a real problem exists, but to overlook many problems. The tradeoff between these approaches to evaluating organizational performance depends on the relative costs of errors of omission and commission, which are unknown to managers because they are borne in the future and depend on the types of errors made.

Another tradeoff is seen in the choice of how specific the performance measurements should be. It is possible to have rough measures of overall performance that will tell a manager that something is amiss, but not exactly what. The overall profitability of an organization would be such a measure. It is also possible to have very specific measures that suggest which organizational process is causing the problem. Testing the quality of inbound parts and outbound products in a factory, for example, gives specific measures on the quality of the production process. Current advice to managers is to have many specific measures so that problems can be identified and solved quickly (Kaplan and Norton 1996), which represents a return to the roots of cost accounting after a period of management by overall financial measures (Johnson and Kaplan 1987). There is a tradeoff here, however, because very specific measures could signal a problem in a different part of the organization's operations than the one with the actual problem. Organizations are bundles of interdependent activities, so problems in one process can affect the output of related processes. For example, the quality of outbound products is not determined by production management alone, but also by factors such as product design and human-resource management. The tradeoff between general and specific performance measures depends on how the costs of not knowing where to search for problems compare with the costs of searching for problems in the wrong places.

A third dilemma lies in the different uses of performance feedback systems in organizations. Throughout this book, performance feedback is analyzed as a diagnostic tool that managers use to discover problems in the organization and initiate search and decision-making activities. Performance feedback as a diagnostic tool relies on a theory of managers as boundedly rational actors who are seeking to improve the organizations under conditions of uncertainty. There is also another view of performance feedback. Performance feedback systems in actual organizations are often found as a part of incentive schemes that reward managers for reaching certain performance levels, as in stock-option grants and bonuses linked to accounting measures of performance. Performance feedback as an incentive device relies on a theory of managers who are rational enough to know how to improve the organization, but will only do so if they are rewarded for it. Theories of incentive systems design exist (Milgrom and Roberts 1992), but have difficulty incorporating issues of bounded rationality. The result is that the diagnostic and incentive views of performance feedback yield conflicting advice, so managers need to make choices between these two uses of performance feedback.

It should be clear that performance feedback theory speaks to important issues in the management of organizations. Before drawing more detailed implications, however, we need to get into the core of the argument. The book is organized as follows. In chapter 2, the foundations of the theory of performance feedback are discussed. The theory is an outgrowth of the behavioral theory of the firm (Cyert and March 1963), and section 2.1 explains this theory and its concepts of organizational goals, aspiration levels, and search. These are central concepts in the explanation of how organizations respond to performance feedback. The theory has also benefited from psychological theories of goal-oriented behavior, which are reviewed in section 2.2. These theories reinforce the ideas of the behavioral theory of the firm, but they have inspired an additional concern with the role of risk taking in organizational change. Learning from performance feedback is also becoming an important issue in economics, and some recent economic experiments are reviewed in section 2.3.

Chapter 3 develops the theory in detail, and explains why aspiration levels are important and how they are formed (section 3.1) and affect organizational change (section 3.2). This chapter integrates the ideas of chapter 2 and develops a single model of organizational response to performance feedback that will be used to interpret the research in chapter 4. In addition, simulation models of how aspiration levels affect organizational change and performance are covered in section 3.3. This section introduces an important idea of this book: learning based on performance feedback and aspiration-level adjustment can help the organization adapt to its environment. Section 3.4 completes the theory by describing how managers select goal variables for the organization.

Chapter 4 reviews research on the effect of performance feedback on important organizational behaviors. First, the direct effects of performance relative to aspiration levels on risk taking by managers and organizations are reviewed in section 4.1. Next, processes that reflect organizational search are treated. Research and development intensity, which is the most direct organizational indicator of search, is considered in section 4.2. The launching of innovations results both from successful organizational search for alternative behaviors and from managerial acceptance of risk, and is thus a good opportunity to see how these processes work in tandem. Effects of performance feedback on the rate of innovation are shown in section 4.3. Similarly, investments in production facilities reflect both search processes and risk preferences, and are treated in section 4.4. Finally, change of the organization's product-market strategy is one of the most fateful decisions a manager can make, and should strongly reflect risk preferences and search processes. It is treated in section 4.5.

Chapter 5 treats some advanced topics of interest to researchers on performance feedback in organizations. Section 5.1 reviews the basic methods for estimating performance feedback effects directly from data on aspiration levels or indirectly from data on organizational changes in behavior. Section 5.2 discusses how to estimate social aspiration levels based on the performance of other organizations and historical aspiration levels based on the focal organization's past performance. It also introduces the problem of estimating how quickly the organization updates its historical aspiration level and presents methods for solving this problem. Section 5.3 gives a general discussion of how performance feedback studies should be designed, and sections 5.4 and 5.5 describe the radio station and shipbuilding data used in chapter 4.

Chapter 6 gives concluding remarks. In section 6.1, the practical implications of the theory are developed further with reference to the empirical findings. This section covers the important questions of how adaptive the observed behaviors are and how organizational decision making can be designed to take advantage of learning from feedback. The dilemmas mentioned earlier in this chapter are again addressed there, but now with the added knowledge from empirical research on performance feedback. Section 6.2 discusses the links between the theory of performance feedback and other theories of strategy and organizational change. Performance feedback theory predicts the timing and form of organizational change, which are important issues in other theories of organizational learning and cognition, as well as in institutional theory and population ecology. These theories can be developed by incorporating the insights of performance feedback theory, and performance feedback theory can also learn from them. Section 6.3 discusses gaps in our current knowledge and makes suggestions for research needed to fill them. It gives a road map for how performance feedback theory can be improved by better theory and additional empirical research.

The book contains a variety of material, and there are many ways of reading it. Chapter 3 is the core of the argument, and some readers may wish to read it first. The cost of doing so is the loss of chapter 2's introduction to the theoretical problems that chapter 3 seeks to resolve, but the benefit is to reach the main argument more quickly. The sections in chapter 4 are ordered according to my judgment on how the behaviors studied fit on the search and risk dimensions. Pure risk and pure search are treated first, followed by outcomes that incorporate both of these dimensions. The sections of chapter 4 do not build on each other, so they can be read in any order. Readers with a strong interest in one of the subjects can go directly from chapter 3 to their favorite section. Chapter 5 is rather technical, and is put before chapter 6 mainly to follow the convention of placing conclusions last. Many will wish to look at chapter 5 after reading chapter 6. Especially impatient and practically oriented readers may wish to go directly to section 6.1, but will probably find this discussion easier to follow after reading chapter 3.

2   Foundations

The theory of learning from performance feedback has deep roots. These roots can be traced historically as a sequence of contributions or described analytically as a foundation of assumptions and findings upon which the theory can be built. In this chapter, I will take the analytical approach of selecting and ordering material based on how it fits with the theory developed in chapter 3. Along the way, I hope also to show some of the intellectual history. The goal of this chapter is to show how the theory of organizational learning from performance feedback is built on a set of independent research traditions that have produced related findings. These research traditions have developed along their own paths and have also examined issues that are not relevant to performance feedback theory, but parts can be selected from them that form a coherent body of theoretical propositions and empirical support.

The research traditions described in this chapter underpin the theory of organizational learning from performance feedback, but are not a substitute for it. Much of the theory and evidence they have amassed is on individual learning from performance feedback. Such findings increase our confidence in theory positing similar effects at the organization level. Individuals and organizations are different, however, and the differences mean that the theory has to be modified and then tested again. Chapter 3 develops the theory of organizational learning from performance feedback, and chapter 4 presents tests of it.

The first tradition is the behavioral theory of the firm (Cyert and March 1963), which is the direct antecedent of performance feedback theory. It is the only theory of organizations in this introductory chapter, and has a broad set of propositions on how organizations react and adapt to their environment. The behavioral theory of the firm launched the concepts of a goal variable that managers attend to, performance feedback on this goal variable, and an aspiration level for judging whether the performance is satisfactory or not. It then derived a process of performance feedback triggering search, and search leading to organizational change. The theory was induced from a series of case studies on organizational change processes, and its concepts and processes are recognizable to anyone who has participated in organizational decision making, which means practically everyone in a modern society. One does not have to be a theorist to take the behavioral theory of the firm as a realistic description of how organizations work.

The behavioral theory of the firm contains numerous mentions of "decision makers," that is, managers or others who make decisions on behalf of their organization. These decision makers are individuals, and we can learn more about their thinking and behavior from psychological research. First, goal-setting research offers a direct test of some propositions from the behavioral theory of the firm taken down to the level of individual persons. It shows that individuals search for ways to improve their performance when they receive information on their own performance relative to an aspiration level. Second, risk research shows that low performance can increase a decision maker's propensity to take risks. Third, escalation of commitment research shows that low performance triggers a variety of defensive reactions in a decision maker.

The first three theories show that performance relative to an aspiration level affects an individual in several ways; the next two answer questions related to these effects. First, if aspiration levels are important, then we need to know how they are made. The fourth line of research on social comparison theory shows that individuals use a variety of social clues to form aspiration levels. Second, individuals are not organizations but components of organizations, leaving a levels-of-analysis gap between theories of individual behavior and the behavioral theory of the firm's propositions on how whole organizations behave. Research on group decision making bridges the gap by showing how individual intentions aggregate to group decisions.

Finally, economists have also been interested in learning processes. They have conducted experimental research on how individuals learn from performance in order to test whether the theory of rationality fits actual decisions. Many findings reinforce those of the psychologists, especially on how individuals use clues in the situation to set aspiration levels. This is reassuring because two research traditions on similar questions ought to produce consistent results even though the approaches differ somewhat. It also brings the chapter on foundations to a full circle, because the behavioral theory of the firm was built on the same critique of the rational decision making paradigm that modern experimental economists are seeking to investigate empirically.

2.1   Behavioral theory of the firm

Researchers' interest in how organizations learn from performance feedback can be traced back to the behavioral theory of the firm (Cyert and March 1963; March and Simon 1958). This theory has had wide-ranging impact on the theory of organizations and cannot be fully reviewed here (see the postscript of Cyert and March 1992; Schultz 2001), but I will note the parts that directly antecede the theory of learning from performance feedback. March and Simon (1958) and Cyert and March (1963) made propositions on the formation and effect of goals that are largely preserved in current theory of learning from performance feedback and aspiration levels, making the theory of organizational learning from performance feedback an outgrowth of the behavioral theory of the firm.

March and Simon (1958) made a behavioral theory of internal organizational structure and behaviors, and discussed such intra-organizational processes as productivity, rewards, and conflict. Their most important contribution to the theory of organizational learning from performance feedback was the introduction of bounded rationality and satisficing as theoretical concepts. Bounded rationality means that human decision makers have limited information, attention, and processing ability that make them unable to perform the maximization tasks assumed in many economic treatments of the firm. Instead of maximizing, decision makers are likely to satisfice, which means that they set a goal that they try to meet and evaluate alternatives sequentially until one that satisfies the goal has been found.

Bounded rationality is a modification of the rational choice paradigm that underpins most economic theory. Rational choice means that the decision maker compares all consequences of all alternatives with respect to their value to him or her, and chooses the alternative with the highest value. Uncertainty about the consequences of different alternatives is solved by taking the highest expected value or adjusting the expectation by the risk. What cannot be changed without leaving the rational choice paradigm is the concept of maximizing, which is trying to find the best alternative. Bounded rationality with satisficing is different because it creates the possibility that a decision maker is content because the goal has been fulfilled. A rational decision maker is never content – the concept has no meaning for a maximizing individual.

The idea of decision makers seeking to fulfill a goal is pervasive in the theory of organizational and individual decision making, as the next section will show. Though they rarely use the word, theories of goal seeking and risk taking can be recast as theories of satisficing behavior making specific assumptions on how individuals react to falling short of their goals. Social comparison theory can be viewed as a theory answering the question left open by satisficing theory: what goal will be chosen? These lines of research have filled important gaps in our knowledge of how a satisficing decision maker behaves. It is now possible to make good estimates of goal levels and good predictions on what alternatives will look appealing to a satisficing decision maker currently below the goal level, which are the two most important questions raised by satisficing theory. The resolution of these issues has transformed bounded rationality from a critique of rationality to an alternative to rationality.

Although the concept of bounded rationality is widely accepted in management, economics, and psychology, it is interpreted in different ways (March 1988). The most restrictive interpretation views bounded rationality as a loosely specified statement of limits to knowledge that leads to minor adjustments to rational behavior. This interpretation is clearly made to avoid modifying rational choice theory too much, and it differs starkly from interpretations made by some cognitive researchers. The most literal interpretation of bounded rationality is found in work measuring the cost of information collection, processing, and errors when decision makers use decision rules such as rationality or satisficing (Bettman, Johnson, and Payne 1990). An important finding from this research is that rationality is costly. Using rational rules on problems with many alternatives or many attributes of each alternative leads to great increase in cognitive effort. Bounded rationality suggests that these cost differences cause individuals to simplify the decision-making procedure when the problem is complex, and experiments show that they indeed do so (Payne, Bettman, and Johnson 1988). The implication is that rational choice is a good theory of how individuals approach simple decision problems.

Managerial decision making is filled with complex problems that have many alternatives and many attributes of each alternative. Suppose, for example, that a production manager has identified a problem with the quality of the finished products coming from an assembly process. Possible solutions include quality control by specialists at the end of assembly, quality control by regular workers throughout, redesign of the assembly process or product, change in the reward system for workers, and so on. Now consider the relevant attributes of the decision. The problem arose because of low quality, but choosing a solution requires consideration of assembly cost, worker satisfaction, production scheduling, and product performance. It would be nice to be fully rational when facing problems of such complexity, but this requires calculating through many alternatives and many consequences per alternative, with some of the consequences involving outcomes that are difficult to compare because the timing or metrics of the consequences differ. The decision maker has to compare the effects on cost of production and worker motivation, which are on different scales, and to compare these with customer satisfaction, which is on a different scale and occurs in the future. It seems more likely that simple decision-making rules will be used. Such rules involve satisficing, which makes them very sensitive to the aspiration level that the decision maker seeks to satisfy.

Cyert and March (1963) turned their attention to how the organization adapts to its external environment, emphasizing decisions of strategic importance such as price, quantity, and resource allocation. They continued to view intra-organizational decision making as an important part of the explanation, thus avoiding the temptation to simplify the theory by predicting how the organization reacts to the environment solely from the opportunities and threats in the environment. Instead, the theory states that the organization interacts with the environment through the performance feedback process. The environment gives performance feedback on goals determined by the organization, and managers use this performance feedback to control search and decision making.

The process of performance feedback in the behavioral theory of the firm is portrayed in simplified form in figure 2.1, which is based on figure 6.1 in Cyert and March (1963, p. 126; see also March, 1994 p. 33) but removes some paths that are not treated here. The decision maker observes feedback from the environment and compares it with a goal, and starts searching for solutions if the goal is not met. The search is originally local to the organizational unit where the problem occurs, but is expanded if the local search does not uncover acceptable solutions. Solutions are fed into decision rules that take into account whether the goal has been met or not, with changes likely to occur if the goal has not been met. Both the search rules and the decision rules are evaluated based on their success in finding solutions and implementing them (this link is not shown in the figure).

This theory made several innovations based on the concept of bounded rationality. First, attempts to improve the organization do not happen continuously, but rather are initiated by performance shortfalls. Second, alternatives to the current set of activities do not suddenly appear on the decision maker's desk, they have to be generated through a process of searching for solutions. Third, this search needs to be directed by some rule, and a set of rules that seems to fit observation of organizations and bounded rationality was proposed. These were "proximity rules" specifying that the search initially would occur in the proximity of (1) the problem, (2) the current state of the organization, and (3) vulnerable areas of the organization. The search would expand later if it failed to yield solutions. The rules imply a highly conservative response to

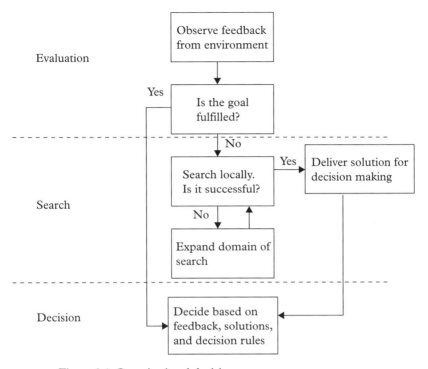

Figure 2.1 Organizational decision process

performance feedback. The proximity to problem rule will favor changes in the organizational unit that first reports a problem over more wide-ranging changes, the proximity to current state rule will favor solutions that make minor changes to current routines, and the proximity to vulnerable areas rule will favor changes in organizational units that are unable to claim that preservation of their current routines is essential to the organizational functioning. Later we will see how concerns with risk in the decision making stage amplify this conservativism in the search stage.

Implicit in this perspective on organizations was a redirection of researcher effort. In the behavioral theory of the firm, organizational structures faded in importance as organizational decision making and change took center stage. Problems of internal management such as authority and division in labor became secondary to the concern of responsiveness to the organizational environment. In short, researcher attention shifted to organizational change of activities in response to environmental demands. This focus was long a distinctive feature of the behavioral theory of the firm, as the environment only gradually moved into organizational theory during the 1970s (Scott 1987). The behavioral theory of the firm still has quite distinctive ideas on how organizations react in response to the environment. Recent theories of environmental effects on organizations place less emphasis on organizational decision making and more on absorption of innovations found in the environment or selection of organizations with characteristics favored by the environment.[1]

A theory of organizations responding to the environment faces the important questions of how decision makers assess environmental demands and react to them (Pfeffer and Salancik 1978). It is cognitively easy for a decision maker to divide feedback into dichotomous judgments of success and failure (March and Simon 1958), but it is rarely obvious when an organizational activity should be called a success and when it should be called a failure. It is clear that performance feedback interpreted as a failure could cause change in the organization, but how organizations choose an appropriate solution to failures to reach performance targets is less clear (Cyert and March 1963). In the behavioral theory of the firm, the resolution to the first problem was to assume that organizations make aspiration levels by adjusting the existing aspiration level towards the most recent performance of the focal organization and of comparable organizations (Cyert and March 1963). That is, organizations learn what performance to expect by drawing on their experience and the experience of referent organizations. This learning is anchored on the previous-period aspiration level, so it does not instantly adapt to new experience.

The second problem of how problems lead to behavioral change has proved more difficult, and is a matter of dispute today. The most direct answer is given by the problemistic search model. This model states that failures spur search that is initially local to the current symptom and the current set of activities, and thus may quickly result in some small change in the organizational unit to which the performance failure is attributed (Cyert and March 1963). Local search can easily lead to the organization adopting minor changes as solutions, such as greater commitment of resources to the original strategy or minute changes in operations. To outside observers, organizations pursuing such local solutions appear totally rigid even though they are actively engaged in problem-solving activities (Meyer and Zucker 1989; Starbuck and Hedberg 1977). Failure to find a satisfactory local solution will usually cause the search to spiral outwards, however, and it may eventually cause changes that are large or distant from the original symptom.

---

[1] Perhaps because the firm is the causal locus, the behavioral theory of the firm has strong appeal to researchers in the field of strategic management, with many papers recently appearing in strategy journals.

A model of less directed search is the garbage can model of decision making (Cohen, March, and Olsen 1972), where problems can wander freely around the organization and become matched with solutions that are currently under consideration. This model puts less causal force on the problem and more on the availability of solutions, and removes the assumption of a local bias in the search process. It does not have the proximity biases that make problemistic search so conservative, and could in principle lead to large organizational changes even when the problem is small. Because large responses are rare in real organizations, it has been suggested that the garbage can model should be supplemented by mechanisms that prevent large changes, such as the professional norms of decision makers or constraints from actors in the environment (Levitt and Nass 1989).

Neither model of search makes clear predictions on what will happen when multiple solutions are available but only one problem is. It seems likely that only one or a few solutions can be matched to a given problem, as the garbage can model specifies, which means that decision makers need to select from the set of solutions. The problem of how decision makers winnow down a solution set cannot be answered by search theory, but later work has proposed that it is highly dependent on the perceived risk of each solution. This will lead to a role of risk in the theory of organizational learning from performance feedback.

While the behavioral theory of the firm is the direct origin of aspiration level learning as an organizational theory, it is useful to view its contribution in a broader context. The behavioral theory of the firm was part of a general movement towards viewing organizations as open systems (Scott 1987) whose interaction with their environment is of primary theoretical importance. Some theorists saw self-regulation in response to the environment as a shared characteristic of human and natural systems and viewed it as a possible route to unify the social and natural sciences (Bertalanffy 1956; Boulding 1956). Other theories of open systems viewed the environment differently, emphasizing the political aspects of negotiation with important constituents of the organization (Selznick 1948). Both self-regulation and politics are important aspects of organizations that have affected the behavioral theory of the firm and later thinking about organizations.

Self-regulation is an idea with broad appeal, and it has proven its value especially in the field of psychology (Carver and Scheier 1982; Powers 1973). Its application to organizations is not straightforward, however, but involves problems that were foreseen by the behavioral theory of the firm and have been amplified in later work. A very important problem in organizational decision making is the uncertainty of means-ends relations in organizations (Lindblom 1959; March 1994). Simply put, organizations are so complex that activities undertaken to solve a performance problem may give no result or a result opposite of the intention. A second problem is that the regulator seems to be getting stuck in the "off" position. It is easier to stop search activities when the organization does well than it is to start them when the organization does poorly (Milliken and Lant 1991).

Thus, the image of organizational self-regulation as a process akin to a climate-control system regulating the temperature by controlling a heater and a cooler (Swinth 1974) is a little too efficient to be a good description of the processes we study here. It is clear that a regulator is in action, but this regulator may respond to high temperature by making irrelevant changes such as turning on the CD player. Alternatively, it may respond to high temperature by turning on the cooler but make no response to low temperature. My car runs the signals of the climate control and CD player (as well as all other electronics) along the same wires, and would behave this way if it were incorrectly programmed. Fortunately for me, automotive electronics are easier to control than organizations.

Political aspects of organizations enter the behavioral theory of the firm through the selection of the goal variable. Saying that organizational behaviors are regulated by comparisons of performance and an aspiration level presumes that some agreement exists on the organizational goal and variables for measuring progress along that goal. Cyert and March (1963) devoted one chapter to the problem of defining goals, starting with the stark statement that "People (i.e., individuals) have goals; collectivities of people do not" (26). Their solution to this problem was to view the organizational goal as formed by a coalition of its members and other actors with an interest in the organization's operations and ability to influence it. This dominant coalition does not consist of all interested parties, but only of participants with sufficient authority to enforce the agreement in the short run. In the longer run, the dominant coalition may change through the introduction of new problems or changes in the power distribution.

This solution was known from political theories of coalition formation and game theoretic models of negotiation, but the behavioral theory of the firm took bounded rationality into account by making several additional suggestions on how dominant coalitions were formed and maintained (Cyert and March 1963; March 1962). First, many participants have individual goals that can be fulfilled simultaneously, so the coalition formation process is different from fixed-pie bargaining. Many of the goals can be phrased as policy commitments, such as a focus on certain markets, or as constraints, such as minimum allocation of resources to certain activities. Such goals are easier to form coalitions around than maximization goals. Second, the bargainers are unable to calculate the optimal size and composition of the coalition and predict the future problems of the organization. They will err on the side of caution, which leads to coalitions that are larger than the minimal possible size and place multiple constraints on the future behavior of the organization. Strategic plans and budgets are examples of such constraints generated by dominant coalitions in order to stabilize the agreement, and hence the organization.

The concept of the dominant coalition as the arbiter of organizational goals is important for the theory of learning from performance feedback. First, it alerts the researcher to the problem that common assumptions of which goals organizations pursue may be incorrect in any particular case. Most research takes for granted that business organizations pursue profitability goals, and we will later see that there are good reasons for making this assumption as a first approximation. Organizations may have multiple goals or goals that change over time, however, so profit goals are not the sole determinant of organizational changes. Second, the mechanisms for stabilizing the agreement of the dominant coalition are sufficiently effective that it may be difficult to make certain changes to the organization. Thus, organizational inertia is partly caused by the ability of members of the dominant coalition to prevent changes that violate past agreements (Hannan and Freeman 1977). Indeed, stabilization mechanisms such as budgets do not have an obvious link with the bargaining process that established the dominant coalition, so a manager may find it difficult to discover which organizational changes are allowable within the present agreement and which changes require renegotiation and a new dominant coalition. As a result, learning from performance feedback is done in fits and starts rather than as a smooth process of immediate adjustment to each problem that occurs.

The next section discusses related research traditions that primarily emphasize the decision making of individuals and small groups. This research usually takes the organizational goal variable as given, but asks questions on how individuals accept the goal variable, make aspiration levels for their performance, and change their behavior in response to performance feedback. The research has produced findings that are very important to the theory of organizational learning from performance feedback. The findings converge across the different research traditions and with the predictions from the behavioral theory of the firm, and thus give it a good micro-level foundation. They also provide new ideas that are helpful in developing the theory of organizational responses to performance feedback.

2.2   Social psychology

Social psychologists have long been interested in issues of performance feedback and goals (Lewin et al. 1944), and this has led to research traditions emphasizing different parts of the process of setting and pursuing goals. Goal-setting researchers work on how goals set by managers affect the behavior of workers, and have a strong interest in finding goal-setting mechanisms that improve organizational productivity. In this work, high goals are functional because they inspire effort and problem solving that increase individual and group performance. Researchers on risk taking are interested in the quality and consistency of individual decision making. In their work, goals are more problematic because they appear to reduce the consistency and often also quality of the decision making. Escalation-of-commitment researchers have a similar interest in how decision-making quality can degrade as a result of goal-seeking behavior. Social comparison researchers investigate how individuals set goals by observing the performance of others, but also do some work on the effects of goals. It is obvious from these research traditions that goals exert powerful effects on individual behavior, but less clear how these effects translate into organizational action. Some suggestive answers to this are given by the work on group decision making, which examines how groups of decision makers with different preferences make decisions.

Goal setting and performance

Individuals seek to fulfill goals (Locke and Latham 1990). This behavior can be strengthened by attaching rewards to goal fulfillment, but appears not to be driven by rewards alone (Hogarth et al. 1991). Efforts to reach goals with no tangible rewards attached have been observed in experimental and organizational contexts, and it has even been suggested that goals without rewards result in better behaviors (Locke and Latham 1990). Goal-seeking behavior occurs because individuals directly value the goal variables (Heath, Larrick, and Wu 1999), derive secondary intangible rewards such as pride or social esteem from goal fulfillment, or simply use goals as guides to what performance is possible. In the latter case, individuals are behaving like satisficers (March and Simon 1958) who view the goal as an acceptable level of performance. They seek to improve when their performance is below the aspiration level, but are content with the current performance level when it is above the aspiration level.

That goals and feedback together accelerate learning has been shown by comparing the performance of individuals given goals and performance feedback with that of individuals given feedback only, goals only, or neither goals nor feedback (Kluger and DeNisi 1996; Locke and Latham 1990). These comparisons are important because individuals will improve their performance on unfamiliar tasks even if they are not given goals and feedback, and improve even faster if they get goals only or feedback only. The combination of assigned goals and feedback is especially powerful, however, because it focuses attention on the shortfall in performance and makes attempts to improve the performance more likely than other coping strategies such as avoiding feedback or rejecting the goal (Kluger and DeNisi 1996).

A long string of studies on goal-fulfillment behavior has revealed some important variations on the main findings. Goals and performance feedback give the greatest performance improvement on tasks that can be reached through brute force, such as increasing effort. Complex tasks where analysis of the situation is needed for high performance show a weaker performance improvement but still a significant one (Wood, Mento, and Locke 1987). The higher performance in complex tasks is at least partly a result of making higher quality decisions, as individuals appear to concentrate better and use more sophisticated problem-solving strategies when they are seeking to fulfill a goal and given performance feedback (Bandura and Jourden 1991; Chesney and Locke 1991).

Individuals seem to know when the barrier to high performance is lack of knowledge about the situation or poor coordination of related tasks. Managerial behaviors such as information collection and coordination start spontaneously when workers or experimental subjects are given goals and performance feedback (Campbell and Gingrich 1986; Latham and Saari 1979). Individuals are also more persistent in working on the task and show a greater ability to focus on task-solving information and ignore irrelevant information when they are seeking to fulfill a goal (Rothkopf and Billington 1979; Singer et al. 1981), so "mental effort" is spent more readily and effectively when individuals are oriented towards a goal. Remarkably, goals can even be used to increase creativity, which is an outcome that most people would attribute to personal ability rather than situational factors such as goals (Shalley 1995). Goals thus have wide-ranging effects on human performance.

In organizations, group goals are more common than individual goals, especially at top management levels where the total performance of the organization is at stake. The switch to group goals could potentially weaken individual attempts to fulfill goals, since each individual has less responsibility for and effect on a group goal as the size of the group increases (Earley 1993; Latane, Williams, and Harkins 1979). Surprisingly, the results of many studies indicate that group goals have as strong effects as individual goals do (O'Leary-Kelly, Martocchio, and Frink 1994). It is thus realistic to consider goal-fulfillment behavior to be a characteristic of groups as well as individuals.

Managers assign goals to groups and individuals, just as researchers on goal seeking do to their experimental subjects. These goals are not necessarily accepted and used as the actual goal of the individual, however, and will fail to affect the behavior when they are rejected (Earley 1986; Erez, Earley, and Hulin 1985; Podsakoff, MacKenzie, and Ahearne 1997). Individuals adjust the goals that they are given by making some compromise between assigned goals and the available information on what goals are realistic (Locke et al. 1984; Martin and Manning 1995; Meyer and Gellatly 1988). Information sources used to adjust the goal include the individual's past performance and the performance of others on the same task (Bandura and Jourden 1991; Locke, Latham, and Erez 1988; Martin and Manning 1995; Vance and Colella 1990). Thus, individuals who are adjusting a goal assigned by a manager use the same mechanisms that decision makers use to generate aspiration levels according to the behavioral theory of the firm.

In organizations, the effects of individual behaviors on group goal fulfillment are often difficult to judge. If everyone in a group does the same task, a group goal is easy to divide into individual goals. Organizations divide labor by creating specialized and differentiated tasks, however, complicating the translation between individual and group goals. When sub-goals interact to form the total goal, goal fulfillment requires complex tasks of coordination (Simon 1957). This complicates the goal-fulfillment process and increases the time required before the goals affect the total group performance (Wood and Bandura 1989). Many field studies of goal-seeking behavior have recognized this limitation, as it is mainly tasks with modest interdependence among workers that have been targeted for improvement through goal setting. Still, complex interdependence of tasks does not preclude group goals from improving performance (Locke and Latham 1990).

At higher levels of management, conflicts among multiple goals and determination of behaviors in ambiguous situations are likely to be the order of the day (Badaracco 1988; Pfeffer and Salancik 1978; Selznick 1957), so the theory should take the existence of a unitary goal and knowledge of how to fulfill the goal to be problematic. Goal-setting research has examined this issue indirectly through observation of how workers adjust goals given to them by managers, but has not made goal conflict a major research issue.

These differences between the situations studied in goal-setting research and the decision-making tasks facing managers caution against overly direct transfer of its conclusions to managerial work, but it is still clear that goal-setting research has provided important support and extension of the behavioral theory of the firm. The ideas of satisficing and of search in response to low performance have been amply confirmed both for individuals and groups. They have been observed in a wide range of behaviors, including complex problem-solving behaviors that closely resemble managerial decision making. The research includes experimental studies that clearly demonstrate causal relations and field studies showing them to hold in real organizations. The main piece missing from the puzzle is how goals affect behavior when one course of action is more risky than the other, as is often the case when managers choose between strategic change and persistence with the current strategy. Most goal-setting research concerns situations where risk differences between alternatives are not a salient part of the problem, and thus cannot directly answer this question. Fortunately, a separate research tradition on risk taking has addressed it.

Risk taking and goals

A core managerial task is to make decisions when the alternatives have uncertain consequences. The consequences of different alternatives may be uncertain by nature, by insufficient information, or by insufficient understanding of the relation between cause and consequence. For example, a managerial task involving consequences that are uncertain by nature is the resource allocation by a farmer. The productivity of a land plot will differ depending on the crop the farmer decides to sow and the weather, but the weather is unpredictable. A managerial task involving insufficient information is product-design decisions such as features or appearance. There are good methods for measuring consumer preferences for different designs, but cost considerations often preclude collection of the necessary data. Insufficient understanding of the relation between cause and consequences occurs in many decisions involving the reactions of other actors with conflicting interests, such as when entering the markets of other firms.[2] The profitability depends on how the focal firm's entry affects the incumbents' behavior, but this cause-effect relation is not well understood by the entrant (and may not even be known in advance by the incumbents).

---

[2] An alternative analysis of organizational uncertainty uses the categories environmental state, organizational uncertainty, and decision response uncertainty (Christensen and Bower 1996; Milliken 1987). The last of these is the same as cause-effect uncertainty; the two former collapse uncertainty by nature or insufficient information and subdivide them depending on whether the uncertainty regards events in the environment or the effect of such events on the organization. This division has had some empirical application (Miller and Shamsie 1999).

Researchers distinguish between risk, which is uncertainty that can be quantified as probabilities, and uncertainty, where such quantification is not possible.[3] There is some indication that individuals view uncertainty and risk differently and are more averse to uncertainty than to risk (Camerer and Weber 1992; Ellsberg 1961), but most research has emphasized how individuals make decisions when the probabilities are known. Some work has suggested that risk and uncertainty are processed similarly by individuals except for the greater aversion to uncertainty (Hogarth and Einhorn 1990). Choosing among risky alternatives involves issues of risk perception, or how individuals understand risk, and of risk attitudes, or how individuals value risk (Mellers, Scwartz, and Cooke 1999). Since risk is an essential component of managerial work, research on risky choice is important for understanding how managers make decisions.

The leading behavioral model of risk taking is prospect theory (Kahneman and Tversky 1979). According to prospect theory, individuals evaluate possible future outcomes differently depending on whether they are above or below a reference point, which is usually taken to be the status quo. Thus, the consequences of a given alternative (a prospect in this terminology) are discounted according to how likely they are, as in rational models of choice under uncertainty, but they are evaluated differently depending on whether they involve gains or losses. The additional value of an extra unit of gain decreases as gains increase, as in the usual model of rational risk aversion, but the additional value of an extra unit of loss also decreases as losses increase, contrary to risk aversion. This leads decision makers to avoid risk in the domain of gains and seek risk in the domain of losses. Various inconsistencies in decision making follow from this, since problems can be divided into sub-problems or presented so that the reference point is shifted, with different decisions resulting depending on how the same problem is presented to the decision maker.

Such inconsistent choices have been demonstrated by asking subjects questions that are substantively the same but differ in being phrased as gains or losses, and observing that the risky choice was much more prevalent among subjects who saw the loss phrasing than the gain phrasing (Kahneman and Tversky 1979; Schoemaker 1990). This apparent reversal of preferences has been extensively studied, and later work has supported the risk aversion for gains, but revealed that subjects choosing among losing prospects show clear signs of conflict and inconsistent choices, which are sometimes risk averse and sometimes risk seeking

---

[3] The terminology is not completely standardized. Some use ambiguity to refer to uncertainty that cannot be quantified, but others reserve ambiguity for situations in which the criteria for making decisions are not clear.

(Schneider 1992; Schneider and Lopes 1986). The inconsistency does not seem to be a result of failing to understand the questions, as individuals are capable of distinguishing the loss and gain potential of complex gambles and reason through their choices (Lopes 1987). Rather, acting like satisficing decision makers, individuals view the reference point as a goal that ought to be achieved, but they also consider other risks such as that of disastrous losses (March and Shapira 1992).

One indication that the satisficing interpretation of observed risk-taking behaviors is correct is to note that satisficing requires knowledge of the goal and the means-ends relations for meeting it. This suggests that the reversal of preferences should be strongest when both the goal and the probability of reaching it are clearly understood by the decision makers, and should be weaker when they are ambiguous. Consistent with this, a meta-analysis of several studies has shown that the reversal of risk preferences is strongest when the decision maker chooses between a risky alternative and an alternative with a certain outcome (Kuehberger 1998). The analysis showed that the reversal is weaker when the goal or the probabilities are not specified clearly, or when complex probability assessments are required to understand which action will be most likely to meet the goal. Presenting information in formats that encourage a focus on either long-term or short-term goals also affects the decision, as a focus on long-term goals can shift the outcomes or the goal so that individuals accept risks even for gains (Benartzi and Thaler 1999).

Individuals also differ in risk-taking propensity (Atkinson 1983; McClelland 1961). Although individuals readily adjust risk taking by contextual factors (MacCrimmon and Wehrung 1986), it is still possible to identify different levels of risk taking in individuals (Schneider and Lopes 1986). These interpersonal differences make the relation from the risk inherent in the problem to the decision harder to predict without knowledge of the individual risk propensity. Change in preferences for gains and losses holds for risk seekers and risk avoiders alike (Schneider and Lopes 1986), however, so risk preferences have both interpersonal differences and contextual variation. This has led to the proposition that decision makers choose between uncertain prospects based on goals of either achieving security (risk avoiders) or high potential (risk seekers) and an aspiration level for how much security or potential they want in a given situation (Lopes 1987).

What is the origin of individual risk preferences? They can be viewed as results of shared and stable human traits that may have genetic origin, as results of learning from one's own experience, or as a result of socialization into a set of cultural beliefs. These explanations explain different parts of the behavior. Researchers struck by the interpersonal consistency of choices in the same situation favor explanations rooted in stable traits regarding how humans perceive the world or value outcomes (Kahneman and Tversky 1979). Researchers noting the effectiveness of learning explanations for a wide range of human behaviors favor explanations based on learning from direct experience with risky decisions (March 1996). Researchers finding cross-national differences in risk taking have come to favor cultural explanations (Weber, Hsee, and Sokolowska 1998). We do not know enough to choose among these explanations, and, as they are not mutually exclusive, it is important to be aware that risk taking may differ across individuals based on inheritance, socialization, or direct experience with the consequences of taking risk.

The difference in risk behavior depending on whether potential outcomes are above or below the reference point of the decision maker is an extremely important finding. It extends the effect of goals from situations involving choices with relatively certain performance implications to situations involving choices among alternatives with stochastic rewards. This fills a gap left by goal-setting theory, which does not consider risk. Since performance below a goal spurs problem-solving activities, as goal-setting theory shows, and increases risk tolerance, as risk theory shows, it is clear that major organizational changes are more likely when the organization has performance below the aspiration level. Thus, the behavioral theory of the firm links up with these theories to form an explanation of how performance affects strategic change in organizations. What remains to cover is one research tradition that directly deals with decisions to change organizations and one research tradition that studies how goals are made.

Before doing so, it is perhaps worthwhile to comment on one practical implication of risk-taking theory that the alert reader may already have noted. While decision makers seem capable of making sophisticated probability judgments, the sensitivity of risk preferences to a reference point makes the resulting decisions vulnerable to manipulation. A shrewd assistant to a CEO could in principle influence decisions by taking risk-theoretic principles into account when preparing decision-support materials. Since prospect theory has been widely taught in business schools in the last decade or so, such manipulation has probably been attempted already.

Escalation of commitment

A series of experiments related to risk theory have looked at how decision makers react to receiving negative performance feedback on an earlier decision (Staw 1976; Staw 1981; Staw and Ross 1987). The experiments were done by letting the subject choose to allocate organizational resources to one of two alternative activities, informing the subject that the choice turned out badly, and then asking for a new resource allocation. This small manipulation is enough to stress the subjects, and tends to result in decisions to commit more resources to the activity that caused the loss, in effect escalating their commitment to a decision that appears to be faulty. These findings are closely related to the risk-taking literature because the alternatives usually are to increase investment in an activity that has caused losses but has a chance of giving future revenues (a risky prospect) or not to invest, which gives no more gain or loss (a prospect with no risk). Escalating the commitment after negative feedback thus has been interpreted as risk seeking in a situation framed as a loss (Bazerman 1984; Northcraft and Neale 1986; Whyte 1986).

Viewed as a risk-seeking behavior, the choice between a certain loss and a chance of recovery is a situation that encourages escalation more strongly than a choice of different risky options, as a choice of risky options might include one that would allow recovery of the loss with lower risk for further losses than reinvesting in the project that caused losses. Consistent with this suggestion, individuals seem to avoid escalation if an alternative with lower risk level is present, showing that the risk level of different alternatives is more important for choices than whether a given alternative has been chosen earlier and given negative feedback (Schaubroeck and Davis 1994). This effect hinges on the potential for the low-risk prospect to recover the past losses, however, since a low-risk prospect that cannot give high enough rewards to provide a net gain is nearly as unattractive as a sure loss (Thaler and Johnson 1990). In another parallel with risk theory, individuals seem to have a dual focus on both the potential to recover losses and security against disastrous losses. Individuals in escalation situations stop investing when their losses reach a sum close to the potential win (Heath 1995), which indicates that they set a limit of maximally acceptable losses similar to the security motive in risk taking.

A purely risk-theoretic interpretation of escalation processes is not possible, however, as findings show that other mechanisms also contribute to escalation of commitment (Staw and Ross 1987). Consistent with a cognitive dissonance explanation, individual feeling of responsibility for the decision and need to justify past behavior result in a stronger escalation tendency (Bazerman, Giuliano, and Appelman 1984; Staw and Ross 1987; Whyte 1993). High self-efficacy also strengthens escalation processes, presumably because individuals confuse efficacy in skill-related tasks with control over chance outcomes (Whyte, Saks, and Hook 1997). High self-esteem has a similar effect (Sandelands, Brockner, and Glynn 1988). Reinforcement processes also contribute, as seen in the greater escalation tendency when the investment occasionally gives some rewards (Hantula and Crowell 1994). Just like occasional prizes make gamblers less sensitive to the accumulating losses, small rewards along the way can deepen managerial commitment to an investment that yields an overall loss.

Escalation of commitment leads to a "sunk cost" effect where managers overuse expensive assets that perform below expectations. An especially clear demonstration was given in research showing that players with a high position in the NBA draft order[4] get more playing time, even after controlling for their performance (Staw and Hoang 1995). The coaches commit to past draft choices so much that they ignore the safer option of letting the actual performance determine playing time. The strength of this effect has been disputed, but not its existence (Camerer and Weber 1999). Escalating commitment and sunk costs can bias decision makers towards continuing current activities rather than replacing them with new ones. This generally leads to risk aversion in organizational decision making since new activities tend to have more risk than current ones, but reversals can occur when the current activity is risky (Schaubroeck and Davis 1994).

Overall the escalation literature is consistent with the risk-taking literature, and can be seen as complementary since it covers a couple of weak spots in risk-taking research. The strong emphasis on managerial decision-making tasks gives the experiments a very realistic flavor, and the demonstration of sunk-cost effects in real organizational decisions further demonstrates its applicability to managerial work. It thus takes risk-theoretic considerations a step closer to the problem of organizational change. It also shares a limitation with risk-taking research. It tends to assume a status quo (zero profits) aspiration level where commitment or risk-taking processes start when the decision maker has faced a loss. This is clearly one possible aspiration level, but it seems fair to ask whether managers really would be content with not losing. One mechanism for making aspiration levels higher than the status quo is given by the next literature, which treats goals as resulting from comparison among actors.

Social comparison

While risk and escalation research is about how people make choices under uncertainty about future outcomes, the literature on social comparison processes is about how people handle uncertainty in the evaluation of current outcomes. According to social comparison theory,

---

[4] In the NBA (National Basketball Association), new players are picked sequentially by teams according to an order determined by a lottery. Because a team that picks a player early (high in the draft order) has signaled that the player is valuable to it, such players have considerable negotiating power and get higher pay than players lower in the draft order.

individuals have a need to evaluate their own opinions and capabilities. They do so by comparing themselves against objective standards whenever possible, and by comparing themselves with others when objective standards are unavailable (Festinger 1954). They choose similar others as referents in order to make accurate comparisons, but also seek to improve themselves so that they exceed the standard, thus competing with their peers. Clearly, social comparison theory specifies one way for individuals to set aspiration levels.

Social comparison theory has been extensively tested and to some extent revised by unexpected findings (Kruglanski and Mayseless 1990; Wood 1989). Individuals do indeed use social comparison to interpret their own performance, and show responsiveness to the degree of uncertainty by choosing different performance targets depending on their prior knowledge. When they know little about the performance variable under evaluation, they look for information on its range by comparing with the most dissimilar others, but they prefer comparison with similar others for familiar variables (Wheeler et al. 1969). The selection of referents also uses social similarity, as individuals prefer to compare themselves with others who are similar on attributes such as gender, appearance, and group affiliation (Miller 1982; Wheeler and Koestner 1984). While the original theory specified that attributes that predict task performance would be preferred, social similarity on attributes unrelated to task performance also affects social comparison (Tesser 1986). Individuals are particularly likely to use distinctive attributes that define a small reference group (Miller, Turnbull, and McFarland 1988).

These findings have been interpreted as suggesting that people prefer to compare themselves with others who are most relevant to their identity, but could also reflect use of cognitive shortcuts to bring the number of referents down to a manageable number by applying a simple but possibly arbitrary relevance rule. It is difficult to distinguish between these explanations. Identity may be involved when students compare their math scores with others of similar race or physical attractiveness despite knowing that these characteristics are irrelevant, but we need to know the intensity of this preference before concluding that this is so. Individuals who are indifferent between different social referents and merely wish to make a small comparison set might apply a frequently used (but irrelevant in this situation) comparison characteristic as a tie-breaking rule.

Social comparison processes are directed by the goals of the individual, and these goals are not limited to accurate assessment of one's own ability. Individuals use social comparison to pursue goals of self-assessment, self-improvement, and self-enhancement (Wood 1989). Only the first of these goals consistently leads to comparison with the most similar others. Self-improvement leads to comparison with similar but slightly better performers, and self-enhancement leads to comparison with similar but lower performers (Wood 1989). Self-enhancement can also be achieved by distorting information about the performance of others, such as by inaccurately judging that many others show the same undesirable behavior as oneself, but few others show the same desirable behavior as oneself (Goethals 1986). Another form of self-enhancement through distortion involves comparison with higher performers, who are then inaccurately judged to have approximately the same performance as oneself (Collins 1996).

Self-enhancement leads to selection of comparison targets and processing of the information that are inconsistent with accuracy and improvement goals, raising the question of when individuals are more likely to pursue self-enhancement goals or self-evaluation or improvement goals. The answer seems to be that this is guided by the self-relevance of the given performance dimension to the individual: performance dimensions that are important to the individual's self image are most likely to yield self-enhancing comparisons (Tesser 1986). A problematic implication is that professional accomplishments have high self-relevance and thus are likely to be inaccurately judged (Salovey and Rodin 1984). For top managers, the performance of the organization they manage is clearly a form of professional accomplishment, which could mean that they have difficulty making an unbiased assessment of their organization's performance.

The similarity judgments that underlie social comparison processes are also subject to biases (Kruglanski and Mayseless 1990). The most important bias occurs when an individual seeks to compare a subject with a referent other across multiple features. Multiple-feature comparison is done by taking a subject, such as oneself or one's own organization, as the baseline and mapping all salient features of the subject onto the referent, reducing the judgment of similarity whenever a difference is found (Tversky 1977). This procedure causes bias whenever the subject and reference have different salient and unique references, as the two will be viewed as less similar when the one with the most unique reference is chosen as the referent. This is a bias because they obviously have the same similarity regardless of the basis for comparison. As a result, comparison with oneself as the subject will yield too high differences due to the greater knowledge that individuals have about themselves than about others, and comparisons that managers make of organizations will yield too high differences due to the greater knowledge that managers have about their own organization than about other organizations. This process could prevent social comparisons from becoming influential by reducing the perceived relevance of all potential referents. At the very least, it suggests that closeness to the referent not only affects the informational basis for making social comparisons, but also the perceived relevance of the comparison.

Sociologists have also been interested in social comparison processes, and have noted that social networks make persons who have informal contacts with a given individual easily available for social comparison (Erickson 1988; Marsden and Friedkin 1993). This supports psychologists' finding that individuals often let the situation determine the comparison group (Wood 1989), and suggests that networks of social interaction are an important situational determinant of social comparison (Hogg, Terry, and White 1995). Social comparison through networks can also influence concrete organizational behaviors such as allocation of resources and change of strategies (Galaskiewicz and Burt 1991; Kraatz 1998). For example, managers use comparison with others to decide how much the organization should give to charity, causing organizations in similar network positions to have similar charity giving (Galaskiewicz and Burt 1991).

Individuals often use social comparison to crosscheck information received from other sources. Researchers in the goal-seeking literature have noted that workers do not necessarily accept goals given by a manager, but will instead change them by using available information on what can and should be achieved in a given situation (Earley 1986; Locke, Latham, and Erez 1988). The performance of other workers is often used for this purpose. Information about how well others do on the same task is an important influence when workers set their goals, since it allows goals set by social comparison to affect problem-solving behaviors (Martin and Manning 1995; Meyer and Gellatly 1988).

There are even some hints that social comparison directly affects the risk taking of decision makers. In a managerial decision-making simulation, Bandura and Jourden (1991) found that subjects who received false feedback that they were doing progressively worse than others started doing multiple changes simultaneously, which is a more risky strategy than changing one decision at a time or making no changes at all.[5] The strategy of changing one decision at a time was followed by subjects just below their social aspiration level, and the strategy of making no changes at all appeared to be more common among subjects just above their social aspiration level, which is also consistent with a link from social comparison to risk taking. Doing worse than others may cause individuals to take more risks.

[5] The authors interpreted multiple changes at once as degraded decision-making quality, since multiple changes at once makes it more difficult to learn from experience. This interpretation is clearly correct, but it is also the case that a strategy of making multiple changes takes higher risks than a strategy of one change at a time.

A parallel theory to social comparison theory is temporal comparison theory, which states that individuals interpret their performance through comparison with their past performance outcomes (Albert 1977). This theory has not been given nearly as much attention as social comparison theory, but is consistent with some experiments in economics that are reviewed in the next section. Recently, researchers have started re-examining temporal comparison theory, and have found that young people make temporal comparisons as often as they make social comparisons (Wilson and Ross 2000). This is in part because learning of new tasks often leads to quick improvements but not high performance compared with others, so temporal comparisons are more gratifying than social comparisons for inexperienced individuals. Social comparisons are more accurate, however, and are still preferred when the individual seeks to make a precise assessment of the performance (Wilson and Ross 2000). It is likely that joint examination of social and historical comparison processes will become more important in future research.

The findings on social comparison among individuals are complemented by research on social comparison among organizations, which is treated in chapter 3. While the findings are much less specific in the organizational version of this research, they do suggest that organizational performance can be compared in similar ways as individual performance. Thus, there is some confirmation of the suggestion that managers set aspiration levels by observing the performance of other organizations (Cyert and March 1963). This adds another piece to the theoretical puzzle on how performance affects organizational change, leaving only a question of levels of analysis. The behavioral theory of the firm made propositions at the organizational level of analysis, and performance feedback theory likewise investigates how organizational performance affects organizational change. The confirming evidence from social psychology most often concerns individual behaviors, which are at least two levels removed from organizations. In between comes group behavior, which is important in organizations since both search and decision making may be done in groups. The full answer to this question will have to wait for chapter 4, which reports research on how organizational performance affects organizational change, but a preliminary answer is provided by research on group decision making.

Group decision making

An important feature of organizations is that decisions are often discussed and made by groups rather than individuals. Even when managers make decisions on their own, they are influenced by information and advice from other members of the organization. Often such information and advice is aired in meetings of advisory groups, so individual decisions are preceded by group discussion and influence processes. The prevalence of groups in advisory or decision making roles in organizations means that caution is needed when transferring results from the literature on individual risk taking to organizational contexts, and suggests a need for investigating how groups make decisions.

Research on how individual preferences aggregate to group decisions has given a number of important findings that help our understanding of how group decision making happens. The simplest case of groups of people with similar aspiration levels leads to decisions similar to an average of what the individual decisions would have been, but more extreme – the so-called risky shift (Davis 1992). The explanation is that the discussion process brings out more supporting arguments than objections, which shifts the group decision and the post-discussion individual preferences. Hearing that others agree with one's opinion but do not voice one's doubts will reinforce that opinion.

The problems start with the recognition that when organizational change is considered as a response to performance feedback, the members of the decision-making group may have different aspiration levels (Kameda and Davis 1990; Tindale, Sheffey, and Scott 1993). Historical aspiration levels differ because members' individual histories are not equal to the organization's history, and their job experiences outside the organization are likely to affect their aspiration levels. Social aspiration levels differ because different functional backgrounds are likely to give different reference groups and possibly even different goal variables (Schurr 1987).

Differences in aspiration levels can lead to groups in which some members are above their aspiration level and others are below it, and the resulting decision-making process has proven difficult to model. Simple and fairly successful models include voting rules (Crott, Zuber, and Schermer 1986; Davis 1992; Kameda and Davis 1990), which means that extreme opinions do not affect the decision, but shifts towards more risky alternatives are also found (Isenberg 1986; Tindale, Sheffey, and Scott 1993; Whyte 1993). The shifts towards more risky alternatives is part of a general process of opinion polarization in which greater exposure to information supporting the majority opinion and pressures towards conformity cause greater opinion shifts in group members far from the original central opinion than in those near it, leading to a shift in the central opinion of the group (Isenberg 1986; Myers and Lamm 1976). It is different from the risky shift seen in groups with similar pre-discussion preferences, but relies on the same processes.

While group-decision research suggests that the aggregation of individual preferences can be modeled as voting rules, possibly with a polarization effect, translating this to organizations is problematic because of the differences between experimental settings and organizations. Experiments generally use temporary groups with no a priori differences in power or status characteristics that might lead to unequal influence in the decision making. Members of organizational decision-making groups often differ in general status characteristics, such as age, gender, and education, and specific status characteristics, such as abilities or skills relevant to the task. Differences in status create shared expectations that some members of the group will perform better than others (Berger, Rosenholtz, and Zelditch 1980). In discussions, the members that are expected to perform better are deferred to, allowing them to dominate the decision making (Ridgeway, Diekema, and Johnson 1995). Groups in which members have unequal status may make decisions that are similar to the decisions the highest-status members would have made individually, because they are allowed to set the aspiration level and determine what alternatives are acceptable (Whyte and Levi 1994). Such processes are clearly a possibility in organizational decision making, where differences in hierarchical position reflect real power differences and are connected with general beliefs about competence and performance. As a result, organizational decision making could follow rules somewhere between voting-style group-decision rules and domination by high-status or powerful individuals.

The tension between group-based and individual-based explanations of decisions is high in case studies of group-decision making, which is an active field especially in political science. While it is common to note the contribution of group heterogeneity in power as well as in preferences, some explanations clearly emphasize the emergent properties of the group. The best-known group level explanation is "groupthink" (Esser and Lindoerfer 1989; Janis 1982; McCauley 1989), which posits that groups have a tendency to seek consensus. Consensus seeking can lead to restrictions on the collection of information that might contradict the prevailing view and to dissenters failing to voice their opinion or even changing it towards the majority view. While groupthink processes have been shown to occur in some settings, recent work has argued for a greater role of the preferences and decision-making style of the group leader (Kramer 1998) and situational characteristics such as organizational routines for collecting information (Vertzberger 2000).

The organizational context of the decision-making group adds another layer of complexity to the process, as organizational communication, timing, and participation in decision making greatly affects the decision (March and Olsen 1976; Ocasio 1995). It is difficult for organizations to ensure that interested and knowledgeable participants will be available for all its decision making, since so many decisions need to be made and it is not always clear a priori which decisions are most important. The result is fluid participation (Cohen, March, and Olsen 1972), with organizational members allocating varying amounts of time to different decision domains depending on their preferences and time constraint. Fluid participation makes the set of participants present at a given decision-making occasion unpredictable. This adds variability to the decision-making process, and can result in delayed decision making and decisions made through matching a smaller set of problems and solutions than full participation would give (Cohen, March, and Olsen 1972).

Fluid participation may cause organizational decisions to be more like those of individuals by reducing the number of interested and knowledgeable decision makers present to the point where others will defer to the manager with the greatest interest in the decision. Who this manager is will vary, so the end result is not necessarily predictable, but a notable feature of fluid participation is its potential for creating organizational inertia. Organizational changes often cause a few to suffer for the benefit of the whole, such as when poorly functioning organizational units are reorganized in order to raise overall competitiveness. Clearly members of the unit targeted for change have intense preferences against change proposals, and others may have only mild preferences in favor, leading to inertia in organizations where participation in a given decision-making situation is determined by the intensity of preference for or against the alternatives under consideration.

Group decision-making work provides some confirmation that the ideas of the social psychological literature and the behavioral theory of the firm link up. There are mechanisms that can make a group aspiration level behave like an individual aspiration level, and mechanisms that can make a group decision behave like an aggregate of individual decisions plus some process-induced variability. This work also adds the complication that members of decision-making groups may have differing goal variables or aspiration levels. Some theoretical attention has already been given to this problem in the literature on organizational responses to performance feedback, and is described in section 3.1, when the creation of aspiration levels is discussed. It is still an issue with little empirical work on organizational behaviors, so it is high on the list of unsolved problems in the literature.

2.3   Economics

Economics is built on the rational choice paradigm, which differs from bounded rationality in having a maximization assumption. Rational actors do not satisfice, and thus do not need goals to know whether to be content. Because of this assumption, one does not expect much research relevant to performance feedback theory in economics. Nevertheless, it can be found. A small but growing literature on goal-seeking behavior is found in the work on learning in experimental games. Game theory (Fudenberg and Tirole 1991; Kreps 1990) uses assumptions on rationality to deduce the optimal choice in situations where the benefits to each actor is a function of their own choice and that of the others. Its theoretical branch uses reasoning of the form "if I do x and my opponent does y, then neither of us can do better by unilaterally changing our action" (i.e., a Nash equilibrium), which allows the analyst to find a set of actions that form a unique equilibrium, no set of single actions that does so, or many that do, depending on the nature of the game. The equilibria are usually viewed as predictions of behavior in economic situations with the same characteristics, but this view has been criticized by scholars who view the form of reasoning leading to Nash equilibria as too remote from actual human decision making (Radner 1996). Selten has argued that aspiration level theory is a good foundation for making economic models of boundedly rational decision making (Sauermann and Selten 1962; Selten 1998a, 1998b)

A diverse set of experiments has been conducted to find out how decisions are actually made in games and similar decision-making situations (Camerer and Ho 1999; Crawford 1995; Roth and Erev 1995; Selten 1998b), and work has advanced enough that distinct approaches have crystallized. The first distinction is whether the situation involves strong conflicts of interest between the parties, as in bargaining over fixed pies, or a stronger aspect of coordination, as in production where coordinated efforts maximize productivity. Games often involve both conflict and coordination, so this distinction is a matter of degree. The second distinction is whether the decision making is modeled as pure reinforcement learning, goal-directed learning, or optimization with learning of opponent behavior. This level of strategic sophistication in the decision making is important to game theorists because the lower levels lead to behavior that can differ appreciably from the game-theoretic optimum (Costa-Gomes, Crawford, and Broseta 2000; Crawford 1997; Roth and Erev 1995). To students of performance feedback, the mid-level theory of goal-directed learning is of special interest because it corresponds to the use of aspiration levels to explain individual behavior in social psychology and organizational behavior in the behavioral theory of the firm.

This literature has revealed considerable use of aspiration levels and great flexibility in how individuals form aspiration levels. Some experiments have shown effects of goals based on the player's own experience in much the same way as historical aspiration levels are formed in the behavioral theory of the firm (Crawford 1995, 1997; Ostmann 1992; Van Huyck, Battalio, and Rankin 1997). The crucial feature of these experiments is that the game was repeated, making past outcome information available to the subjects. When past outcomes are not available to subjects but other kinds of information are, subjects use a diverse set of alternative information sources to form aspiration levels. Social comparison or assigned goals are used when available (Pingle and Day 1996), analysis of the game payoff structure can be used (Costa-Gomes, Crawford, and Broseta 2000), loss/gain framing effects suggest that zero can be used as an aspiration level (Cachon and Camerer 2000), and general norms of fairness are invoked in situations where they are seen as applicable (Hennig-Schmidt 1999). A caution in interpreting this variability in goal sources is that the experiments usually make only one source of goals available (or at least most salient), so they show flexibility in using different kinds of goal-relevant information rather than variability in which kind of information is preferred. Unlike the social comparison literature, most of these experiments are not designed to show which information is preferred. An interesting exception is that an experiment with both a historical aspiration level and a loss frame showed that the prospect of a loss affected choices so greatly that the effect of the historical aspiration level disappeared (Cachon and Camerer 2000).

As in the psychological work on goal fulfillment, aspiration levels have been shown to affect behaviors in a variety of situations. In bargaining situations, groups of negotiators with high aspiration levels had higher level of demands, longer duration of negotiations, and higher rate of failing to reach agreements (Hennig-Schmidt 1999). In coalition-formation games, individuals with high aspiration levels were more active in seeking to influence others and obtained higher payoffs (Ostmann 1992). In repeated joint production situations with a reward for high group-level (median or lowest) choice but disincentives to contribute more than the group choice, the individual choices were controlled by historically updated aspiration levels (Crawford 1995). All these experiments showed that individuals used aspiration levels to determine their choices, as in bounded rationality.

Some experiments introduce interesting methods for studying aspiration levels. Hennig-Schmidt (1999) videotaped decision-making groups as they considered which offer to make in a bargaining situation, and found that aspiration levels were spontaneously mentioned during the discussions. This procedure verifies that individuals use aspiration levels in their decision making even when they are not prompted (by researcher instructions or other manipulations) to do so. It is still possible to interpret the results as indicating that aspiration levels are needed to *explain* suggested strategies but not to make them, but that explanation raises the question of why aspiration levels rather than some other explanation should be used. It seems more natural to suggest that the discussion reflects the actual reasoning of the subjects.

Experimental economics seems to reinforce performance feedback theory in three ways. First, the experiments show that many subjects prefer performance feedback to analysis of the structure of the game, as bounded rationality would predict. Second, the experiments reveal such a wide range of sources of aspiration levels that they suggest that individuals need aspiration levels so much that they are prepared to cast a wide net in their search for them. Finally, experiments in economics often use cover stories that mimic managerial decisions such as negotiations or production decisions, so they are another research tradition that seeks to give results that easily transfer to real organizations. In the next chapter I will integrate the theory and findings of these foundation pieces, and in chapter four I will go through the evidence from organizational decision making.

3   Model

A central idea of performance feedback theory is that decision makers use an aspiration level to evaluate organizational performance along an organizational goal dimension. An aspiration level has been defined as "the level of future performance in a familiar task which an individual . . . explicitly undertakes to reach" (Frank 1935), as a "reference point that is psychologically neutral" (Kameda and Davis 1990: 56) or as "the smallest outcome that would be deemed satisfactory by the decision maker" (Schneider 1992: 1053). It is a result of a boundedly rational decision maker trying to simplify evaluation by transforming a continuous measure of performance into a discrete measure of success or failure (March 1988; March and Simon 1958). The aspiration level is the borderline between perceived success and failure and the starting point of doubt and conflict in decision making (Lopes 1987; Schneider 1992).

Aspiration levels are the center of the theory. Before the aspiration level can take effect, some cognitive process must form it. Once the aspiration level is set, comparisons with performance guide organizational change processes. Here I develop the theory in the same order, starting with how aspiration levels are made and continuing with how they affect the organization. The origins of aspiration levels include learning from the performance of oneself, learning from the performance of others, or direct learning of the aspirations of others (Lewin et al. 1944). Aspiration levels have both direct behavioral consequences such as risk-taking or innovations and outcome consequences such as the performance or survival that results from making appropriate changes. Behavioral consequences will be discussed first, followed by a discussion of simulation studies on how aspiration-level learning contributes to organizational adaptation. Finally I discuss how organizational goal variables are chosen.

3.1   How aspirations are made

Natural aspiration levels

Though most of this book will treat the determination of aspiration levels as problematic, we should first consider whether there are situations in which decision makers naturally choose a given aspiration level. Choosing an aspiration level would be easy if there were strong clues in the situation as to what aspiration level is appropriate or if decision makers had been taught to prefer certain aspiration levels to others. We would know that a natural aspiration level were present if it were interpersonally consistent and temporally stable, that is, if we could see different decision makers choose the same aspiration level and stick to it over time. A variation of this would be if the aspiration level tracked a piece of information that varied over time but was available to all decision makers (the prime lending rate, for example). A natural aspiration level is cognitively simpler to process and requires less information than the socially constructed aspiration levels that are treated later. We would expect a decision maker who rations cognitive effort to choose a natural aspiration level whenever possible, as would a decision maker who lacks the information to build an adaptive aspiration level.

Are there natural aspiration levels in reality? Arguably, the status quo is often a natural aspiration level. Many of the experiments on prospect theory phrased potential outcomes as gains and losses relative to the status quo (Kahneman and Tversky 1979), and this proved to be enough to show adjustment of the risk level in the study population. Later work has also shown that individuals naturally pay attention to the loss or gain dimension when evaluating past or future outcomes (Schneider 1992; Schurr 1987). Using the status quo as an aspiration level literally means that the aspiration level is zero, that is, no gain or loss. Zero is certainly cognitively simple to process, and the corresponding loss/gain frame is familiar and capable of evoking strong reactions in decision makers.

Despite its simplicity, the status quo is often not a useful aspiration level in organizational decision making. When decision makers look at variables measuring profits, a positive value is normally expected, but the question of how high this value should be is not easy to answer. This leaves the decision makers with no natural aspiration level and a need to form their own aspiration level. Fortunately, organizational decision makers are better equipped to form aspiration levels than experimental subjects. The experiments using the status quo as the aspiration level typically concerned one-shot decision making or learning over the short term, and the subjects were often unfamiliar with the types of problems presented. They lacked prior knowledge of the situation and had little opportunity to incorporate information received during the experiment. By contrast, organizations face repeated decisions with a long time to learn, and organizational decision makers either have some familiarity with the decision or build it up in the course of learning their job. Managers almost cannot help receiving information that gives opportunities to build adaptive aspiration levels.

Certain types of education can create aspiration levels that seem natural to the decision maker. For example, financial methods of evaluating risky prospects typically rely on discounting budgeted expenses and income by a discount rate set to reflect the perceived risk of these income streams. This procedure has two noteworthy features. First, if the calculations are done correctly, then the correct aspiration level for the result (the net present value) is zero. All prospects above zero should be accepted, and all prospects below should be rejected. This is an appealing decision rule because it corresponds to a natural aspiration level of zero and the corresponding coding of prospects with positive or negative net present values as gain or loss prospects, respectively. It is not clear whether such decision rules are fully accepted by managers (Shapira 1994), but they would be one way of restoring zero as a natural aspiration level in management. Second, it will probably bother statisticians that risk is put into the denominator (as the interest rate) instead of by calculating how the enumerator (the income) varies. It is difficult to justify such a procedure except by assuming that the person preparing the analysis is unable to calculate the variance of the income or the person making the decision is unable to interpret the variance. Thus this method is a compromise between a desire for full rationality and recognition that the user of the method is boundedly rational.

Cruder ways of creating an aspiration level of zero are sometimes found. When decision makers look at variables measuring various forms of production loss, a stated goal of zero is often used as a management device. Zero defects, zero production line stoppages, zero radioactive leaks, and zero postoperative deaths are slogans that may improve work performance as predicted by goal-setting theory. It is less clear whether they are completely accepted as realistic, or even if they should be. The role of loss situations in generating risky behaviors suggests that it could be problematic to have aspiration levels that can never be exceeded in organizations where safety requirements are present. We may conclude that natural aspiration levels are most likely rare in organizations, so managers need to make their own aspiration levels. It turns out that there are multiple ways of doing so, with historical and social aspiration levels being the most important.

Historical aspiration levels

An aspiration level is necessary to assign performance levels to the success and failure categories favored by boundedly rational decision makers. When a natural aspiration level is not available or meaningful, the decision maker needs to generate an aspiration level from available information. One way to generate an aspiration level is to use the experience of the focal organization. The past performance is an indicator of how well the organization *can* perform and can easily become a standard for how well the organization *should* perform. Managerial aspiration levels are pushed up by the norm of achieving the highest possible performance but held back by uncertainty about what the highest possible performance is. The past performance of the same organization can be used to resolve this uncertainty, resulting in a historical aspiration level. Alternatively, the current performance of other organizations can be used to resolve this uncertainty, resulting in a social aspiration level.

A historical aspiration level can be formed by a rule that takes the historical performance as its input and produces an aspiration level used to evaluate the future performance. Before discussing what such a rule might look like, we should note that an important feature of a historical aspiration level is its modest information requirements. If managers view a given goal variable as important enough to evaluate, which creates a need for an aspiration level, they will also keep records of it and discuss it, and they should be able to recall or look up its past values. The conditions that produce a need for an aspiration level also produce the information necessary to make a historical aspiration level.

Since a historical aspiration level relies on information generated inside the organization, it is based on information with properties that are better understood by the decision makers than external information would be. An organization's accounting system may not produce information that its managers take as error-free and unbiased, but they are likely to have a guess about the magnitude and direction of its errors and biases. The manager may not even have a good guess of the properties of information generated by the accounting system of other organizations. It follows that a historical aspiration level would be most useful when external sources of information are absent, unreliable, or deemed irrelevant. It should thus be prevalent in organizations whose competitors are secretive or whose business is too different from their competitors' to allow easy comparison of performance across organizations. It would also be used in organizations that are in fact similar to other organizations, but whose managers erroneously judge to be unique.

Historical aspiration levels also have good forecasting properties. Because they are based on the same organization's performance, they incorporate information regarding relatively stable characteristics of the organization such as its knowledge or resource base that are likely to determine the performance in subsequent periods as well (Barney 1991; Wernerfeldt 1984). Historical aspiration levels are less useful for forecasting effects of the environment on the organizational performance, and they can produce misleading aspiration levels if the environment undergoes change that lowers the relevance of past capabilities and strategies for predicting future performance. Discontinuous environmental changes (Tushman and Anderson 1986) reduce the usefulness of historical aspiration levels.

Even more important, however, is that a good forecast is not necessarily a good aspiration level. Suppose that an organization has few valuable capabilities and, as a result, has had low performance for some time. A historical aspiration level will be low, which is a good forecast of the future performance if major changes are not made to the organization's set of capabilities or strategy. Precisely such an organization would seem to need major changes, and would be better served by a high aspiration level that clearly signaled a need to change. Which form of aspiration level is more adaptive to the organization is discussed in detail in section 3.3, but it is worthwhile noting already that exclusive reliance on a historical aspiration level can cause managers to be content with long stretches of performance below that of comparable organizations.

An easy rule for generating a historical aspiration level is by gradually updating the most recent aspiration level when new performance measures become available. This rule can be formalized as an exponentially weighted average model (Levinthal and March 1981) such as this:

$$L_t = AL_{t-1} + (1 - A)P_{t-1} \tag{3.1}$$

Here, L is the aspiration level, P is the performance measure, t is a time subscript, and A gives the weight of the previous-level aspiration level when making the new aspiration level. A is between zero and one. If A is high, the decision maker is confident of the previous aspiration level and thus puts a low weight on new information. Low A means that the decision maker lacks confidence in the previous aspiration level and puts a high weight on new information.

Note that by recursively inserting the previous-period aspiration level and collecting terms, equation 3.1 can be expressed as a sum of all previous performance levels:

$$L_t = (1 - A) \sum_{s=1,\infty} A^{s-1}P_{t-s} \tag{3.2}$$

This equation shows that the adjustment parameter A can be viewed as a discount rate for evaluating the relevance of the past performance when setting aspiration levels, with a high A giving a greater weight to past performance relative to the most recent. This functional form corresponds to the Bayesian approach of updating an estimate of a stochastic variable as new information becomes available (Crawford 1995), except that Bayesian updating requires adjusting A upward as more information is incorporated into L, while the behavioral studies reviewed here assume that A is a constant. It also corresponds to a cognitive heuristic of anchoring on the old aspiration level and adjustment by the new performance information (Tversky and Kahneman 1974). This updating rule resembles both a normative rule and a cognitive heuristic. It is too good to be wrong, but we still have to test whether decision makers really follow it.

Experimental and field studies have provided evidence on historical aspiration levels (Lant 1992; Lant and Montgomery 1987; Mezias and Murphy 1998). In these studies, informants reported their expected performance, received real or manipulated feedback on their actual performance, and reported their expected performance again. This was repeated over several periods, giving suitable data for estimating how aspiration levels were updated. In the experiments (Lant 1992; Lant and Montgomery 1987) the subjects were MBA or executive Master's students making decisions in a simulated market environment (the Markstrat game), while the field study was based on unit sales goals in a large retail bank (Mezias and Murphy 1998). The researchers estimated the following updating rule:

$$L_t = \beta_0 + \beta_1 L_{t-1} + \beta_2 (P_{t-1} - L_{t-1}) \tag{3.3}$$

The first of these terms is a constant that allows for the possibility of bias in the aspiration-level adjustment process, such as would result if the decision makers were persistently optimistic or pessimistic despite receiving information that should help them make an unbiased aspiration level. Such biases do not seem entirely logical, since, for example, a positive intercept corresponding to persistent optimism would be added in each period, causing the aspiration to spiral out of control. Nevertheless, findings suggesting that optimism sometimes overrides logic (Einhorn and Hogarth 1978; Langer 1975) make it worthwhile estimating whether a bias is present. The two last terms are just a rearrangement of equation 3.1 that allows easy testing of whether the weights assigned to the previous aspiration level and performance sum to one, as they should.

The experimental studies (Lant 1992; Lant and Montgomery 1987) found that the intercept was positive, consistent with persistent optimism. They also found the weights of the performance and past aspiration to exceed one, which will also induce aspiration levels that are higher than the data warrant. The difference from one could be viewed as minor (it was less than 10%), but when such a difference occurs in each period the aspiration level quickly escalates. These results suggest that the simple weighted average rule may overestimate the rationality of decision makers. The field study found a nonsignificant intercept, however, and weights of performance and past aspiration levels that barely exceeded one (Mezias and Murphy 1998). Thus, the organizational decision makers appeared to have a more sophisticated rule than the students, as one might expect from their greater experience and perhaps also from the greater accountability attached to their aspiration levels. Fulfillment of budgets usually enters into evaluations of managerial performance, giving good reasons not to report unreachable aspiration levels.

Social aspiration levels

An alternative rule for making aspiration levels is to use information on other organizations that are viewed as comparable to the focal organization. Because it resembles social comparison processes in individuals, this is called a social aspiration level. A decision maker forming a social comparison level needs to choose a suitable reference group and observe its performance. Managers appear to solve the first of these tasks easily. When asked who their competitors are, managers will give a list of other firms whose size and proximity make them important to their firm (Gripsrud and Grønhaug 1985; Lant and Baum 1995). More detailed questioning reveals that managers discern differences in organizational structure and operations and use them to further differentiate the reference set of organizations, while retaining a preference for organizations that are easily observed (Clark and Montgomery 1999; Porac and Thomas 1990; Porac, Thomas, and Baden-Fuller 1989; Porac et al. 1995; Reger and Huff 1993). For managers, making reference groups of similar organizations does not seem appreciably harder than making reference groups of similar persons is for individuals (Wood 1989).

   Collecting information on the performance of other organizations is more difficult. The most informative performance measures concern details of organizational operations that are not reported externally, such as productivity in specific plants or sales broken down by region or product. Some of these performance measures are not even made available to high-level decision makers in the focal organization, as accounting conventions and delegation of responsibility have led to top managers receiving increasingly aggregated and summarized information (Johnson and Kaplan 1987). This could cause top managers to fall back on measures that are less informative but readily available when evaluating the organizational performance. The traditional measures of profitability reported to stockholders (operating profits, return on assets, and the like) are especially easy to obtain. Since their computation relies on a set of general principles that are familiar to managers, they are likely to be viewed as interpretable and comparable across similar organizations. These characteristics could make them more influential than they perhaps deserve, especially when considering that any single measure of the performance of a firm loses its meaning when the firm has a variety of business activities (Kaplan and Norton 1996). Even standardized accounting measures suffer from some comparability problems across organizations,[1] however, so one may wonder whether any measures of the performance of other organizations is deemed sufficiently valid that managers will form a social aspiration level. As social comparison research has shown, individual drive for external evaluation is so strong that a decision maker may decide to ignore validity problems with the information at hand.

It is also likely that decision makers will pay attention to performance measures that are collected and made public by some well-known and trusted third party. Mass media generate and publish rankings on many forms of organizational performance, since magazine and newspapers readers have an interest in rankings in general, and in particular rankings on a product or service they intend to buy. Such measures also have reliability problems, which partly stem from the difficulties in finding objective criteria and collecting data on them, and partly stem from the low incentives media have to produce accurate measures. Beyond the basic requirement of face validity, it is not clear that improvements in methodology help the sales of magazines reporting firm or product rankings. Nevertheless, such measures get attention and respect from consumers accustomed to the product testing advocated by consumer watchdog organizations (Rao 1998), and there are clear signs that managers also view them as important (Elsbach and Kramer 1996). Some of these rankings use highly informative performance outcomes such as the measures of defects in car models published by J. D. Powers.

When third-party measures are not available, organizations sometimes collaborate to make social comparison possible. In the radio industry, the market shares of other stations in the market are readily available to managers through the market share reports issued by the Arbitron ratings agency. These reports are costly, but viewed as essential to managing radio stations and are found on some bookshelf in nearly every radio station. They are also issued electronically for quicker access and easier analysis.

---

[1] This is not a reference to the Enron scandal, which broke after this passage was written. Application of accounting principles varies among organizations even when deception is not involved, so the measures are not completely comparable. Naturally, any hint that the books may be cooked will only increase this concern.

As if that were not enough, radio stations in some markets collaborate to have an accounting firm collect reports of advertising sales in all commercial radio stations and report back to each station their sales share to market share ratio (called the "power ratio"). Radio stations do not have to release sales figures since they are usually privately owned or sub-units of larger corporations. Their managers view sales as highly confidential information, but the ability to compare sales across stations is so important that they have agreed to release them to a trusted third party who computes the information they need to form their social aspiration level. This may be a rare agreement, but it does suggest that managers are willing to go to great lengths to make accurate social aspiration levels.[2]

Once performance measures of a set of referent organizations are available, they can be combined into a social aspiration level according to rule such as this:

$$L_t = \sum_{a \in R} \omega P_{at} \qquad (3.4)$$

Here, R is the set of referent organizations and ω is a set of weights giving the importance of each member of the reference group in making the social aspiration level (scaled to sum to one). This general form takes into account that managers may recognize grades of relevance of other organizations, just as individuals recognize grades of relevance of other people. Although such differentiated reference groups seem realistic, they are difficult to verify empirically. Just as theoretical statements have so far concentrated on simpler rules of taking the unweighted average performance of the members of the referent group (Levinthal and March 1981), so has empirical work been content with defining a set of referents and taking their unweighted average performance as the social aspiration level (Fiegenbaum and Thomas 1988; Greve 1998b).

The validity of social aspiration levels for judging the organizational performance springs mainly from their effectiveness in taking into account environmental influences common to all organizations in the comparison group. For organizations in turbulent environments, this feature makes social aspiration levels more valuable than historical aspiration levels, since rapid changes in the environment make the history of the focal organization less diagnostic for judging its performance than the contemporary performance of comparable organizations. The weakness of a

---

[2] Other examples of information release quickly come to mind, suggesting that radio stations are not unique in releasing information for the purpose of making social aspiration levels. The MIT auto manufacturing study obtained access to cost information that one would normally expect firms to keep secret, presumably because the firms were interested in its goal of comparing cost levels across plants and firms (Womack, Jones, and Roos 1990).

social comparison level is its inability to account for organizational heterogeneity in capabilities or niches. To some degree this problem can be solved through careful definition of the referent group. Thus the ability of managers to make fine-grained distinctions among organizations based on organizational or market differences is useful, but biases in similarity judgments and preferences for easily available information are not.

Direct measure of social aspiration levels has so far been done mainly in the goal-setting literature, where the concept of group norm is used to refer to the influence of the performance of others on individual goals (Locke and Latham 1990). The naming suggests norm-setting reasons for social influence, which is probably due to an early experiment showing that subjects set goals that were greater than the performance of low-status others, similar to the performance of similar-status others, and lower than the performance of high-status others (Festinger 1942). Whether social aspiration levels represent norms or just predictive information is not clear, but the evidence suggests a clear effect of the performance of others on the aspiration level of individuals (Garland 1983; Martin and Manning 1995; Meyer and Gellatly 1988).

Interestingly, individuals use social information less as their experience with a given task increases (Weiss, Suchow, and Rakestraw 1999). Normative reasoning would suggest that managers should not apply the same learning rule to organizational performance, since the aspiration level for organizational performance should reflect the organizational environment. This environment may change, making past experience obsolete and suggesting a continued need to use the performance of others to evaluate one's own performance. There are, however, suggestions that experienced managers make less use of social information than inexperienced managers. Managers with high tenure are less likely to change their organizational strategy in response to environmental changes than managers with low tenure, suggesting less collection of environmental information (Miller 1991). The preference for social versus historical sources of aspiration levels may thus depend on the experience of the focal decision maker as well as the availability and validity of information.

Direct learning

Finally, aspirations can be learnt directly from others (Lewin et al. 1944). Rather than organizations using the performance of others to make a performance level for themselves, they may be able to get direct information on the aspiration level of other organizations and use it to set their own. Such a mechanism places much greater demands on information collection than the other two. Indeed, if aspiration levels are viewed as cognitive constructs that only exist inside a given decision maker's head, it is not possible for managers to be influenced by the aspiration levels of others. Individual aspiration levels may be purely cognitive constructs, but organizational aspiration levels are not. Because organizations require joint action and coordination, aspiration levels tend to become tangible figures that are printed in internal documents such as budgets and sales quotas, and that leak to the outside through press releases, reports to shareholders, stock analyst briefings, and interviews of managers. When General Electric CEO Jack Welch decided that all GE business units needed to be one of the top two firms in their industry, this intention was widely announced both within the company and to external audiences (Slater and Welch 1993). Earnings estimates are regularly released by firms and the stock analysts who follow them, and failure to meet earnings estimates are problematic for managers. Infectious aspiration levels are thus not as unrealistic as they seem at first glance, but they are at least as demanding in terms of information collection and processing as social aspiration levels, and are not necessarily more useful for the organization. We know little about direct learning of aspiration levels, however.

Multiple sources

The original formulation of aspiration-level learning suggested that historical and social aspiration levels were combined to form one aspiration level (Cyert and March 1963), and this can be extended to give directly learned aspiration levels a role. In such a model, the three sources of learning the aspiration levels are given weights that reflect their relative importance to the decision maker, giving a formula like this:

$$L_t = (1 - \beta_h - \beta_s - \beta_d)L_{t-1} + \beta_h P_{t-1} + \beta_s L_{st} + \beta_d L_{dt} \qquad (3.5)$$

Here, L_t is the aspiration level in time t, as before, and L_{st} and L_{dt} are the social and direct-learning aspiration levels, respectively. The formula makes the new aspiration a weighted sum of the past aspiration level, most recent performance, and social and direct-learning aspiration levels. It assumes that the decision maker incorporates all available information, but is not restrictive about how this combination is done. Since each β can be small, it is possible for a decision maker to show little evidence of influence from one of the sources. A small β_d would imply that direct learning had little effect, for example, which could occur because such information was not available, or was not used because the organization's own experience or social referents provided more salient information.

A second proposal is that multiple aspiration levels are active simultaneously and jointly affect the behavior (Greve 1998b). In that case, the performance relative to each aspiration level enters as an independent factor in determining whether the organization changes in the same way as effects of different variables jointly influence a response variable in a regression framework. This relation is a little harder to justify behaviorally, since it is difficult to imagine decision makers simultaneously comparing a performance variable relative to two different aspiration levels. It is a little easier to justify cognitively, since it does not involve the step of integrating information from different sources that the weighted formula does. If changes are determined by multiple managers, this proposal is easy to justify both cognitively and behaviorally since each manager may focus on a different aspiration level.

A third proposal is that the decision maker shift attention among different aspiration levels depending on the performance (March and Shapira 1992). This theory was originally developed to suggest that decision makers are influenced either by an aspiration level point or by a survival point (an asset level that would lead to bankruptcy). Attention could then switch between these points according to some rule, such as a stochastic rule or one that is guided by the importance of each goal. Because survival is an overriding goal, it is natural to suggest that managers will pay attention to the survival goal first, and then switch attention to the aspiration level if the prospects for organizational survival are not in danger (March and Shapira 1992). The finding that declining organizations pay attention to asset growth (Wiseman and Bromiley 1996) supports this theory. Another suggestion is that aspiration levels become salient when they are proximate to the current performance. An organization near the mean performance of its competitors might pay attention to the social aspiration level, while an organization close to failure would pay attention to the survival point. Thus, different aspiration levels of performance can be maintained and paid attention to depending on importance or proximity. This is a cognitively simple and behaviorally realistic rule; after all it is easy to imagine a manager complaining that sales fell last year being told that all is well because the sales are still higher than those of the competitors.

The combining rule and joint consideration rule are behaviorally similar to each other and to a simple rule of randomly switching between aspiration levels. Suppose an organization switches between two aspiration levels and has a probability π of paying attention to the first of these aspiration levels at any period of time and an identical response to each rule. This behavior is equivalent to a combining rule with weights π and $1 - \pi$ assigned to the aspiration levels. It is also the same as a joint consideration rule where the ratio of the estimated effects of the two aspiration levels is $\pi/(1 - \pi)$. The main difference between the combining rule and the two others is that the combining rule disallows different response patterns to different goals, so it would require that the response curves (see figure 3.2) be identical.

The joint consideration rule and the switching rule are behaviorally identical as long as the switching rule is random, but random switching is not the most interesting form of behavior. Rather, switching rules are interesting because they allow the decision maker to choose between aspiration levels when the organization performs above one aspiration level but below another. Nonrandom switching rules can be influenced by the level of the performance or the characteristics of the performance measure. Among the levels-based switching rules, two are of special interest (Greve 1998b). A "fire alarm" rule shifts attention to the aspiration level above the current performance, just as people pay attention to a ringing fire alarm but not a silent one, making change responsive to the most exacting standard. A self-enhancing rule shifts attention to the aspiration level below the current performance, making change responsive to the least demanding standard. These rules have been investigated in one study without clear evidence for levels-based switching rules (Greve 1998b).

An interesting family of measure-based switching rules involves decision makers paying attention to aspiration levels in descending order of importance, with the aspiration level indicating a problem getting more attention. A sequence of checking for survival risk before worrying about the social or historical aspiration level would be one example of such a rule (March and Shapira 1992). A second would be for firms that are viewed as comparable by stock analysts to attend to the social aspiration level first, since it is a bellwether for difficulties with investors, and then attending to the historical aspiration level. A third would be to attend to goal variables with legal implications (pollution, hazardous products) before profit variables. Such ranked rules are called lexicographic rules because they correspond to how we sort words. They mimic the behavior of a manager who makes a ranked priority list of goals and then goes down the list checking each goal until finding one that has not been fulfilled. Lexicographic rules are cognitively simple and behaviorally easy to justify, but are difficult to analyze statistically because it is hard to tell which rule will be in operation at any given time. They do not seem to have been investigated empirically.

Bias

The historical, social, and direct aspiration-level updating rules all assume that the decision maker makes an unbiased estimate based on the available information. The information may be biased, such as when information is more readily available for high-performing organizations, but the processing of it is not. Switching updating rules according to their rank is an example of an updating rule where the decision maker processes information in a way that gives a bias, which is either upward for the "fire alarm" rule or downward for the self-enhancing rule. This is not the only way of biasing the aspiration level, however. Bias could also be introduced by selecting social comparison targets according to their performance relative to the focal organization; by interpreting the information of one's own performance differently according to how high it is; and by distorting the received information.

Choosing a reference group of other organizations is a task that involves judgment of the similarity of the businesses. Organizations that are more similar to the focal organization will be seen as more diagnostic of the performance it can achieve and thus more important for social comparison. If the research on social comparison among individuals is any guide, the reference group may also be sensitive to how the performance of the focal organization ranks relative to others. Both self-assessment and self-improvement goals may lead managers to compare their organization to other organizations with similar performance, but in the case of self improvement organizations with slightly higher performance will be preferred. Selecting organizations with similar performance as the focal organization will tend to make a social updating rule similar to a historical updating rule, since organizations with performance very unlike that of the focal organizations will be removed from the comparison set. Selecting organizations with similar but slightly higher performance will add a positive bias to the updating rule, driving the aspiration level upwards. The opposite effect will result from a self-enhancement goal, which would lead managers to compare with organizations that have lower performance (perhaps even much lower performance) and thus drive the aspiration level downwards. Self-enhancing rules are likely to be used by managers who are seeking to avoid termination, that is, by managers who are responsible for goal variables that currently show very low performance.

When using a historical updating rule, the decision maker is sensitive to the timing of the performance, with more recent performance being viewed as more relevant. This does not give any bias, but the decision maker may also be sensitive to the level of performance in earlier periods. A rule of giving greater weight to either high performance or low performance will bias the aspiration level. Some intriguing evidence of levels-based bias comes from the interpretations of performance given in the annual reports of corporations. Managers appear to view high performance as more conclusive evidence of the organization's capabilities than low performance, as the explanations given for high performance are usually internally oriented, while the explanations given for low performance concern external and temporary conditions (Meindl and Ehrlich 1987; Salancik and Meindl 1984). Such public statements could be face-saving behaviors that do not necessarily reflect the assessment of the managers (Elsbach and Kramer 1996), but it is a little too easy to dismiss them entirely. If managers really take the level of performance into account when updating aspiration levels, the greater weight attached to high performance drives the aspiration level upwards. By itself, this would lead to more frequent performance below the aspiration level, but since the same discounting of low performance also occurs when evaluating the current period's performance, such apparent failures to reach the aspiration level may not be believed. This will make the organizational behavior insensitive to the level of performance, since the performance is only thought to be accurate when it is high.

Finally, the information received may be processed in ways that lead to systematically higher or lower aspiration levels than the averaging implicit in the historical or social updating rules specified above. Most often, theoretical and empirical treatments use an upward striving rule that adds a constant to the aspiration rule (Lant 1992) or multiply it with an inflation factor greater than one (Bromiley 1991). Such biased updating may result from mechanisms such as drive for self-improvement (Festinger 1954), or they may just be a simple way of incorporating more complex behaviors such as the biased selection of referents or selective interpretation of own behavior discussed above. It is not clear that upward striving rules are correct, however, or whether self-enhancing rules should be used instead.

3.2   How aspirations affect behavior

Search

Search is a central concept in the behavioral theory of the firm. It includes activities such as production workers varying their work procedures to look for more effective ways of working or simply to relieve boredom, engineers going to conferences to pick up news about technologies, marketing staff conducting focus groups to learn about consumer preferences, purchasing departments collecting bids and specifications for new equipment, and managers discussing alternative strategies. Search is not the same as organizational change, since none of the above activities necessarily implies any permanent change of activities. They all give potential to change, however, by generating alternatives to the current set of activities. If such alternative activities are promoted as solutions to organizational problems in an appropriate decision-making situation, permanent organizational change may result. It is for this reason that search is thought to be a precursor of change.

Search is an everyday phenomenon in organizations, and there are multiple processes driving it (March 1981). They are slack search, institutionalized search, and problemistic search. *Slack search* results from extra time and resources that are used for experimentation. Engineers in a product development department often appropriate time for their own projects in addition to the projects they are being told to work on, and some managers let them do so since such "finagling" can lead to important discoveries (Jelinek and Schoonhoven 1990). Other managers may seek to eliminate such own time, but simply be unable to monitor the engineers. Production workers with available time also make experiments. It was probably free time that allowed a pizza franchise worker to find a new way to stack the empty delivery boxes that made transfer of finished pizzas easier, thereby reducing strain and the rate of dropping pizzas on the floor (Darr, Argote, and Epple 1995). Slack search is usually not deliberately managed, but organizational mechanisms such as quality circles are used to encourage development and transfer of new work procedures in factories. These mechanisms increase the impact of slack search on organizational routines. Conversely, slack search responds to the availability of resources such as free time and depends on workers who are motivated to improve the organizational procedures, and thus it can be reduced by "lean organization" practices such as staff cuts and contingent employment (Pfeffer 1994).

Institutionalized search is done by organizational units devoted to search activities, such as Research and Development, Market Research, and Strategic Planning. It is sometimes conducted throughout the organization as a part of periodical planning and budgeting cycles. Unlike slack search, institutionalized search is a planned result of the organizational structure and resource allocation. Although deliberately managed, the rate of institutionalized search is not easy to adjust in the short run since these organizational units are small and devote most of their time to search activities to begin with. Increasing institutionalized search normally requires hiring additional workers in these organizational units, which delays the response to managerial directives. Like slack search, institutionalized search can be viewed as a background process that does not respond to performance feedback in the short run.

Problemistic search occurs as a response to an organizational problem. It is the most important form of search for the theory of performance feedback, since it is governed by performance relative to aspirations. Problemistic search is the middle step of a sequential process of comparing the performance with an aspiration level, initiating search if the performance is low relative to the aspiration level, and making changes if an acceptable solution can be found (Cyert and March 1963). Problemistic search seeks to mend performance shortfalls, so unlike slack and institutionalized search it is a goal-oriented behavior. It is increased when the organization performs below the aspiration level and decreased when the organization performs above the aspiration level. The intensity of problemistic search is highly variable since it is governed by performance feedback and conducted by changing the activities of the regular organization from regular production to search.

Ad hoc research initiatives, task forces, and staff brainstorming sessions are examples of organizational behaviors that constitute problemistic search. Managers initiate these activities by diverting resources from routine production to search, and thus the organization will only perform problemistic search if it managers have judged that the organization faces a problem that is so important that resources are best spent searching for solutions. In practice, low sales and idle production capacity are among the problems that low-performing organizations face, so the resources spent on problemistic search may not have high-value alternative uses. Managers can either use the spare capacity for search or reduce the capacity through layoffs and other downsizing mechanisms. Still, it is important to emphasize that problemistic search is done by diverting resources away from routine production and administrative activites.

Like the intensity of problemistic search, the direction of problemistic search is varied according to managerial judgments. Problemistic search is initially done in the proximity of the problem symptom and the current activities (Cyert and March 1963), which makes it dependent on the current state of the organization. Search in the proximity of the current symptom means that simple rules such as searching for sales solutions to low sales or production solutions to low productivity will be used first. More complex alternatives such as searching for product design solutions to low sales or low productivity are likely to be attempted after the simple search has failed. As a result, the early phase of problemistic search is unlikely to generate appropriate solutions to problems that span departmental boundaries, which may explain why organizations are slow to solve problems that incorporate multiple specialties (Henderson and Clark 1990).

Search in the proximity of the current activities means that solutions that are minor variations on the current activities will be considered before major changes to the organization, and solutions that the organization has recently applied elsewhere are likely to be considered before novel solutions. Such search behavior results in organizational momentum (Amburgey and Miner 1992; Kelly and Amburgey 1991; Miller and Friesen 1982): the organization keeps moving in the same direction. Since the organization may recently have done changes that have little resemblance to the problem currently under consideration, repetition of recent actions can yield surprising solutions such as acquiring another firm in response to reduced sales or productivity. While momentum can dissociate the result of search from the problem that initiated the search, momentum results in changes that are easily predicted from the history of the organization. Some patterns of momentum are seen in many organizations. It is common to continue improving an existing technology beyond the point where a switch to a competing technology would have been better (Miller and Friesen 1982) and to escalate resources committed to the current strategy (Noda and Bower 1996).

Problemistic search is initially conducted near the problem symptom or the current activities, but it may expand over time. Problemistic search will continue until a solution has been found, and can be restarted if failure continues after a solution has been implemented. In such cases more distant solutions will be sought. Problemistic search can also be drawn away from the current symptom by "solution entrepreneurs"– organizational members or external actors who view the problem as an opportunity to steer the organization in a direction they desire. Successful solution entrepreneurship may be seen through such large-scale changes as the tendency of the CEOs of major corporations to be recruited from the functional backgrounds currently in vogue according to management rhetoric (Fligstein 1990; Ocasio and Kim 1999). It is probably more prevalently seen in the collusion of equipment vendors and production engineers in turning productivity problems into equipment purchase solutions.

Risk taking

Organizations conduct slack search, institutionalized search, and problemistic search. All three forms of search can create organizational change, and problemistic search is especially likely to do so. Problemistic search is conducted in response to a problem, and thus occurs when managers have already decided that organizational change may be necessary. Other forms of search may produce solutions at times when managers do not judge that the organization needs to change. The lack of a mechanism to transfer solutions generated through search into organizational change wastes the search effort, but it is a normal result of managers doing their job. Proposals to change the organization are evaluated for their costs and benefits, and risk is central in this consideration.

Whether a solution will be implemented and what kind of solution will be chosen depends on the risk preferences of the decision makers, making risk theory an important component of the theory of organizational reactions to performance feedback. Risk theory predicts that risk preferences change in response to performance feedback. Risky alternatives are more acceptable when the decision maker is in the loss domain, so performance below the aspiration level should make major organizational changes more acceptable to managers. It is still worthwhile considering some important details on how organizational risk taking differs from individual risk taking.

Organizational risk taking is decided by managers, who are professional risk takers. Selection, socialization, and incentives all contribute to give managers different risk preferences than the general population, and in general they seem to take greater risks (Wehrung 1989). This does not necessarily make them risk seekers, however. There is an important conceptual difference between being risk averse with a high level of acceptable risk and being risk seeking, since risk aversion means rejecting fair bets while risk seeking means accepting fair bets.[3] A risk-averse decision maker with high level of acceptable risk will reject a fair bet, but may accept a bet of positive expected value even if the stakes are high. When managers evaluate prospects in the gain domain, risk aversion with high levels of acceptable risk is more common than risk seeking, but risk seeking becomes more frequent in the loss domain, as prospect theory predicts (Wehrung 1989). Risk seeking in the domain of losses may lead to sharp increases in the probability of making changes or the risk of the chosen alternative when the organization is below the aspiration level.

The acceptance of risk by individual managers has a counterweight in organizational processes favoring small changes over large ones. Organizational scholars have discovered a sizable set of organizational processes that prevent major changes, making organizations structurally inert (Hannan and Freeman 1977, 1984). Among these, intra-organizational politics and inter-organizational constraints are especially important (Barnett and Freeman 2001). Although lines of authority formally go from the top down in most organizations, there are usually sufficient independent power bases that lower-level managers may be able to resist changes that go against their individual interests or those of the

---

[3] Fair bets have an expected value of zero. If the cost of playing is one, the fair-bet reward to calling a coin flip correctly is two and the fair-bet reward to calling a dice roll correctly is six. Risk seekers accept fair bets as well as some losing bets.

organizational unit they head. Intra-organizational politics result in a need to make changes acceptable to a broad coalition of managers. Otherwise, dissenting managers can resist in the decision-making process and stall the implementation process. Inter-organizational constraints result from the need to maintain stable exchanges with the environment. The organization has access to necessary resources as long as its managers can structure exchanges that also fulfill the needs of its current exchange partners (Pfeffer and Salancik 1978). This dependence on other actors makes changes intended to reorganize current exchanges less likely, since current exchange partners have a voice in the decision-making process through the organizational members who manage the exchange, while alternative exchange partners are likely to lack such representation and thus are a weaker voice in the decision-making process than their economic potential warrants (Christensen and Bower 1996).

These sources of inertia create constraints that decouple financial and organizational risk. While managers are quite capable of taking financial risks, and may become risk seeking when the performance is below the aspiration level, they are less capable of taking organizationally risky actions. Many changes that are large financially are also large organizationally, such as changing the product or market strategy, so for such changes the distinction is not important. Other changes have unequal organizational and financial risks. Managers are likely to favor changes that are large financially but not organizationally. Changing the organization by budding or grafting new elements onto the existing structure have this characteristic, making new product development (without dropping existing products), acquisition of other organizations (leaving the current intact) or divestment of weak organizational units (leaving the rest intact) very attractive solutions for managers who seek financial risk but not organizational risk. These are financially risky but organizationally piecemeal approaches to change.

Organizational change

The effects of performance feedback on organizational search and managerial risk preferences combine to yield the effect on the rate of making organizational change. To see how this happens, consider the following propositions derived from the discussion above:

P1 Slack search and institutionalized search are not responsive to performance feedback.

P2 Problemistic search is increased when the organization performs below the aspiration level and decreased when the organization performs above the aspiration level.

P3 Managerial preference for financially risky actions is increased when the organization performs below the aspiration level and decreased when the organization performs below the aspiration level.

P4 Inertial factors reduce the rate of adopting organizationally risky actions regardless of the organizational performance.

To integrate these suggestions, we may consider the organizational decision-making process as a flow of solutions resulting from search. This search has one component that is regulated by performance, problemistic search, and two that are not, slack and institutional search. The solutions are risky alternatives to the current behaviors, and are accepted or rejected depending on whether they can be attached to a problem and whether their organizational and financial risks are acceptable to the managers. Thus we have a flow of solutions which is partially regulated by performance feedback and which passes a decision-making filter regulated by performance feedback. Figure 3.1 shows the relation (compare with figure 2.1).

How performance turns into organizational change thus depends on what kind of organizational change we consider. In general, we should expect change to be less likely to occur when the organization performs above the aspiration level, since problemistic search is at a low level, few problems are available to attach a solution to, and managers are risk averse. We should not expect changes to completely vanish, however. Slack and institutionalized search will continue to feed solutions into the decision-making process, and some of these may have risk levels that are acceptable to the decision makers.

For financially risky actions with low organizational risk, we should expect a much greater rate of change when the organizational performance is below the aspiration level since problemistic search is conducted and risky actions are acceptable. For actions that are organizationally as well as financially risky, we should expect the rate of change to increase less sharply since it is counteracted by organizational inertia, but it should still increase through the effect of the search and decision-making processes.

Figure 3.2 illustrates some ways to integrate the effects of the risk and decision-making processes on organizational change. Figure 3.2(a) shows a very simple model that assumes that decision makers classify outcomes into two categories, success and failure, and that the probability of change is higher in the failure category (March and Simon 1958). This figure is consistent with the arguments above, but may be too simple since it treats a small performance shortfall as equivalent to a large one. Figures 3.2(b) through 3.2(d) show models with continuous adjustments of the probability of change. In figure 3.2(b) the probability of

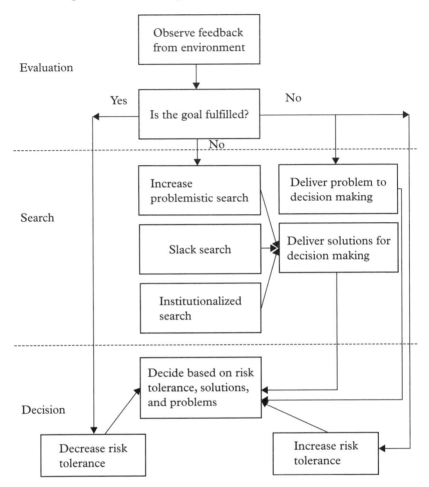

Figure 3.1 Performance-based adjustment of search and decision making

change decreases as the performance increases, but the probability decreases faster above the aspiration level than below the aspiration level. This figure is completely consistent with the arguments above. It incorporates the adjustment of search and risk preference in the downward slopes of the curves, and the resistance to major organizational changes in the flatter curve below the aspiration level than above it. Like figure 3.2(a), it incorporates the possibility that changes may occur even at high levels of performance, which is consistent with continuing slack and institutionalized search even when the performance is high.

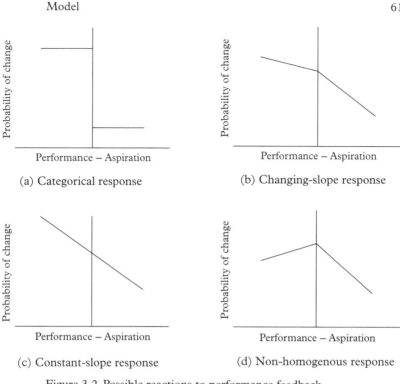

(a) Categorical response   (b) Changing-slope response

(c) Constant-slope response   (d) Non-homogenous response

Figure 3.2 Possible reactions to performance feedback
Source: Greve (1998b). Copyright © 1998 Cornell University.

In figure 3.2(c) these inertial factors are absent, leading to a constant decrease in the probability of change over the entire range of performance. Figure 3.2(c) shows no effect of aspiration levels, since there is no discontinuity or change in slope anywhere in the curve. Such a slope might be proposed for changes with no organizational risk, only financial risk, because such changes do not face the managerial resistance that causes inertia.

Finally, in figure 3.2(d) change is most likely near the aspiration level and declines away from it. Such a relation is not consistent with the above arguments, but might happen as a result of another process. If low performance is interpreted as a threat to an organization, then threat rigidity can cause decision makers to reduce the level of organizational change (Staw and Ross 1987; Staw, Sandelands, and Dutton 1981). Threat rigidity is different from regular performance feedback because it happens as a result of the decision maker changing the focus from the hoped-for aspiration level to the feared failure level of performance (Lopes 1987; March and Shapira 1992). Such a change in focus is most likely when the performance is very low, and an experiment has indeed shown that threat rigidity occurred for very low levels of performance while problemistic search occurred for performance just below the aspiration level (Lant and Hurley 1999).

The curve in figure 3.2(b) thus is most consistent with the theory of performance feedback interpreted by aspiration levels. This curve is characterized by two properties: (1) decline in the probability of change when the performance increases, both above and below the aspiration level; and (2) higher sensitivity above the aspiration level, as the decline in probability of change is more rapid then. The second property gives the curve a kink – a change in the slope – at the aspiration level. Finding this kinked-curve relation in empirical data is a strong confirmation of the theory because it shows that the aspiration level changes the behavior by modifying the relation from performance to organizational change.[4]

In empirical studies, the kinked-curve relation can be tested against a variety of alternative relations. The most fundamental test is against the traditional null hypothesis of no effect, that is, a horizontal relation from performance to change. This is tested by examining whether the estimated slopes above and below the aspiration level are below zero. It is possible for inertial forces to be so strong that the relation is horizontal below the aspiration level; in such cases the organization does not react differently to different levels of losses. A second important test is whether the curve really has a kink, that is, whether it declines more rapidly above the aspiration level than below it. This is tested by examining whether the estimated slopes above and below the aspiration level are significantly different from each other. It is possible for the response curve to decline at the same rate above and below the aspiration level, and in such cases it would be hard to argue that the aspiration level is behaviorally important.

Figure 3.3 shows one way to interpret the slopes in figure 3.2(b). In this figure, the hypothesized relation is shown by a solid line, and dotted reference lines are drawn to illustrate how the causal factors influence the response to performance feedback. As before, the horizontal axis is the performance with the aspiration level set to the origin, and the vertical axis is the probability or extent of organizational change. The horizontal

---

[4] I have tried to discuss the curves without using mathematical jargon, but should clarify three terms. Figures 3.2(b)–3.2(d) are continuous, which simply means that all points are connected. Put more formally, at all points the limit of the function taken from the right is the same as the limit taken to the left. Figure 3.2(a) "jumps", so it is not continuous. Figures 3.2(b) and 3.2(d) are kinked, which means that the slope changes at the aspiration level. Put more formally, they are non-differentiable at the aspiration level, which means that the right derivative and left derivative are different. Figure 3.2(d) is also non-homogeneous (it goes up and down). I'll refrain from giving the formal definition of homogeneity since it is likely to be confusing.

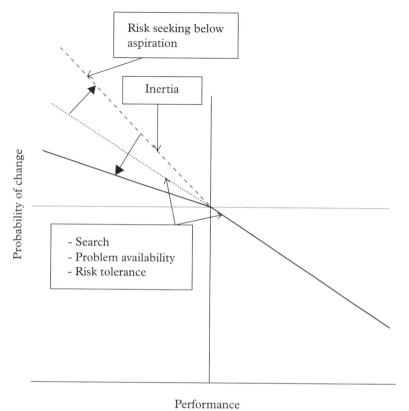

Performance

Figure 3.3 Determinants of response to performance feedback

dotted line represents a relation where there is no effect of performance on change. The three processes of organizational search, increased availability of problems in the decision-making process, and increased tolerance of risk when the performance is low rotate the curve so that the probability of change increases when the performance is lower, as shown by the two arrows and the dotted line that decreases to the right. This line is also different than the hypothesized relation, however, because of two additional effects. The greater risk taking below the aspiration level predicted by risk theory twists the curve up below the aspiration level, yielding the upper dotted line to the left of the origin. Organizational inertia partially cancels out the greater probability of changing when the performance is low, twisting the curve back down and yielding the solid line to the left of the origin. Thus, organizational search, problem-solution matching and increased risk tolerance cause the declining curve, and the aspiration-level effect on risk taking and organizational inertia cause the kink in the curve.

The timing problem

Before describing how these processes affect organizational behaviors, a problem of timing should be discussed. The basic drivers of organizational change in response to performance feedback are the processes of organizational search, availability of problems, and tolerance of risk. It would be easier to show that performance feedback affects organizational change if these processes operated at similar speed, but unfortunately we cannot assume that they do. It seems clear that changes in risk tolerance can happen very rapidly, and indeed may have nearly instant and perhaps temporary effects. Risk tolerance is affected by the current performance and aspiration level, and the effect is strongest at the moment when performance feedback becomes available and is discussed in the organization. As risk research has shown, such framing effects are highly context-specific and unstable. They may not linger in the mind of the decision maker for long. The availability of problems can also have rapid effects since a decision can be made as soon as a solution is matched with a performance problem. Organizational decision theory argues that problem availability depends on the timing of organizational agendas and decision-making routines, as problems need to be raised at the appropriate decision-making occasion in order to result in decisions (Cohen, March, and Olsen 1972). Thus, organizations with highly formalized and rigid decision-making procedures may show delayed responses to the availability of performance problems.

The most problematic process is organizational search, as some search processes, such as research and development, can be very lengthy. Depending on the technology used, the usual duration of R&D projects ranges from one to ten years (Jelinek and Schoonhoven 1990; Nichols 1994).[5] Other search processes may be quick. R&D projects that have been completed but not launched as products are found in many organizations with productive R&D departments and risk-averse top management, and can quickly become proposed solutions to low performance. Also, when managers search for generic solutions such as currently popular management practices (Abrahamson 1991) or industry recipes (Spender 1989), short response times can be achieved. Radio stations made format changes within a year after experiencing low performance,

---

[5] The ten-year figure is from pharmaceuticals, but is seen in some projects of other industries as well. Honda's walking robot project Asimo has lasted ten years at the time of writing, and has resulted in a prototype capable of going up and down stairs and slopes but no product announcement.

which may have been possible because the managers could easily find alternative formats based on their knowledge of about two dozen well-established formats and four innovative formats that diffused through the population of radio stations during the study (Greve 1998a, 1998b).

A possible consequence of the varying lags of search processes is that organizations initially show generic responses to low performance, such as the currently popular downsizing programs (Budros 1997), but later show more differentiated responses such as innovations created through research and development. Differentiated responses will occur if the generic responses fail to improve the performance, causing the search process to restart. Another possible consequence is that research and development processes can be initiated by low performance but not result in innovation launches until after the search process has been completed *and* the organization experiences low performance again. Organizations may store innovations whose implementation gets rejected during periods of high performance, and re-examine them for possible launching when low performance occurs again.

The timing problem suggests that we should think of the effect of low performance on organizations as being similar to the effect of dropping a stone into water. The result is not a single response but multiple waves of responses. These waves start at the point of impact and spread outwards. If a second stone is dropped, the effect of the first may be canceled out or amplified, depending on the timing and point of impact. Similarly, organizations may respond to performance problems quickly with proximate or generic solutions. They may also respond later, with more distant solutions, but the effect of low performance is less the further away it is temporally and organizationally. Additional performance problems may distract the attention of management from the original problem or may reinforce the push for change. The potentially widespread effect of performance feedback means that it is easy to argue that performance feedback is important for the organization, but it can sometimes be hard to predict exactly when and how the organization will respond.

3.3   Aspiration levels and adaptation

Is it helpful or harmful for organizations that managers use performance feedback and aspiration levels to manage change? As noted earlier, historical and social aspiration levels have some good forecasting properties, since they correctly incorporate effects of organizational and environmental factors, respectively. They also have biases. Historical aspiration levels track the actual performance of the organization, and thus may let the aspiration level lose alignment with what is actually achievable in a given environment. Both positive and negative deviations are possible, each with consequences that could be maladaptive. Too high aspiration levels cause unnecessary change, and too low aspiration levels prevent timely responses to problems. Social aspiration levels ignore how the organization differs from other organizations, and may become almost irrelevant for organizations that differ greatly from other organization or decision makers who have dissimilar organizations in their reference group. This can also cause the aspiration level to lose alignment with what the organization can achieve. The consequences are the same as for misaligned historical performance levels: unnecessary and possibly harmful change, or failure to change when necessary.

Simulation studies have examined the effect of aspiration-level learning on outcomes such as wealth and survival. Herriott, Levinthal, and March (1985) analyzed a model of organizations allocating resources between two activities with unequal expected rewards but variable actual rewards. The simulated rewards changed over time through competition, learning-by-doing, and stochastic variation, just as the returns to different products would for an actual organization. The resource allocation decisions were implicitly risky because the potential profits from each activity and the competition from others caused organizational performance to depend on the choice of activity. Herriott, Levinthal, and March (1985) examined the effects of both historical and social aspiration levels. Rapid adjustment of historical aspiration levels gave a high probability of specializing in the best alternative if the change in organizational allocations was slow, but a high probability of specializing in the inferior alternative if organizations rapidly changed their resource allocations. Social aspiration levels caused low specialization, as did imitation of the activities of others. The simulations showed that historical aspiration levels created more self-centered learning and thus greater variation among organizations, but this learning could lead to suboptimal resource allocations. On the other hand, social aspiration levels gave less specialized resource allocations and more similar resource allocations across organizations. Because spreading the resources over alternatives slows down learning-by-doing, the unspecialized resource allocations caused by social aspiration levels were less optimal than the specialized ones obtained by historical aspiration levels.

The choice between just two technologies was a limiting feature of the Herriot-Levinthal-March model. Later the model was generalized to involve a choice of searching for a new technology or investing in improving the old (Levinthal and March 1981). Historical updating of aspiration levels were used, and performance below the aspiration level caused reduced search for innovations and increased search for improvements. The reason for this search rule was the tendency for high performance to give organizational slack, which makes innovations more likely, while problemistic search follows failure and gives local improvements. It should be noted that the prediction of more innovations when performance is high contradicts current risk theory, which would suggest that risk aversion above the aspiration level point prevents adoption of risky innovations. The simulations showed that the model leads to mixes of search for innovations and improvements rather than specialization in one, and the mix was close to the optimal value. The adaptive aspiration level was very important in determining the performance of organizations since performance influenced search choices so strongly. Aspiration levels that quickly adjusted to the recent performance gave the highest performance because such quick aspiration-level adjustment created subjective failures that caused the organization to continue searching for improvements.

An important feature of the Levinthal-March model was that the organization could observe the benefits of the innovative technology (with some error) before implementing it, and thus could avoid adopting a new technology that was worse than the current. In a study of radio stations changing their market differentiation strategies, I found that the performance after the change showed regression to the mean, suggesting that the managers were choosing strategies under high uncertainty and were likely to choose worse strategies if their current strategy was good (Greve 1999). Because a study of performance feedback on the same data had suggested that historical aspiration levels were adjusted slowly (Greve 1998b), I became interested in simulating an environment with a risk of performance-reducing changes. Such an environment might give selection pressures towards slow updating of the aspiration level instead of the fast updating shown by Levinthal and March (1981). A simulation model with the same reactions to performance feedback as the empirical estimates but varying speed of aspiration level updating showed that slow updating of historical aspiration levels allowed organizations to change at more appropriate times (Greve 2002). This resulted in selection pressures in favor of slow updaters, who significantly increased their proportion of the population when each period had a high failure rate or the replacement of organizations was in proportion to their performance. Under other conditions, the selection worked too slowly to affect the composition of the population.

These models did not explicitly consider risk, though they implicitly included risk through the specification of the stochastic search and performance functions. March (1988) analyzed a model of risk taking where the level of risk depended on the ratio of the aspiration level and the wealth of the decision maker. He used a historical aspiration level and accumulated wealth as the goal variable. This model had a linear adjustment of risk instead of a kinked curve, so very low performance would yield very high risk levels. When the aspiration level adjustment

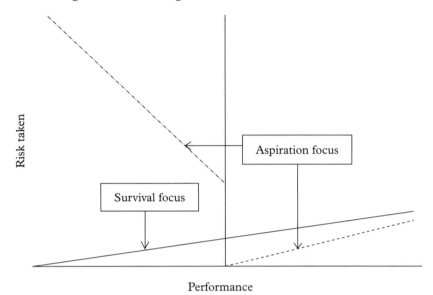

Figure 3.4 Risk as a function of cumulative resources
Source: March and Shapira (1992). Copyright © 1992 the American
Psychological Association. Adapted with permission.

was gradual, this model gave low risk levels for decision makers who had
experienced an increase in wealth and high risk levels for decision makers
who had experienced a decrease in wealth. The adjustment of the aspiration level led to risk-taking levels that gave higher rates of ruin (all wealth
spent) than a fixed aspiration level, but it also gave greater total wealth.
Thus adjusting the risk level by performance feedback and historical aspiration levels is a good strategy for a population of risk takers, but some
individuals will go broke following this strategy.

   A model of risk taking with a shifting focus between a survival point and
an aspiration level was examined by March and Shapira (1992). In this
model, the decision maker adjusted the risk level to give a fixed probability
of an outcome in excess of the focal point, which was either survival
or a historical aspiration level with an upward bias. If the performance
was expressed as the total accumulated resources, this model gave risk
preferences such as those depicted in figure 3.4. The acceptable risk
level gradually increased above each of the two goals of survival and
aspirations, reflecting the lower probability of falling below each goal
when the resources increase. The acceptable risk level increased below the
aspiration level, reflecting the greater risks necessary to bring resources
back to the aspiration level.

Simulations of this model showed that the adjustment of the aspiration level was very important for the risk taking. As in the previous models, rapid adjustment of the aspiration level generated failures that increased risk taking. If social aspiration levels were added to the model, the risk taking also increased. Since risk taking directly influenced the probability of survival, this lead to a selection process that removed quick adjusters of the aspiration level at a higher rate than slow adjusters. When the focus of the risk taker randomly shifted between the aspiration-level point and the survival point, the total risk taking and survival also depended on the probability that either of these would be the focus of attention. The risk taking resulting from mixing these two foci was always intermediate to the risk taking resulting from using just one of them, so an even mix of the two foci meant that there were no levels of performance where the risk taking was low. As one might expect, such even shifting of focus resulted in greater risk taking than an exclusive focus on survival or on aspiration levels, and thus greater failure risk. A non-random rule shifting the focus to the nearest goal would have yielded higher survival rates.

When risk takers using different rules were pitted against each other in competition, March and Shapira (1992) found that the survival rule did well under conditions where the competing rules gave too high risk levels, such as when failed organizations were replaced by new ones in proportion to the number of each form in the population and social aspiration levels with an upward bias were used. The conditions that favored an aspiration level focus seem more general, however, since aspiration levels did well when replacement was in proportion to the resources accumulated by each form or when historical adjustment of aspiration levels were used.

These simulation models differ in a number of details, reflecting the researchers' wish to emphasize some features of the learning process and market environment over others. Naturally, the conclusions from the models also differ in some details, but they agree on the main conclusion: adaptive aspiration levels can improve organizations under a wide range of conditions. Choice between two alternative technologies, search for either incremental improvements or radical innovations, and choice of risk levels all give broad conditions where aspiration levels that adjust to the experience of the organization (and sometimes, its competitors) give high performance and survival chances. There are also conditions where adjusting the aspiration level causes problems, such as when too quick adjustment gives high risk levels or too great focus on incremental search. Variation in the parameters of aspiration level adjustment seems to give sufficient difference in performance and survival that environmental selection might push the rules used in a population of organizations towards robust rules that give a high chance of survival. These are not necessarily the rules that are strongest in the long term, because short-term survival can be traded against long-term efficiency. Nor are organizational selection processes so efficient that an improved rule necessarily defeats an entrenched rule (Carroll and Harrison 1994).

The rules favor experimentation and risk taking to different degrees, and these tendencies affect the adaptiveness of the rules. The most appropriate rule in a given situation depends on how the environment rewards experimentation. Environments where organizational changes give positive rewards on average favor failure-generating rules such as upward social adjustment of the aspiration level or quick historical adjustment of the aspiration level, but environments where the rewards have regression toward the mean favor conservative rules such as slow historical adjustment of the aspiration level. These contingencies aside, environments penalize rules where experimentation is not adjusted by the performance.

3.4   How goal variables are chosen

So far I have described the interpretation and reaction to performance on a given goal. I have assumed that the organizational members know what the goal variable is and how to measure performance on it, but not how to interpret different levels of performance along a goal variable. This is the core of the theory and the situation usually faced by organizational decision makers. It is not, however, the whole theory of goals in organizations. Behind it lies a larger agenda of goal selection, goal acceptance, and goal attention that also has to be included among the problems that managers face when seeking to learn from performance feedback. The reason is that goals are no more nature-given than aspiration levels are – organizational goals are constructed by managers and assigned to other managers or workers. They in turn construct their own goals that may differ from the assigned ones. Even if top managers announce that profitability is important and assign goal variables such as return on assets, sales managers may still believe that market share is more important. Sometimes they are encouraged to do so through evaluation and incentive systems that reward sales managers for sales and other functional managers for their functional goals, leaving top management to worry about how these subunit goals all add up to profitability (Andrews 1971; March and Simon 1958). The process of selecting goals for the whole organization or a unit of the organization is a complex mixture of precedence, politics, payoffs, and proselytizing. Goals define the character and strategic direction of the organization (Selznick 1957), so the stakes are high.

Goals are an integral part of the firm's strategy. A classic definition states "strategy is the pattern of decisions in a company that determines and reveals its objectives, purposes, or goals...and the nature of the economic and noneconomic contribution it intends to make to its shareholders, employees, customers, and communities" (Andrews 1980: 18). Within the theory and practice of strategy, goals are found in two forms. One is a firm's mission, which is often is phrased in terms of how its products and services benefit society. For example, the pharmaceutical firm Eli Lilly has the mission posted on its top web page: "Eli Lilly and Company creates and delivers innovative medicines that enable people to live longer, healthier and more active lives." On its web page, DaimlerChrysler announces its intention of "Harnessing our expertise, energy, experience and global resources...to build the best cars, trucks and buses." The other form of goal is a firm's "numbers," a variety of commonly accepted measures of success along such dimensions as profitability and size. The web page of Eli Lilly contains numbers indicating its size, profitability, and investment in research. DaimlerChrysler posts accounting and stock data prominently, as do other automakers such as GM and Ford. Indeed, I quoted DaimlerChrysler's mission because I could not easily locate the mission statements of the two other automakers when going through their web pages in November 2001.

A quick check of how firms present themselves to others will suggest that "numbers" goals are currently more widespread than mission goals. The mission concept is actually the older of the two, and has long been an integral part of teaching in strategy (Andrews 1971). It was weakened during the 1960s as firms grew to conglomerates and used the "numbers" through portfolio-planning techniques to evaluate what their mission should be (Fligstein 1990). The see-saw pattern of mergers, acquisitions, and divestitures displayed by many firms since then has been driven largely by financial goals, and suggests that firms are much more flexible in their choice of activities than the concept of mission suggests (Davis, Diekmann, and Tinsley 1994; Fligstein 1990). Often activities are changed in response to low performance along financial goals, but firms that have seemingly arbitrary groupings of activities are likely to refocus around a mission that is easier to justify (Zuckerman 2000). Thus, firms experience ongoing negotiations among mission and "numbers" based conceptions of strategy. There are also ongoing negotiations about which numbers should count, which involve a struggle among managers with different functional backgrounds, such as accounting, marketing, and finance, for the use of goal variables that they are trained to favor (Fligstein 1990). Firm goals are clearly contentious.

The many actors who can negotiate over firm goals include owners, board members, managers, workers, the state, and lobby groups (Freeman and McVea 2001). Organizational theory has particularly emphasized negotiations among managers of different organizational subunits, because they have direct access to the organization's decision-making process and resources (Cyert and March 1963; Pfeffer and Salancik 1978). Although the main participants of the process are managers, actors outside the organization also influence the negotiation. They can provide managerial rhetoric in favor of specific goals (Barley and Kunda 1992; Fligstein 1990; J. W. Meyer 1994) and give resources to organizations that pay attention to goals that they favor (Pfeffer and Salancik 1978). Managers acting on behalf of themselves or their organizational subunits can thus become agents of environmental actors that have transactions with that subunit (Pfeffer and Salancik 1978) or can provide justification for it (Dobbin et al. 1993; Edelman 1990).

The theory of the dominant coalition (Cyert and March 1963) was discussed in section 2.1 and can help us understand how the negotiation process works. It states that goals are negotiated with the prior agreement as an anchor, managers with direct access to the decision-making process as the main actors, and the environment providing problems, rhetoric, and resources that can be used by managers in the negotiation process. The result is an agreement not too different from the previous one, but adjusted towards emphasizing the goals of actors who have gained power since the last round of negotiation (Boeker 1989a; Cyert and March 1963; Ocasio and Kim 1999; Pfeffer and Salancik 1978). The agreement is likely to involve multiple goal variables, with some serving as constraints and others as variables to maximize. Thus, firms have multiple goals of unequal importance. The most important goals are usually attended to, and managers shift attention among less important goals depending on which goal is in danger of not being met. Shifting attention can be viewed as a self-regulation mechanism that emphasizes problem solving over the pursuit of opportunities. This view of shifting attention is similar to the view of aspiration levels as diagnostic tools for discovering problems. Shifting attention also has a political aspect, however, since failure to fulfill goals that are important to some coalition members can force a renegotiation of the dominant coalition, which may destabilize the organization. This threat shifts the incentives so that over-fulfilling a given goal is far less valuable than reaching another goal that is in danger of not being met.

The choice of certain goals by the dominant coalition of an organization is not the end of the story. Just as the degree of goal acceptance is an important variable in explaining whether an individual member of an organization will react to his or her performance on that goal variable (Locke 1978; Locke, Latham, and Erez 1988), so is the degree of goal acceptance by a subunit manager important in explaining whether the subunit will act according to the organizational goals given to them. This is sometimes treated as a problem of agreement implementation. It is easy to show that managers are more sensitive to actual rewards than to stated goals (Kerr 1975), so much energy is spent designing incentive systems that are aligned with goals (Milgrom and Roberts 1992; Tosi and Gomez-Mejia 1989; Wiseman and Gomez-Mejia 1998). Incentive systems treat goal acceptance as a problem of designing side payments to managers that ensure compliance with the goals of the dominant coalition. Pay for performance is essentially a form of side payment where members of the organization are directly compensated for performance along a goal variable, which presumably is different from the goals that they would have pursued without pay for performance. Pay for performance is increasingly used for both managers and other categories of employees (Ledford, Lawler, and Mohrman 1995; Useem 1996).

Critics of the implementation perspective do not doubt that side payments affect individual behaviors, but take issue with their effectiveness relative to other techniques such as socializing new members and maintaining an organizational culture focused on specific goals (Pfeffer 1997). Socialization means that new members of the organization are subjected to experiences that instill a feeling of commitment to the organization's goals (Pascale 1985). It relies on techniques that trigger psychological processes leading to commitment (Cialdini 1993). For example, an onerous selection process will cause new employees to commit to the organization as a way of justifying their investment in being selected, immersion in the organization isolates them from other opinions, and group training creates a community feeling among the new employees and fertile ground for using group influence tactics to make them accept goals (Pfeffer 1997). Some firms make extensive use of socialization to achieve goal acceptance.

Socialization of new workers can be combined with practices that reinforce traditions, shared meanings, and values among existing workers to create organizational cultures focused around certain organizational goals (Ebers 1995; Kunda 1992). Seemingly small decisions can be imbued with cultural meaning. A software firm that lets workers decorate their cubicles as they wish is sending signals that individuality is welcome, and also suggesting that the cubicle is similar to home and thus a place where they might stay all day. Allowing futons in the cubicle, as some Silicon Valley firms do, reinforces both of these messages. Socialization into organizational cultures does affect commitment to goals and values, as well as other variables such as satisfaction, so it clearly is an alternative way of making employees pursue given goals (Ashford and Saks 1996; Chatman 1991; O'Reilly and Chatman 1986). Because it is done through a set of techniques that impose few limitations on what goals can be taught, it is a flexible method. It is effective only when members of the dominant coalition can agree on a small set of consistent goals, however, so socialization fails in organizations where the goals are in dispute (Meyerson and Martin 1987).

The mechanisms used to imbue managers with goals can fail to work as intended, leading to low goal acceptance. Two kinds of behaviors are likely to follow. The first is that the subunit members will pursue their own interests instead of the assigned subunit goals or organizational goals (Boeker 1989b; Hooks 1990; Selznick 1948). This is likely to reduce the impact of the assigned goals on search and risk-taking, resulting in inertia through obstruction of change attempts (Hannan and Freeman 1977). Such behaviors may be quite frequent in organizations, and are an important reason that the theory earlier in the chapter predicted a kinked curve effect of performance feedback on organizational change. Second, subunit members who do not accept the assigned goals are likely seek changes in goals, and will attempt to break into the dominant coalition. This can cause the balance of power inside the organization to shift when environmental conditions favor organizational subunits that have been left out of the goal-setting process (Boeker 1989b; Boeker and Goodstein 1991; Fligstein 1990; Pfeffer and Salancik 1978). Even unsuccessful attempts to overthrow the dominant coalition are likely to slow down its pursuit of goals.

These arguments suggest that organizational compliance with official goals can become partial, and that the goals themselves may shift over time. This point is useful to keep in mind when examining research on performance feedback, but it is uncertain exactly how far one can draw implications from it. The reason is that the organizational units least willing to comply with assigned goals are the ones left out of the dominant coalition. Because participation in the dominant coalition is a result of high subunit power, the units with low willingness to comply may also have low ability to resist changes imposed on them, suggesting that they are "vulnerable areas" (Cyert and March 1963: 122) in the organization where changes are particularly likely to happen in response to problemistic search. Willingness to comply and ability to resist thus give opposing predictions on where organizational change will occur.

The concept of shifting attention among goals can be taken even further than the theory of the dominant coalition suggests. According to the theory of the dominant coalition, attention will shift among the goals held by members of the dominant coalition, but other goals will not be considered. One step beyond this theory would be to suggest that any variable appearing in the organizational reporting system could potentially become a goal. Managerial attention may be drawn to one goal or the other depending on the vagaries of organizational routines for reporting results, discussing their implications, and evaluating alternatives (Cohen, March, and Olsen 1972; Cyert and March 1963; Levitt and Nass 1989; Ocasio 1997). March (1994) referred to organizational reports as "magic numbers" because of their ability to draw the attention of managers and set the context for problem solving (15–18). It is clear that organizational routines for reporting performance have powerful effects on managerial attention and decision making. Part of the case for the importance of accounting measures of performance rests on such attention processes, as budgeting and reporting routines ensure that these measures are periodically discussed and taken as summaries of the state of the firm. We know little about what types of other goals may become salient through this process.

A second step beyond the theory of the dominant coalition is to let events in the environment draw managerial attention to new goals. This can happen because events in the environment alert managers to interdependencies with other actors that they were not aware of, or because external advocacy groups campaign to have the organization recognize their goals (Daft and Weick 1984; Dutton and Dukerich 1991; Hoffman and Ocasio 2001). For example, firms now pay attention to the labor management practices of subcontractors in developing countries as a result of news reports on sweatshops with horrid work conditions and pressure from organized labor (Bernstein 2001). Researchers implicitly recognize the role of the environment when entering variables indicating major environmental events into models explaining organizational changes without emphasizing the implications of such models. More work on the interplay between the routine attention to goals embedded in the organizational reporting system and such external claims for attention seems needed (Ocasio 1997).

The process of determining organizational goals and ensuring acceptance of these goals is complex. One may wonder whether all this potential maneuvering and resistance predicts less stability in goals over time and similarity of goals across organizations than what is observed. Maybe the answer is that not all the potential conflict materializes. Many organizations are going concerns where longtime use of goal-enforcing mechanisms has led members to take the goals for granted. The full-scale contention over goals depicted by coalition and incentive theories may be characteristics of recently established organizations and organizations in deep crisis (Stinchcombe 1965).

4   Applications

The theory of performance feedback developed in the previous chapter can be used to understand when and how organizations change their structures and behaviors. According to the theory, performance relative to the aspiration level affects organizational search, risk taking, and change. This broad impact makes performance a "master switch" that controls a range of organizational responses to problems. Because so many kinds of organizational changes involve search and risk taking, we can examine each form of change individually and compare it with others. The theory poses few limitations on what behaviors can change in response to performance feedback, so we expect rather similar results when studying different forms of organizational change. If the results differ, they should do so in ways that the theory predicts. For example, the role of organizational search and risk-taking in the theory suggests that performance will predict strategic changes better than everyday activities. The role of inertia in the kinked-curve relation suggests that this curve should be seen for major organizational changes, such as changes in market strategy or organizational technology. It is less likely for changes in peripheral parts of the organization, where inertia is lower.

Most organizational changes require that managers search for solutions and are willing to accept risk. This means that we cannot separate the effects of performance on search and risk as cleanly as we would like, but comparison of different types of change can yield useful insights. In this chapter, we will look at research on organizational risk taking, R&D expenditures, innovations, facility investment, and strategic change. The two first outcomes can be viewed as nearly pure risk and search, respectively, while the rest involve a mixture of search and risk. All are strategic changes that cause long-term commitment of resources and have long-term effects on the competitiveness of the organization. They are important organizational changes, but other changes are also important and could be studied from the viewpoint of this theory. Change of CEO or acquisition of another firm are examples of strategic changes that could have been examined from the viewpoint of this theory, but are omitted here because little work has been done. They are opportunities left for future research.

4.1   Risk taking

Managerial attitudes to risk are determined both by the general psychological mechanisms discussed in section 2.2 and by the selection, socialization, and experience of managers. Unlike most people, managers frequently make risky decisions with high monetary stakes. They also learn risk attitudes and behaviors from other managers, either by observing and modeling their behavior or from more active teaching. Risk taking increases at higher levels of management, as high-level managers show both greater propensity to take risks (MacCrimmon and Wehrung 1986) and greater inclination to encourage others to take risks (March and Shapira 1987) than low-level managers do. Managers also distinguish clearly between personal and professional risk taking, and take greater risks when making decisions on behalf of their organization than when making decisions on their own finances (MacCrimmon and Wehrung 1986). Clearly, managerial risk taking is consequential for organizations and different from personal risk taking, so it is of interest to study how managers perceive and take risks. Here I will briefly discuss two questions: how managers differ from other individuals and how their risk taking is affected by performance. Books on managerial risk taking are available for readers who are interested in additional details (MacCrimmon and Wehrung 1986; Shapira 1994; Vertzberger 2000).

Managerial risk perceptions and behavior

The first question is how managerial risk taking differs from that of other decision makers. A good start is two studies that presented the same risk problems to either undergraduate students or managers, allowing direct comparison of the responses (Payne, Laughhunn, and Crum 1980; 1981). The studies followed a common procedure in experimental study of risk. Respondents were given a choice between risky prospects with equal expected value but unequal variance, and choosing high-variance prospects indicated a preference for risk. Addition of a constant was used to shift the expected value of the prospects above and below a zero reference point to look for an aspiration-level effect on the risk preference. The managers and students were given the same prospects except that those given to the managers were multiplied by $100,000, giving a range of +/−$8,600,000 for them and +/−$86 for the students. The greater stakes might be expected to increase risk aversion for the managers, but instead a greater proportion of managers chose the risky prospects when asked to choose among pairs of uncertain prospects in the gain domain. Except for this difference, the risk preferences were similar. Managers and students alike showed a greater preference for the risky option in the loss domain, and for these prospects the probabilities were remarkably similar for managers and students. Thus, managers take more risks for gains, but similar risks for losses.

Asking subjects to choose among predetermined alternatives gives evidence of risk preferences, but choosing from a list of alternatives is just one element of managerial risk behavior. Two in-depth studies of managerial risk perceptions and behaviors provide more detail on how managers approach risk (MacCrimmon and Wehrung 1986; Shapira 1994). Shapira (1994) interviewed and surveyed high-level managers on how they approach risks, and found that the most distinctive feature of the responses was their denial of taking risks. The managers reported that their business was to control and reduce the odds of adverse outcomes, not to accept the risks as given to them. The methods for reducing risks varied from simply revising risk estimates to structuring transactions and contracts to divide risks between the organization and its subcontractors and other transaction partners. MacCrimmon and Wehrung (1986) used a questionnaire to investigate how managers reacted to realistic business scenarios involving risk. They found that collection of information, negotiation with actors controlling the risk, and delay or delegation of decisions were important risk-reduction strategies.

The strategies for reducing risk described by these managers are potentially effective, but the managers' claim of having eliminated risk does not seem realistic. It is likely that the managers' perception of risk is susceptible to illusion of control, whereby events that are actually outside their control are perceived as controllable. Illusion of control is common among decision makers with experience in a given situation, because experience with successfully controlling some elements of a situation can cause them to incorrectly infer that other elements are also controllable (Langer 1975). Managers who structure contracts to divide and reduce risk display considerable skill and experience, and they may be prone to generalize this skill element to uncontrollable risk factors as well. Thus, managers react to risk both by exerting real control over risk and by having an illusion of control over the uncontrollable component of risk.

When asked about the decisions that they would take in hypothetical situations of gain and loss, the managers' responses were similar to other decision makers (Shapira 1994). Risk taking was lowest just above the aspiration level and increased slightly in the success region, which reflects normal risk aversion in the domain of gains. In the domain of losses, the average level of risk taking increased, as prospect theory would predict, but this average was generated by a wide range of responses with some managers increasing risks and others preferring unchanged or decreased risks. MacCrimmon and Wehrung (1986) also found wide variation in risk-taking among executives in each of their four decision scenarios. They found highest risk-taking in the scenario involving only large losses, highest risk aversion in the scenario involving only gains, and intermediate risk-taking in two scenarios involving smaller losses. These responses suggest that executives try to avoid losses, and are willing to take considerable risk in return for the hope of getting a positive outcome. Losses are deeply unpopular, even if they are small. The dispersion of risk preferences also seemed to be greater for the scenarios involving losses. Both studies thus produced findings consistent with the risk-seeker/risk-avoider responses reviewed in section 2.2 (Schneider and Lopes 1986). Risk seekers increase the risks taken in the domain of losses while risk avoiders experience a conflict between the goals of avoiding losses and reaching the aspiration level, and show a variety of responses depending on how these goals are weighted.

A useful way of thinking about managerial risk taking is that managers focus on the probability of reaching a performance above an aspiration level, but also consider the probability of disastrous losses that threaten the survival of the firm (March and Shapira 1987). If the goal variable is the total accumulated resources, a dual focus on aspiration and survival will lead to risk preferences such as those depicted in figure 3.4. The acceptable risk level will gradually increase above each of the two goals of survival and aspirations, reflecting the lower probability of falling below each goal when the resources increase. The acceptable risk level will increase below the aspiration level, reflecting the greater risks necessary to bring resources back to the aspiration level. As a result, the aspiration and survival foci of attention lead to conflicting risk preferences everywhere, but the conflict is greatest when the decision maker is below the aspiration level. This model seems to fit well with the conflict between escalating and reducing risks seen in managerial risk preferences and with the conflict between escalating and reducing risks in organizations whose survival is threatened (Wiseman and Bromiley 1996).

To show that this dual foci model of risk taking is correct, the best kind of evidence would be that managers at a given (low) level of performance take greater risk if they focus on the aspiration level. This is exactly what was found in a recent experimental study of evening MBA students with extensive managerial experience (Mullins, Forlani, and Walker 1999). Subjects focusing on the aspiration level took greater risks than subjects focusing on the survival level. The researchers also found that greater risks

were taken by managers who attributed the outcomes of earlier investment decisions to their managerial control, as predicted by the illusion of
control. In that study, the alternatives were presented to the subjects as
probability distributions symmetric around the aspiration level with different dispersion of outcomes, giving no reason for the subjects to believe
that they actually controlled the outcomes.

One experiment examined risk taking in a group negotiation over prices
for goods with uncertain value (Schurr 1987). Groups negotiated face-
to-face with other groups, and could choose from a wide level of risk
levels. Such group negotiation over the division of an uncertain reward
is a very realistic task for organizations, and especially since one experiment used professional purchasing managers whose work includes such
negotiations. The findings show greater risk taking in negotiations over
losses than over gains, as other studies have found. Managers and MBA
students showed only minor differences in risk-taking behavior. A similar
experiment on students reproduced the finding of greater risk taking in
negotiations over losses and showed clearly that the effect was caused by
different risk preferences about the final outcome, not by reluctance to
make concessions in the bargaining process (Bottom 1998). Both studies
reproduced findings known from pen-and-paper studies in quite realistic
experimental settings.

The number of risk-taking studies on students and various professionals familiar with risk (such as managers and medical doctors) is now so
large that it is possible to judge how they differ in risk taking. A comprehensive meta-analysis of fifteen years of research on risk taking showed
no statistically significant difference between students and professionals:
both groups took greater risks below the aspiration level. The author
suggested, however, that students might be slightly more susceptible to
positive and negative framing (Kuehberger 1998). If it turns out to be true
that student preferences change more, the reason might be the greater
risk taking by managers in the domain of gains seen in some of the studies
reviewed earlier. If managers are less risk averse in the domain of gains
and become equally risk seeking in the domain of losses, the manipulation
of the aspiration level affects them less than it affects students.

Willingness to take risks is a value instilled in aspiring managers by their
seniors (March and Shapira 1987), and this socialization seems to work.
Managers take greater risks when acting as managers than when making
private decisions. One study asked managers to choose options in simulated business decisions, simulated personal decisions involving large
amounts of money, and real bets for moderate amounts of money (expected value $10, range $-$274$ to $+$414$) (MacCrimmon and Wehrung
1986). The findings were clear. First, managers often picked high-risk

alternatives in business situations, especially when choosing between a sure loss and a bet between zero and a larger loss. Second, managers chose moderate levels of risk in both types of personal decisions, picking bets over the sure payout in the betting situation and taking risky investments (but not the riskiest) in the investment situation. Although the responses to the investment decisions showed a somewhat higher propensity to risk than non-managers have, the results suggest that managers acting as managers take more risks than managers acting as individuals. This may be because the managers enact the normatively approved risk-taker role in work-related decisions, but not in private decisions (March and Shapira 1987).

Managers also appear to be highly sensitive to context when making risky choices. A study comparing the risk taking of each individual across several private and business choices found that the level of risk taking differed so greatly across situations that it was not meaningful to characterize individual managers as general risk takers or risk averters (MacCrimmon and Wehrung 1986). Dividing the choices into the business and personal domain increased the consistency in each domain and showed that the greatest consistency was found inside the personal domain of risk taking. Within each domain, the responses to situations involving mostly gains differed from the responses to situations involving mainly losses, as one would expect from the use of zero (no gain or loss) as an aspiration level. The conclusion is that managers are sensitive to the context of a risk-taking situation, and this sensitivity is related both to the domain of the risk and to the goals invoked by the situation.

The lower consistency of risk taking in business situations could be taken to imply that managers are less careful when making decisions on behalf of the organization. Although this interpretation is possible, it seems more likely that the inconsistency occurs because they apply experience with similar situations to the choices on the questionnaire. It is unlikely that a manager with experience with union negotiations, for example, will answer a question on a negotiation situation based only on the text of the question, without referring to his or her own experience. But since these experiences may have taught some managers to accommodate and others to confront the union, the answers to the question may reflect their specific track record on this type of problem more than their general risk preference. Thus, the consistency of responses is lower for business questions because managers answer based on their own varying experiences.

Organizational changes usually involve uncertainty that cannot easily be turned into fixed-probability bets, like those used in experiments. It is important to know not just how managers respond to prospects

with well-defined probabilities, but also to prospects where the probabilities of different outcomes have to be estimated. In general, people
are averse to such ambiguous probabilities and willing to forgo some
gains in order to avoid them (Camerer and Weber 1992). Little work has
been done on how managers approach ambiguous problems, but there is
some indication that they are less averse to them than the general public
(MacCrimmon 1986). This could be caused by a general relation between self-assessed competence and ambiguity aversion. Individuals prefer known probabilities to their own estimates in domains where they do
not feel competent, but prefer their own estimates in domains where they
feel competent (Heath and Tversky 1991). Thus, managers show low levels of ambiguity aversion in managerial tasks because they feel confident
in that domain. Shapira's (1994) finding that managers even denied that
their decisions were risky certainly suggests that they are very confident,
so this explanation seems to fit.

Organizational risk taking

The preceding studies used individual attitude measures that do not capture how managers determine organizational risk levels. The image of
the manager as a solitary decision maker may be accurate for some organizational decisions, but managers often need to consult, coordinate,
and negotiate before making risky decisions. Some decision-making rules
bar individual managers from taking risks exceeding certain levels, and
some risky decisions involve coordination even if risk per se can be taken
individually. Product launches, for example, are risky decisions that require coordination among functions such as production and marketing,
and thus lead to collective decision making. As the research on group
decision making in section 2.2 showed, the aggregation of individual
preferences into group decisions is not trivial. Fortunately, researchers
have also made advances on the issue of how organizational risk taking is
determined.

Singh (1986) made an organizational measure of risk by obtaining self-
assessed organizational risk taking from a survey of high-level managers
of sixty-four US corporations, and tested whether risk taking was influenced by performance and organizational slack. The latter variable examines the effect of slack search, and since slack and performance may be
correlated, the inclusion of both in a single model separates their effects
better than a model where one is omitted. In a model with several other
effects included, performance had the strongest effect on risk taking, and
slack had the second strongest. High performance decreased risk taking
and high slack increased it, consistent with the behavioral theory of the

firm and prior findings. Performance was measured both by a subjective measure of how the managers thought the organization performed relative to its competitors and by objective measures of return on net worth and return on assets. The objective measure of return on assets had the greatest weight in the model, which may be surprising since the subjective measure was phrased so that it included a social comparison. According to performance feedback theory, a measure of returns on assets relative to a social or historical aspiration level might have performed even better, but such measures were not made.

Self-reported risk taking is still somewhat subjective, but it is also possible to infer organizational risk taking from observation of actual decisions. Many researchers have found objective measures of organizational risk taking. A series of studies have analyzed how bank lending officers assessed the risk of loans and determined lending rates, thus giving direct measures of risk perceptions and risk tolerance (McNamara and Bromiley 1997, 1999; McNamara, Moon, and Bromiley 2001). They found that decision makers were averse to risk as they perceived it (McNamara and Bromiley 1999), which is consistent with experimental evidence (Weber and Milliman 1997). The risk perceptions were affected by the past performance of the same lender, however, so they were not stable over time. Lending officers appeared to underestimate the risk of lenders with low performance, so the shifting risk perception caused the actual risk taking to increase in response to low loan performance (McNamara, Moon, and Bromiley 2001). They did not take more risks when the performance of the branch they worked in decreased. Lending officers are fairly closely managed with individual goals, however, and the individual goals may have caused them to ignore the organizational goal (McNamara, Moon, and Bromiley 2001).

A study of the precision and spread of financial analyst estimates of firm performance found a creative way of exploring individual risk taking in organizations (Taylor and Clement 2000). Financial analysts take risks every time they release earnings estimates of the firms they follow, since they stake their reputation and career on good predictions of firm earnings. They may get fired for making estimates that turn out to be wrong (Hong, Kubik, and Solomon, 2000). They can, however, reduce the risk by keeping an eye on other analysts. Because analysts release their estimates one by one and know that they will not be blamed for incorrect estimates provided others also made the same mistake, estimates that diverge from other analysts' estimates are riskier than estimates that follow the crowd. Analysis of what caused analysts to give such risky estimates showed a clear increase in risk taking when performance was below the aspiration level: analysts who had been less precise than their peers did not adjust by conforming to others, but instead made additional risky estimates. This finding fits the prediction of risk theory very well.

A study of government bond traders also used a direct risk measure (Shapira 2000). When a trader takes a position in bonds, the risk exposure is proportional to the dollar value of the position multiplied by its duration. Analysis of how traders adjusted their positions showed a clear pattern of increasing the risk exposure in proportion to experienced losses. Most traders kept their risk exposure constant in response to gains, but one trader increased the exposure in proportion to gains (Shapira, 2000: Table 3). Bond traders, who operate in a fast-moving market with numerous transactions in a day, had a high pace of checking the value of their positions and updating their aspiration level, with the updating of aspiration levels appearing to vary from once a day (opening position) to once a trade (most recent position). It is consistent with the theory that decision makers who can choose how often to receive performance feedback elect to ask for it often.

Lending officers, analysts, and bond traders are individuals taking risk on behalf of the organizations, as managers are, and the risk taken by a single trader can be substantial (Shapira 2000). Thus, their risk behaviors are clearly relevant to organizational risk. Still, these employees are not engaged in the prototypical managerial tasks of communicating with and coordinating people and making decisions about long-range commitment of organizational resources. The risk-taking aspect of such everyday managerial decision making is difficult to study directly, but some indirect approaches have been tried.

Variance in income stream is a measure of overall firm risk. It has formed the core of an active area of research on the risk-return paradox. The risk-return paradox refers to the finding that firms with greater variances in income stream also have lower mean incomes, which is the opposite of what rational decision making and risk aversion would predict (Bowman 1980, 1982). Risk theories such as prospect theory and security-potential/aspiration theory would predict such a relation provided that the causal relation was from low income to greater risk taking and not from risk taking to low income. Since Bowman's (1980, 1982) studies were cross-sectional, they could not determine whether the relation was from income to risk or the other way around. He did provide additional evidence from analysis of annual reports showing that managers of low-performing firms were taking additional risks as a result of low performance (Bowman 1984).

Later work has supported these findings and demonstrated the causal relation more clearly (Bromiley, Miller, and Rau 2001). Increased risk taking after low performance has been shown in several multi-industry studies (Fiegenbaum and Thomas 1986; Gooding, Goel, and Wiseman 1996; Miller and Bromiley 1990), and is now an undisputed part of the empirical record. Additional work has shown the causal structure more clearly.

First, a difference in predictions has been resolved. The original risk-return paradox seemed to suggest that risk and returns were always negatively related, whereas risk theory predicts such a relation only in the domain of losses. In the domain of gains, risk and return is positively related if the choices are made according to prospect theory predictions. This is exactly what one study found; risk and returns were positively related for organizations performing above average and negatively related for organizations performing below average (Fiegenbaum and Thomas 1988). Similarly, Bromiley (1991b) found increased risk taking for firms that performed below their industry average.

Second, the choice of aspiration level has been examined. The original findings matched the predictions of risk theory exactly provided managers set the aspiration level equal to the mean performance of comparable firms so that below-mean performers were in the loss domain (Fiegenbaum 1990). This suggests that social comparison theory (section 2.2) provides a good model of how managers interpret organizational performance. They compare it with the performance of other organizations, concluding that it is low if it is below the industry average. Various models of aspiration levels have been used in work on firm risk taking, and studies have so far found support both for comparison of performance with other firms in the industry (Gooding, Goel, and Wiseman 1996) and with the past performance of the same firm (Lehner 2000).

One study measured risk as a loss potential rather than as variance in performance (Miller and Leiblein 1996) in order to align the measure of risk with managers' focus on avoiding losses (Shapira 1994). It also answered a methodological critique that has provoked controversy within the realm of risk-return studies (Bromiley 1991a; Ruefli, Collins, and Lacugna 1999; Ruefli and Wiggins 1994; Wiseman and Bromiley 1991). The critique is that risk measures incorporating high outcomes can produce statistical artifacts in studies of how risk affects performance (Ruefli 1990), and is peripheral to the present issue of how performance affects risk taking. Miller and Leiblein's (1996) concern with measuring how firms manage loss potential is of great interest, however, since the prediction is that managers will avoid the risk that they care about, that is, the risk of losing money rather than the risk of having exceptionally high performance in a given year. They found that performance relative to aspiration levels had a negative relation to subsequent risk, consistent with the theory and earlier findings. This was shown with a five-year lead time between independent and dependent variables, giving firms plenty of time to adjust their risk posture.

A study of aggregate risk taking in a broad sample of firms sought to test the March-Shapira model described earlier (Miller and Chen 2002). According to this model, managers can focus on either a survival point or an aspiration level, and should increase risk taking greatly when falling below the aspiration level, and increase it gradually when being above the survival and aspiration level. Accordingly, very low-performing firms and firms performing above the aspiration level should show a weakly positive relation from performance to risk taking, but firms below the aspiration level should show a strongly negative relation from performance to risk taking. The study found that risk taking declined when the organizational performance or assets increased in all three intervals, which is the opposite of the gradual increase in risk taking above the aspiration level predicted by the March-Shapira model. The finding is consistent with risk models that predict a decline in risk taking as performance increases, including the kinked-curve model derived in chapter 3.

An exception to the negative effect of performance on risk taking was found in a study of declining firms (Wiseman and Bromiley 1996). These firms, which were selected for study because they had experienced several years of declining sales, appeared to take greater risks when their performance increased, contrary to the prediction. The firms showed a tendency to increase risks when their asset value shrank, however, which the authors interpreted as evidence of risk-taking with assets as the goal variable. The argument is that for declining firms, assets are more important than performance since such firms are near bankruptcy. This argument resembles the suggestion that firms monitor both an aspiration level and a survival point (March and Shapira 1992). It is not quite the same, as getting closer to the survival point should reduce risk taking rather than increase it, as Wiseman and Bromiley (1996) found. Declining firms may turn out to have unusual risk-taking patterns.

Proposition P3 in section 3.2 stated that managers have a stronger preference for financially risky prospects when the organization performs below the aspiration level. The proposition is difficult to test directly, because we cannot easily combine the realism of organizational decisions with the strong method given by experimental control, nor can we easily prove that decisions that turn out to be risky were perceived that way when they were made. Indeed, some of the evidence reviewed earlier suggests that actual risk taking increases as a result of duller perception of risk rather than keener preference for risk (McNamara and Bromiley 1997; Weber and Milliman 1997). Keeping that caveat in mind, we can still conclude that the evidence reviewed in this section supports proposition P3 rather well. Greater risk taking in response to low performance was found in managerial responses to hypothetical decision-making scenarios, organizational decisions by individual professionals, and overall risk taking by organizations.

The evidence can best be read as a set of mutually reinforcing studies at the level of the organization and the decision maker. The last set of studies reviewed showed that organizations indeed take greater financial risks after experiencing performance below the aspiration level. To many, this is good enough proof of the proposition, but a skeptic may ask whether the managers knew what they were doing at the time of making the decision. Maybe the organizations with low performance have managers who are inept at estimating risk and who take additional risks in future periods because they are still inept at estimating risks, not because they intentionally increase risks. This is where research on the decisions of individual managers helps fill the gap in the evidence. Most studies show that managers deliberately raise their risk taking after low performance, but some studies suggest that they may also perceive risks differently after experiencing low performance. Conversely, critics of experimental studies measuring managerial decisions in low-stakes or no-stakes (hypothetical) bets may argue that managers are more careful when actual money is at stake. This is where the studies of organizational risk taking can be brought in to suggest that whole organizations show risk-taking patterns consistent with the experiments. It is possible that other mechanisms cause the same pattern of performance effects on risk to emerge at the individual and the organizational level, but it seems more natural to suggest that the same effect of low performance in different settings has the same cause.

Based on the evidence shown here, the risk-taking building-block of the theory of performance feedback seems to be secure. Proposition P3 is just one part of the theory, however, which also contains propositions on when organizations search more intensely and how the search and risk-taking interacts with organizational inertia. Next I examine the search building-block through studies of how performance affects the level of Research and Development.

4.2   Research and development expenditures

An important part of performance feedback theory is the proposal that organizations adjust their level of search in response to performance. Performance below the aspiration level implies an organizational problem and triggers problemistic search. Solutions uncovered by the search are fielded as alternatives in the organizational decision-making process and are evaluated for risk and rewards, with organizational changes occurring if they are viewed as promising. None of this happens if the performance exceeds the aspiration level, because managers will not have a problem that triggers search for solutions. Thus, performance below the aspiration level causing search is the first link in the chain of events leading to organizational change. Investigation of organizational search would clearly help us understand how the process in which low performance leads to organizational change gets started. It is thus a theoretically important issue even though the outcome itself – organizational search – sounds mundane.

To make the theory concrete enough for empirical investigation, we need to specify what is meant by organizational search. Search means that time and attention is spent looking for something, and in problemistic search that "something" is the solution to the problem at hand. This definition introduces two problems. First, organizational problems rarely present themselves in ways that clearly indicate a solution, and low performance on a variable such as profitability is a particularly nonspecific problem. If we start with the definition of profits as revenue less costs, we already have two places to search, and these places are not at all specific. Second, it is not clear who in the organization is responsible for searching, particularly if the problem is not specific to a given organizational unit. The responsibility for high costs, for example, could potentially be anywhere in the organization. Unless we apply more knowledge of how the process works, the location and form of problemistic search is unclear. This is not just a problem with the theory. Unless managers apply routines that guide search, there is no obvious place to search in response to low profitability. The theoretical task is then to model the routines and heuristics managers use to guide search.

We can start by assuming that managers learn how to do problemistic search from their experience. Experiential learning works by connecting current problems with memories of similar problems that were solved in the past. The simple rule of searching in the neighborhood of the problem, as discussed in section 3.2, is easily learnt and likely to be successful for unambiguous problems. This rule fails when the problem is unclear, but a second simple rule of searching in the neighborhood of past solutions can still be applied. This rule implies that search will be most intense in the organizational unit that has solved problems in the past, so that problemistic search is directed by past organizational experience in finding solutions. A third rule of searching in organizational units whose daily responsibilities include search activities can also be applied. This rule suggests that problemistic search will be done in the research and development function, whose responsibility is to search the technological environment, in the marketing function, whose responsibility is to search the market environment, and in the strategic planning function, whose responsibility is to search the overall competitive environment.

From this we can see that a direct but partial approach to show that performance feedback affects search is to study organizational R&D expenditures. The research and development function will search even if there are no pressing problems, and will get increased resources and responsibilities when the organization is seeking to solve a problem. This approach is partial because other organizational units also do problemistic search, and these search activities are omitted because they are hard to trace. Although multiple organizational units can perform problemistic search, it seems reasonable that some problemistic search results in greater research and development expenditures. Still, it should be kept in mind that not all R&D is responsive to organizational performance. Indeed, research and development expenditures are thought to be an institutionalized form of search with a high degree of inertia and industry norms. This suggests that cross-sectional differences in research and development should not be interpreted too strongly, but *changes* in research and development expenditures or methods over time within organizations are meaningful indicators of problemistic search.

There are numerous cases of firms adjusting research and development expenses in response to problems. Anticipating loss of revenue due to competition from generic drugs, the pharmaceutical firm Eli Lilly made significant increases in research and development towards the end of the patent period of its most important drug Prozac (Arndt 2001). The increased research and development led to a number of drugs that are now being tested, but it is too early to tell whether these drugs are enough to solve Eli Lilly's problem of greater competition. Eli Lilly's behavior nicely illustrates how research and development can be used to solve problems, but is not completely supportive of performance feedback theory. Eli Lilly increased research in advance of an anticipated fall in revenue, not after it occurred. Firms can rarely predict revenue falls as easily as pharmaceutical firms with patents that are about to expire, however, so the theorized effect of reacting to low performance may be more common than anticipating low performance. Well-known cases of increasing R&D in response to problems are Intel's 30 percent increase in R&D spending after Apple demonstrated that its computers ran graphics faster than Intel-based machines at the 1993 Comdex trade show (Carlton 1997: 300) and Seagate's increased R&D effort after attributing its low performance in 1997 to being squeezed between the technological leader IBM and the cost-effective Quantum (Tristram 1998).[1]

Interestingly, the hypothesis that firms do more R&D when their performance is high has also been made. Schumpeterian views of the innovation process suggest that research and development results from high profitability and liquidity, giving the most successful firms an advantage in the innovation race (Schumpeter 1976; Young, Smith, and Grimm 1997). Extensive testing of this hypothesis has given mixed results, with many findings suggesting that failure increases research and development expenditures (Kamien and Schwartz 1982). The mixed findings are not easy to interpret since many studies rely on cross-sectional comparisons, which are muddled by the institutionalized component of R&D. Here I will review a few studies that have used the longitudinal designs that are needed in order to separate the problemistic search component of R&D from the institutionalized component.

A study of research and development expenditures in 86 large manufacturing firms in Italy clearly indicated that low performance spurred research and development efforts (Antonelli 1989), as performance feedback theory would predict. Research and development was also influenced by a variety of organizational and environmental variables, with strong effects of organizational size and government subsidies. Firms invested in research and development in response to low performance, thus giving a clear indication of problemistic search through research and development. This effect was seen across a variety of models, including one with a historical aspiration level set equal to the last period's performance. More gradual aspiration-level updating such as by weighting the previous aspiration level and performance was not tested. A comparison of broad samples of US and Japanese firms yielded the same finding for the Japanese sample (Hundley, Jacobson, and Park 1996): declining profits led to an increase in R&D expenditures. For the US sample, no effect of profits on R&D expenditures was found.

An alternative way that problem-oriented search can affect research and development is by changing the way that research and development is done. A study of when firms join research and development consortia suggests a role of performance feedback in this decision as well (Bolton 1993). In a population of the seventy largest US firms in four technology-oriented industries, low-performing firms were more likely to join research and development consortia and joined earlier than high-performing firms did. This association was too weak to yield statistical

---

[1] I am choosing examples from the computer industry because R&D races in that industry are extensively covered by the press. The research reported later in the chapter shows that problemistic search through R&D also happens in other industries.

significance in a full model, however, so the result should be interpreted with some caution.

The preceding studies did not test whether performance above and below the aspiration level has different effects, as the kinked-curve relation specifies. Instead, all of them specified a simple linear relation from performance to R&D. One may wonder whether the risk and inertia effects that cause a kinked-curve relation from performance to change described in section 3.2 are seen for R&D. There are good reasons to question whether the kinked curve will hold for R&D expenditures. Because managers do not launch innovations without first reviewing their profit potential and risk, the research and development process has low risk by itself. When managers quip that R&D expenditures are risk-free because the money is gone for sure, they are describing the process accurately. R&D expenditures can be budgeted in advance and are thus risk-free according to the standard definition of risk as variance in outcomes. Risk enters when innovations are launched in the market. Innovations launched as products can have high earnings if the market accepts them, but products that are rejected cause additional losses through the costs of the product launch. This variance in returns is risky, and managers assess such risk before launching a product based on an innovation. Hence, R&D can be guided by the need to search without interference from risk considerations.

Similarly, inertia may be expected to have minor effects on R&D expenditures. The reason is that R&D can be adjusted without affecting other activities of the firm, so adjusting R&D entails only minor coordination costs. One might expect other departments to resist an increase in R&D expenditures since it would come out of their budgets, but R&D is usually a small expense that can be adjusted without igniting serious conflict within the organization. The main exception is industries that are highly reliant on R&D because of rapid technological progress, but in such industries one would expect R&D to be viewed as a high-priority expense. Because the kinked curve is caused by risk and inertia, both of which are small for R&D, performance should show a nearly linear relation with R&D intensity.

To study the effect of performance on research and development, I analyzed data on R&D intensity (R&D expenses divided by sales) from all the major Japanese shipbuilders for twenty-six years. The details of these data are given in section 5.5, but it is worthwhile noting that these firms had modest R&D intensity (1.4 percent on average) but were still able to launch innovations at a rate of about one per year. This is because the firms were large, so 1.4% of sales was still a significant sum of money. Because R&D budgets are usually adjusted incrementally, the analysis

Table 4.1 *Linear regression models of research and development intensity*[a]

	Model 1	Model 2	Model 3	Model 4
Performance – Aspiration (if <0)		−0.012		−0.012
		(0.009)		(0.009)
Performance – Aspiration (if >0)		−0.018*		−0.019*
		(0.008)		(0.008)
t test of difference of <0 and >0		[0.21]		[0.28]
Absorbed slack			0.052**	0.055**
			(0.018)	(0.018)
Unabsorbed slack			0.0017	0.0012
			(0.0038)	(0.0038)
Potential slack			0.00006	0.00002
			(0.00007)	(0.00007)
R^2	0.310	0.319	0.467	0.478

[†]$p<.10$; *$p<.05$; **$p<.01$; two-sided significance tests.
[a]Based on eleven firms and 230 firm-years. Models include random effects for firms and autocorrelation of disturbances. Controls for number of employees, annual production, growth of shipping income, and oil freight rate are not shown. Standard errors of the coefficient estimates are shown in round brackets; tests of difference of coefficients are shown in square brackets.

incorporated controls for autocorrelation like the R&D studies with longitudinal data reviewed earlier. The goal of the analysis is to find the effect of performance on R&D intensity. In addition, the effect of organizational slack resources is also explored. Slack is included to distinguish problemistic search from slack search, just as Singh (1986) distinguished problemistic and slack risk taking in the previous section.

Table 4.1 shows regression estimates of the R&D intensity of the firms. The models gradually develop the test by first entering the control variables, then tests of performance and slack one at a time, and finally both at once. In this and the subsequent tables, I do not display the coefficients of the control variables, but I do show the fit statistics for the controls-only model and mention the most important findings of the control variables. This is because the control variables are highly industry specific, and do not have much theoretical meaning. For example, model 1 shows a positive effect of the firm size and a negative effect of the industry level of production. The latter effect is not completely intuitive, but could mean that firms ramp up R&D in response to greater competition for orders.

Model 2 tests the effect of performance, and shows negative effects both above and below the aspiration level. Only the effect above the aspiration level is significant, but the two coefficient estimates are very similar in size. A t test for whether the coefficients are different is not significant.

A model entering one variable for performance minus the aspiration level gives an estimate of -0.015, which is significant at the 1 percent level. The conclusion is that R&D intensity declines linearly when the performance increases. Model 3 tests the effects of slack resources, finding that firms with a greater administrative component (absorbed slack) do more research and development. Thus, slack search also exists and has the effect specified in the behavioral theory of the firm. The increase in R squared in model 3 shows that absorbed slack is very important for explaining R&D expenses.

Model 4 enters all variables at once, and retains the results of models 2 and 3. Low performance and high resources increase R&D intensity. The t test of different effects of performance above and below the aspiration is still insignificant. When only one performance variable is entered, its coefficient is again -0.015, significant at the 1 percent level. Model 4 has high explanatory power, as seen by the R-square of 0.478. Clearly, performance and slack are both important in explaining R&D intensity. Managers initiate search when they encounter problems or have abundant resources. The relation from performance to changes in R&D intensity seems to be approximately linear, so the kinked curve is not seen for this outcome. Research and development intensity follows a pure search pattern with no discernable effect of risk taking or organizational inertia.

The research reported in this section is clearly supportive of proposition P2 in section 3.2. Problemistic search increases when the performance is below the aspiration level and decreases when the performance is above the aspiration level. In addition to this, the shipbuilding study was specified to allow detection of the kinked curve where performance has greater effect above the aspiration level than below it. This relation is *not* expected for research and development expenses since they can be adjusted without making major changes in the organization, so finding it would contradict the theory. The estimates instead showed the expected straight-line relation from performance adjusted by aspiration levels to research and development intensity. Other similar studies have assumed a linear relation and found it. The number of studies that examine performance adjusted by aspiration levels is still small, but the evidence is in favor of the search component of performance feedback theory.

With evidence supporting the risk and search components of the theory in place, we can venture into more difficult terrain. The next sections report findings on outcomes that involve organizational risk, and thus bring concerns of organizational inertia into play. The theory of chapter 3 predicts that a kinked-curve relation from performance to organizational change will result. Organizations change more when the performance is low, but organizational inertia causes the effect of performance on organizational change to be greater above the aspiration level than below it. This proposition can be tested on important strategic behaviors like innovations, investment, and change in market niche. All these changes are sufficiently large that inertial forces may affect the organizational response to performance feedback.

4.3   Product innovations

Organizational innovations are interesting to research on performance feedback theory because innovations are strategic actions that organizations may take to solve performance problems or leverage their technological capabilities. If organizations innovate to solve problems, they behave as performance feedback theory predicts. If organizations innovate to leverage capabilities, they behave according to a different logic. Innovations are commonly thought to be something that innovative or competent organizations do. This intuition is a good alternative hypothesis to the prediction that innovations are something that organizations do when seeking to solve performance problems. In the study of innovations, it is not obvious that performance feedback will be a good explanation of the behavior.

Innovations also have high practical importance. Many strategic behaviors affect the focal organization but have modest impact beyond it. For example, in a highly segmented market, a successful change of market niche may save a low-performing organization and please consumers in the new niche, but few other actors are affected. Niche changes are thus important strategic behaviors for the focal organization, but their overall impact on society is small. Innovations are different. Major technological innovations open new areas of economic and social activity or improve existing ones. They can initiate waves of imitation and technology-based competition that reorganize an industry (Tushman and Anderson 1986). Innovations are thus important for the focal organization and for society at large.

Because innovations are so important, researchers have long been interested in explaining when organizations launch technological innovations. Research on how organizations develop and launch innovations has examined many explanations (Drazin and Schoonhoven 1996), but a strong undercurrent is the suggestion that large and established organizations suppress innovative activities (Burgelman and Sayles 1986; Dougherty and Heller 1994; Henderson and Clark 1990; Taylor 1998). Indeed, research on innovative large firms often treats their innovativeness as an aberration from a general pattern of rigidity and draws lessons for large firms in general from their unique management procedures (Jelinek and Schoonhoven 1990). From the viewpoint of organizational theory, the puzzle to explain is not why firms make innovations, but why they don't do it more often.

Theories of innovation failure in organizations can be divided into explanations emphasizing failures in the development process that creates innovations and explanations emphasizing failures in the decision-making process that approves developed innovations for market launch (Fiol 1996). Development process theory argues that the key to successful innovations is the acquisition and management of knowledge and innovative people (Cohen and Levinthal 1990; Leonard-Barton 1995; Nonaka and Takeuchi 1995). Decision process theory notes that innovations are opposed to the organizational requirements of stability and legitimacy, and advocates organizational mechanisms for protecting and promoting innovations (Dougherty and Hardy 1996; Howell and Higgins 1990). These theories place the blame for low innovativeness in the R&D labs and the executive suite; respectively, and thus have different implications for how organizations can increase the rate of launching innovations.

Decision process theory resonates with many qualitative accounts of the innovation process. Both scholarly and popular accounts are filled with stories of managerial resistance causing innovations to fail or become implemented in a different organization than the original innovator (Burgelman and Sayles 1986; Carlton 1997; Johnstone 1999). The most famous story is perhaps when Apple launched the graphical user interface developed by Xerox in the Macintosh computer, thus using an innovation developed by Xerox to launch a major new product line. This story is usually told in a way that omits two important details. At the time, Apple was in deep crisis because its Apple II computer had become obsolete, so its management was prepared to take great risks. Xerox was doing well and not obviously "in need of" an innovation. Thus, the story fits performance feedback theory well except that the decision to launch the development effort was based on anticipation of poor results from the Apple II product line rather than its realization. The ability to anticipate the fall of the Apple II and initiate the innovation process early is widely seen as one of the greatest management successes in the history of Apple computer. After the success of the Macintosh computer, however, Apple experienced a string of cancelled development projects suggesting that its management had become as risk averse as that of Xerox. Indeed, a researcher working for Apple at that time described his organization as "a pond with a lot of bubbles [R&D projects] coming up from the scum. And the executives all stood on the sidelines. They would shoot down the little bubbles when they got too scary" (Carlton 1997: 86).

Because the launching of innovations requires linkages among organizational units and to the overall strategy of the firm, innovative proposals need to clear numerous intra-organizational hurdles. At each step, support from the management is a key contingency (Dougherty and Heller 1994). Outright cancellation is one possible result of such intra-organizational hurdles, and so are compromises with current product lineups that reduce risks at the cost of eliminating the distinctiveness that characterizes truly innovative products. Again, the computer industry contains good examples. After the IBM PC was launched, both Digital Equipment Corporation's and IBM's product development efforts sought to tie the PCs into the larger strategy of the firm, which distanced these products from the core market of microcomputers at the time (Anderson 1995). Both firms were successful at the time. Firms seeking to solve performance problems can also end up compromising innovations. General Motors' Aztek sport-utility vehicle was faulted for containing too many compromises between design and manufacturing concerns, among other things (Welch 2000). There is a slippery slope from the peak of fully innovative products to compromises that reduce the impact of the innovative features of the product.

It is possible to recognize that innovations are always difficult to make, but still maintain that they are even harder to make in firms with high performance. The decision process theory of innovation leads to the proposition that organizations launch innovations following performance below the aspiration level. In this view, an innovation is a solution that will be implemented if it is matched with an organizational problem, but not if a suitable problem cannot be found. Moreover, an innovation differs from alternative solutions by its substantial financial risks for the organization and career risks for its backers. Innovations are new activities with unpredictable revenue, so they are inherently risky for the organizations. Decisions to launch innovations are vivid events that will be remembered for future assignment of credit or blame. Thus, launching an innovation requires that the organization has a problem that the innovation can be claimed to solve, and that the decision makers have sufficient tolerance of risk to choose the innovation over less risky alternatives.

While innovation launches require a problem and managerial risk tolerance, innovation generation results from organizational search only. As discussed in chapter 3, organizations search habitually through institutionalized search, playfully through slack search, and deliberately through problemistic search. Organizations with a high level of institutionalized and slack search will tend to have easy access to innovations that can be launched, making the existence of a problem the main constraint in the innovation process. Such organizations should be able to swiftly launch innovations in response to low performance. Organizations with a low level of institutionalized and slack search will rely much more on problemistic search to generate innovations, which means that they are less capable of quickly rolling out innovations in response to low performance. The time needed for innovation generation stretches the duration from low performance to innovation launch.

Organizations that rely on problemistic search to develop innovations will experience a timing problem in responding to performance feedback. Low performance is needed to start the search process, which is likely to be lengthy when the goal is to develop an innovation. Low performance is also needed to launch the innovation as a product, but since the performance varies over time, there is a chance that it will be above the aspiration level once an innovation has been developed. The likely result is failure to launch the innovation. Even worse, problemistic search may need continued low performance to be sustained, so that high performance at any point before the innovation has been completed can choke off the necessary resources and attention to complete the innovation. Historical aspiration levels result in such interrupted search processes because they adapt to the recent performance, reducing the aspiration level for an organization that experiences low performance over time. The perceived low performance needed to sustain problemistic search can disappear simply by gradually lowering the aspiration level over time.

The role of search processes in determining whether innovations occur is a significant challenge when trying to explain innovation launches by performance feedback. Organizational differences in how the innovation process is managed can result in inter-organizational differences in innovativeness, so cross sections of organizations will give less meaningful results than changes in the organizational rate of innovating over time. Institutional and slack search can contribute strongly to the generation of innovations and can change over time within a single organization, so their effect on the rate of launching innovations should be measured. Once these other causes of innovations have been accounted for, however, the effect of performance feedback on the rate of launching innovations can be estimated.

To meet these requirements, I analyzed data on innovations launched as products from the same set of Japanese shipbuilding firms that were used to analyze research and development intensity in the previous section. The advantages of these data are that innovations are known over a period of twenty-six years from third-party sources, so changes in the rate of launching innovations over time can be investigated, and measures of organizational slack and search effort are also available over time. Thus,

Table 4.2 *Selected innovations in 1972, 1982, and 1992*

Date	Innovating firm	Description
1972/1	Ishikawajima Harima HI and Toshiba	Automated ship control system
1972/2	Fuyo Ocean Development	Twin-hull type ocean research vessel
1972/3	NKK and Nippon Kayaku	World-first launch of ship by explosives
1972/5	Marine Ship Machinery Development Association	New type of highly efficient diving chamber
1972/8	Volcano	Inert gas generator for LNG ships
1972/11	Sasebo and Osaka Jack Inc.	Device to attach and detach rudder and propeller
1982/1	Mitsubishi HI	Super high-pressure seawater pump
1982/5	Kawasaki HI	Variable-pitch propeller of 11m diameter
1982/7	Kobe Steel	World's largest combination crane/grab ship
1982/8	Ishikawajima Harima HI	AT Fin, an energy-saving propulsion device
1982/9	Mitsubishi HI	New technology for preventing adhesion of marine growths
1982/11	Mitsubishi HI	Coal-burning ship, first time in thirty-two years one has been made
1992/2	Sumitomo HI	Prototype superconducting electric propulsion ship
1992/9	Mitsubishi HI	5500HP water jet propulsion system which can propel a 350 ton boat at a speed of 40 knots
1992/10	Ishikawajima Harima HI	Container ship without a hatch cover
1992/10	Tokiwa Shipbuilding	Weather observation boat; the hull was constructed with aluminum honeycomb for the first time in the world

HI = Heavy industries

it is possible to isolate the effect of performance relative to the aspiration level from other drivers of innovation launches.

Table 4.2 lists selected innovations made in 1972, 1982 and 1992 to show the kinds of innovations that are entered in the analysis. The wide range of innovations should be clear. Even in this small selection, they range from new configurations such as the twin-hull ship launched in 1972 to improved basic technologies such as the two propulsion systems launched in 1992. A new configuration of systems is a difficult innovation to make organizationally, as it involves architectural choices that can only be made by coordination across organizational units. It has been argued that established firms are less adept at producing architectural innovations than newly established firms (Henderson and Clark 1990).

This proposition is unlikely to hold in the shipbuilding industry since ship design is an inherently architectural problem that the organizations have long experience solving.[2] The Japanese shipbuilders were adept at making new configurations, with whole-vessel innovations constituting 30% of the innovations in the data. Improvements in component technologies are easier to produce organizationally because they involve less interdependence, but can present serious engineering problems when the technology is exotic or has already been extensively tweaked. Technologies at an intermediate stage of development, like the water-jet propulsion system in the table, are thought to be the easiest to improve (Foster 1986). Component innovations seen in the data include engine (17%), propulsion (7%), communication and control (13%), and accessories (24%). The rest of the innovations were improvements of the production process (9%).

The large shipbuilders made most of the innovations, but small firms also innovated now and then. Two innovations were made by individuals. Many innovations were made by firms supplying parts to the shipbuilding industry. These innovations are not analyzed as outcomes in the models because the firms making them are not shipbuilders, but they were entered into an annual count of innovations in the industry. Such a count controls for the effect of innovations in catalyzing additional innovations that extend their idea (Greve and Taylor 2000).

Table 4.3 shows the results of the first analysis. The dependent variable is zero-one for whether the firm made no innovations or one or more innovations, and the table shows models with different sets of predictor variables. Model 1 has the control variables only, and shows positive effects of size and oil freight rate. Large firms launch more innovations, and promising economic signals cause more innovations to be launched.

Model 2 adds the performance variables, and shows that higher performance reduces the probability that innovations will be launched, as predicted by performance feedback theory. Successful firms launch fewer innovations. This relation holds only above the aspiration level, though. Below it the relation is not significant and the slope is positive, which is opposite to the prediction. Model 3 enters slack variables and finds a very strong positive effect of unabsorbed slack on innovation launches. Resource-rich firms launch more innovations, as slack search would predict. Model 4 gives an important result for interpreting how slack and

---

[2] I have observed the final stages of such a design process where a new type of naval vessel was "put on a diet" because it was too heavy. It involved very close coordination between groups responsible for interdependent parts of the design, but was handled in the course of a few weeks.

Table 4.3 *Logit models of whether innovations were made*[a]

	Model 1	Model 2	Model 3	Model 4
Performance – Aspiration (if <0)		4.130		3.413
		(7.474)		(8.215)
Performance – Aspiration (if >0)		−28.408**		−24.902**
		(7.072)		(7.305)
Wald test of difference >0 and <0		[8.28]**		[5.30]*
Absorbed slack			13.578	13.859
			(9.592)	(10.388)
Unabsorbed slack			9.078**	4.597
			(3.480)	(3.729)
Potential slack			−0.064	−0.018
			(0.072)	(0.077)
Efron (residual) R^2	0.406	0.472	0.431	0.478

†p<.10; *p<.05; **p<.01; two-sided significance tests.
[a]Logit models based on eleven firms and 296 firm-years, of which 115 had innovations. Control variables for innovations in industry, employees, annual production, shipping income, and oil freight rate are not shown. Standard errors of the coefficient estimates are shown in round brackets; tests of significant difference of coefficients are shown in square brackets.

performance interact: at least in these data, the results are nearly unchanged when these variables are entered jointly. The estimates lose some precision, as is usual when many variables are entered at once, but their values show no systematic change.

Table 4.3 uses a robust method, but also an imprecise one since multiple innovations in one year are treated as equivalent to one. Table 4.4 adds precision by analyzing the number of innovations a firm makes in a year, but at the risk of bias if the statistical distribution used is not correct. Here a standard distribution for analyzing count data, the Poisson distribution, is used, and the results do not appear to be sensitive to the choice of distribution. The coefficients in table 4.4 are estimated with lower standard errors than those in table 4.3, but no new significant effect appears. Two old results are strengthened, however. The relation from performance to the rate of launching innovations is still negative and is now more significant above the aspiration level. Below the aspiration level, there is still no clear effect. Unabsorbed slack significantly increases the rate of launching innovations, as slack search would predict, and is now significant also in the full model 4. The results from the two methods of analyzing the data are reassuringly similar.

It is possible to calculate the predicted number of innovations based on this analysis. Figure 4.1 shows the predicted effect of performance,

Table 4.4 *Poisson models of the number of innovations*[a]

	Model 1	Model 2	Model 3	Model 4
Performance – Aspiration (if <0)		1.604		0.662
		(3.673)		(3.713)
Performance – Aspiration (if >0)		−16.895**		−14.086**
		(3.913)		(4.060)
Wald test of difference of <0 and >0		[9.54]**		[5.61]*
Absorbed slack			1.687	2.510
			(3.610)	(3.625)
Unabsorbed slack			5.742**	3.577*
			(1.332)	(1.506)
Potential slack			−0.035	−0.008
			(0.036)	(0.037)
Maximum likelihood R^2	0.630	0.668	0.654	0.675

[†]$p<.10$; [*]$p<.05$; [**]$p<.01$; two-sided significance tests.
[a]Poisson models based on eleven firms and 296 firm-years with a total of 262 innovations. Control variables for innovations in industry, employees, annual production, shipping income, and oil freight rate are not shown. Standard errors of the coefficient estimates are shown in round brackets; tests of significant difference of coefficients are shown in square brackets.

slack, and innovations in the industry on the number of innovations a firm will make in a year. The curve is drawn as follows. First, the number of innovations at origin is set to one, which is close to the average in the data. Next, the three variables are given values that differ from the mean from minus 2.5 to plus 2.5 standard deviations (keeping the others constant), and the results are graphed. The figure shows that both slack and performance relative to the aspiration level are important for the probability of launching innovations, but the number of innovations in the industry during the past year only had a small effect effect. Note that the kink in the performance feedback curve occurs below zero in this graph, as the average performance was about one-half standard deviation below the aspiration level during this time interval.

It is also valuable to keep in mind that in models such as the logit in table 4.3 and the Poisson in table 4.4, changes in multiple variables at the same time are incorporated by multiplying the effects. Thus, based on figure 4.1 we can predict that if slack and performance both increase from the average to one standard deviation above the mean, the predicted number of innovations will stay constant. If performance and innovations both increase from the average to one standard deviation above the mean, the predicted number of innovations will drop considerably. High performance can suppress the effects of other variables, reducing the number

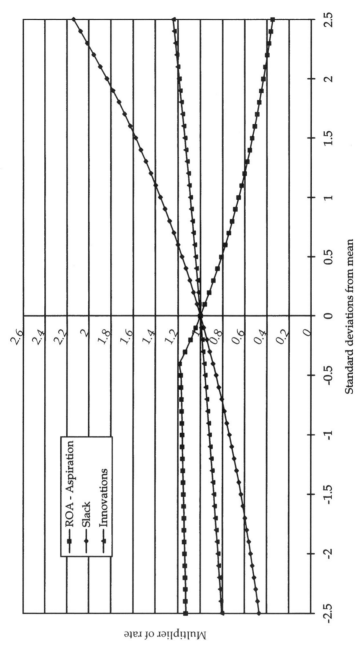

Figure 4.1 Determinants of innovations

of innovations from firms that would be likely to launch innovations for other reasons such as high slack or many innovations in the environment.

The analyses shown here indicate that performance feedback has passed its first test based on strategic changes. Consistent with propositions in section 3.2, organizations launch more innovations when the performance is below the aspiration level than when it is above the aspiration level, and the effect of performance on the innovation rate is stronger above the aspiration level than below it. Indeed, the findings suggest that organizational inertia is a formidable roadblock to launching innovations, as there was no discernable difference in the innovation rate of an organization with performance just below the aspiration level and one with performance far below the aspiration level. Success suppresses innovations more effectively than failure spurs innovations.

I discussed innovation launches before other strategic behaviors because innovations are a natural continuation of the study of R&D reported in the previous section. Innovation launches are not the cleanest possible test of the theory, however, because they are a complex behavior where long-term firm capabilities and investments in research affect the outcome. Firms may well have varying ability to produce innovations and varying portfolios of completed or nearly completed research projects, and these factors affect their rates of launching innovations. Although this concern turned out to have little effect on the results, it is still useful to eliminate the capability issue by studying a simpler strategic behavior. For maximum simplicity, let's examine how firms go shopping. The next section reports research on the acquisition of production assets by firms, a behavior that requires substantial tolerance for risk but little firm-specific capabilities.

4.4   Facility investment

Two prominent features of firms are the production efficiencies they can achieve and the resources that they assemble to do so. Automobile manufacturing is remarkably efficient compared with what it was a few decades ago, and semiconductor manufacturing has progressed significantly within the last decade. Yet the factories that turn out these products are enormously expensive, and may be made obsolete by technological change or redundant by overcapacity. Thus, the pursuit of greater efficiency can lead firms to waste resources as well. The recent woes of the telecommunication carriers and firms that supply them are a good example of resource acquisition that, at least for now, seems to have been a poor bet (Reinhardt 2002), and it is just the latest of many such races to build capacity that ended badly for some participants. Because the resources they hold are the source of a good portion of the production efficiency of modern firms but also a risky investment for the individual firm and for society, we should be interested in how firms acquire resources. We should also be interested because resources play an important role in current theory of strategy management.

First, let us define a resource as follows (Barney and Arikan 2001: 138): "Resources are the tangible and intangible assets firms use to conceive of and implement their strategies." Organizations acquire resources to operate and make profits, and use some of their profits to acquire additional resources. A central task of managers is to make decisions on the acquisition and use of resources that are useful in the long term, that is, to acquire organizational assets. Strategic management researchers treat assets in two different ways. One is to view assets as commitments that shape interactions between firms by giving competitors of firms with assets committed to a given market incentives to avoid competitive battles (Caves and Porter 1977; Ghemawat 1991). Firms engage in confrontations such as price wars for the sake of gaining market share that gives future profits, and may avoid confrontations when the opponent has committed so many assets that it is unlikely to back down. The other is to view assets as giving the firm capabilities that make it a better supplier of its goods than other firms, increasing the likelihood that competitors will lose confrontations they engage in (Wernerfeldt 1984). Both views predict that a good strategy for acquiring assets can lead to high performance over the long run by making other firms reluctant to compete with the focal firm.

Theory stating that resources held by the firm give competitive advantage has led to the resource-based view of the firm (Barney 1991; Lieberman and Montgomery 1998; Wernerfeldt 1984), which is an active research tradition currently (Barney 2001; Barney and Arikan 2001; Priem and Butler 2001). The resource-based view considers resources that are valuable and unique to the firm to be sources of competitive advantage, and studies the role of such resources in giving high performance (Brush and Artz 1999; Makadok 1998, 1999; Miller and Shamsie 2001) and shaping strategic decisions such as diversification strategies (Hitt, Hoskisson, and Kim 1997; Silverman 1999). Resources are interpreted broadly to include nonmaterial assets such as knowledge, which has given the resource-based view of the firm an affiliation with learning theory (Barnett, Greve, and Park 1994; Collis 1991; Hamel 1991; McGrath, MacMillan, and Venkataraman 1995; Noda and Bower 1996).

Given the interest in strategic resources spawned by this theory, one might think that the acquisition of assets (physical or otherwise) would be an active area of research in strategic management. Remarkably, it is not (Barney and Arikan 2001). Empirical research from the resource-based view has emphasized the *consequences* of firm differences so strongly that research on their *origins* has been lagging. Researchers examining resource acquisition have mainly worked from a learning-theory point of view, and have examined the acquisition of non-physical assets such as knowledge and routines (Barnett, Greve, and Park 1994; McGrath, MacMillan, and Venkataraman 1995). The problem seems to be that it is difficult to explain why some firms acquire scarce and valuable resources and others do not, as it seems obvious that all firms would be interested in pursuing such resources. The key to solving this problem is to realize that acquiring resources is a risky organizational change that many managers hesitate to make.

We can study the acquisition of assets by pursuing the usual idea that performance below the aspiration level causes organizational change and managerial risk taking. Investment in production facilities is an important strategic decision in its own right, and may be regarded as a test case of how firms approach the more general problem of obtaining scarce and valuable resources. Large or modern assets can give the firm a comparative advantage in the competition, but also give greater fixed costs. For industries with highly variable demand and rigid supply, the scale of production facilities directly determines the effect of fluctuations in the economic macro-environment on the organizational profits. Large facilities allow the organization to take on more work on good times, but give greater losses in bad times. It is thus a type of organizational change with high potential for solving problems of low performance, but also with great risks.

If we view asset acquisition as a risky problem-solving behavior, theory of performance feedback predicts that firms add fewer resources to their production facilities when their performance is above the aspiration level. They add more resources when the performance is below the aspiration level, but organizational inertia makes the link between performance feedback and resource acquisition weaker below the aspiration level than above it. The result is the kinked-curve relation from performance to change predicted in chapter 3. If the theory is correct, then asset buildup works a lot like bicycle races. The leader is slowed by the headwinds of complacency, while those following are pulled along by the leader. Over time, such performance feedback processes act as an equalizing force in resource-based competition.

Some well-known cases of firms adding to their production assets suggest that low performance indeed spurs investments. Upgrading the factories was one of the strategies pursued by GM after the entry of Japanese firms depressed its performance, as discussed in chapter 1. The same strategy is well known from other industries where physical assets are important for competitiveness. For example, Intel's first reaction to harsh competition in the RAM (random access memory) market was to upgrade its factories; only later did it change its market niche to processing chips (Burgelman 1991, 1994). Although Intel reversed its strategy of investments in factories for producing memory chips, the strategy of investing more in times of trouble is still followed by makers of semi conducting devices. For example, the Taiwanese chip foundry TSMC embarked on an ambitious and controversial upgrade of its factories shortly after the demand for semiconductors tanked, giving it a capacity utilization below 50 percent (Einhorn 2001). To see whether there might be a systematic relation from performance feedback to asset acquisition, I turn to evidence from a focused study of an industry where production assets are crucial for competitive strength.

As in the sections on R&D and innovations, I use data from the Japanese shipbuilding industry. Industries producing industrial investment goods, such as production machinery and non-consumer vehicles, experience greatly fluctuating demand and competition partly based on production assets. This makes them good contexts for testing how asset growth is affected by performance feedback. The decision is especially consequential and risky in such industries, fitting our emphasis on decisions of great strategic import and uncertain consequences. The scale and quality of shipyards are very important in the competition for ship construction contracts, so investments in production facilities are strategic moves for these firms.

Table 4.5 shows the results of analyzing the growth of total production assets in each shipyard. This measure might be relatively unresponsive to performance feedback since it includes both strategically important assets such as docks and machinery and less important assets with a high degree of routine maintenance (buildings are a good example). Nevertheless, the table shows clear and strong effects of performance feedback on the growth rate. As before, model 1 only contains control variables describing current economic conditions and leading indicators of shipbuilding activity. The next three models add performance relative to historical and social aspiration levels and slack, respectively, and the final model includes all variables.

Performance relative to the historical aspiration level has a strong effect on asset growth above the aspiration level, and higher performance reduces the asset growth as predicted. Model 2 shows that performance relative to the historical aspiration level is negatively related to asset growth, but only above the aspiration level. Below the aspiration level, the performance does not have a statistically significant effect on the growth rate, and the estimated coefficient is very close to zero. Success reduces

Table 4.5 *Models of shipyard asset growth in response to performance feedback*[a]

	Model 1	Model 2	Model 3	Model 4	Model 5
Performance – Historical Aspiration (if <0)		0.498 (0.414)			0.447 (0.450)
Performance – Historical Aspiration (if >0)		−1.940** (0.494)			−2.028** (0.495)
t test of difference of <0 and >0		[3.299]**			[3.252]**
Performance – Social Aspiration (if <0)			0.113 (0.478)		0.008 (0.522)
Performance – Social Aspiration (if >0)			−0.103† (0.056)		−0.123* (0.058)
t test for difference of <0 and >0			[0.435]		[0.244]
Absorbed slack				−0.784 (0.699)	−1.124 (0.706)
Unabsorbed slack				0.014 (0.048)	0.047 (0.049)
Potential slack				0.0009 (0.0017)	0.0010 (0.0017)
R-squared (unadjusted)	0.93807	0.93866	0.93820	0.93814	0.93894
R-squared (adjusted)	0.93734	0.93786	0.93740	0.93729	0.93796

†p<.10; *p<.05; **p<.01; two-sided significance tests.
[a]Growth models with fixed effects for thirteen firms. Control variables for the growth parameter, oil shock, order reserve, annual production, oil freight rate, and shipping income are not shown.

asset growth, but failure does not increase asset growth. If we compare this finding with the prediction in figure 3.3, it suggests that inertial forces are so strong that the effect of problem-based search below the aspiration level is canceled out. Performance relative to the historical aspiration level seems to be the only variable that strongly affects the asset growth. Models 3 and 4 show that performance relative to social aspiration levels weakly affects the growth of assets, and organizational slack does not affect the growth at all. Model 5 has all variables included, and confirms the results of the preceding models.

Table 4.6 shows the estimates of growth models of shipyard machinery value. This variable omits slow-adjusting assets like buildings, and should be more responsive to managerial decisions. The results are very similar to the analyses of total production asset value in table 4.5. Model 2 shows a decline in investment as performance relative to the historical aspiration level increases, but only above the aspiration level. Performance relative to the historical aspiration level is the only significant feedback variable in

Table 4.6 *Models of machinery growth in response to performance feedback*[a]

	Model 1	Model 2	Model 3	Model 4	Model 5
Performance – Historical		0.039			0.203
Aspiration (if <0)		(0.532)			(0.551)*
Performance – Historical		−1.401**			−1.403**
Aspiration (if >0)		(0.514)			(0.514)
t test for difference of		[1.653]†			[1.822]†
<0 and >0					
Performance – Social			−0.732		−0.614
Aspiration (if <0)			(0.507)		(0.528)
Performance – Social			−0.036		−0.042
Aspiration (if >0)			(0.057)		(0.057)
t test for difference of			[1.325]		[1.046]
<0 and >0					
Absorbed slack				−0.558	−0.704
				(0.688)	(0.687)
Unabsorbed slack				−0.020	−0.017
				(0.045)	(0.044)
Potential slack				0.0005	0.0005
				(0.0017)	(0.0016)
R-squared (unadjusted)	0.95259	0.95286	0.95269	0.95268	0.95303
R-squared (adjusted)	0.95211	0.95232	0.95215	0.95211	0.95240

†p<.10; *p< 05; **p<.01; two-sided significance tests.
[a]Growth models with fixed effects for ten firms. Control variables for the growth parameter, oil shock, order reserve, annual production, oil freight rate, and shipping income are not shown. Standard errors of coefficient estimates are shown in round brackets; tests of difference of coefficients are shown in square brackets.

these models. For machinery growth the social aspiration level is insignificant, and the slack variables are insignificant as before. The models of machinery value show slightly higher explanatory power than the models of shipyard assets. The higher explanatory power suggests that machinery size is adjusted more readily to the economic conditions and the firm performance than total assets are, as one would expect.

A graph helps understand the results better. Figure 4.2 displays the predicted growth rates of assets based on the estimates of model 5 of table 4.5. The curve is made by normalizing the growth rate to one at the origin and computing how the growth rate varies as each dependent variable varies from 2.5 standard deviations below to 2.5 standard deviations above the mean. The actual growth rates will differ depending on the values of other covariates. The growth rate of assets peaks when the performance equals the aspiration level, but since the upward slope below the aspiration level is not significantly different from zero, the relationship

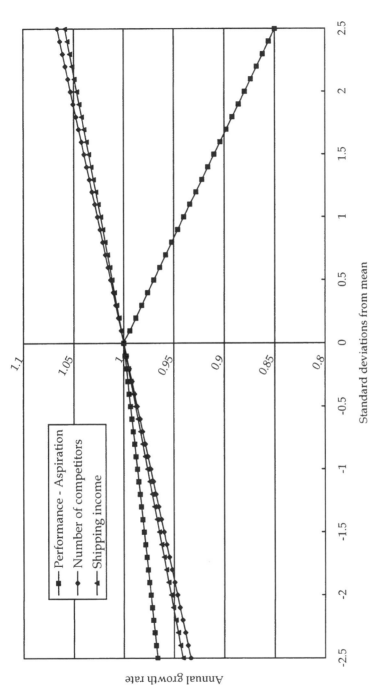

Figure 4.2 Determinants of asset growth

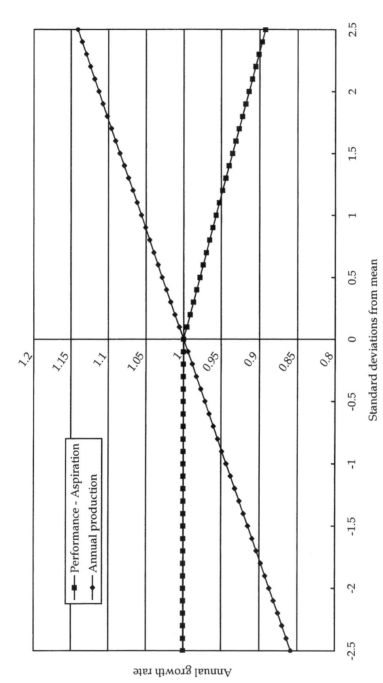

Figure 4.3 Determinants of machinery growth

may in fact be horizontal below the aspiration level. The growth rate declines rapidly above the aspiration level, showing greater risk aversion for successful firms.

In order to compare the effect strength, the effects of two control variables, the number of competing shipyards and the shipping income, are also displayed. These variables have the two strongest effects of the control variables, and their total effects are similar. Their overall effect on asset growth rate is also similar to that of performance feedback, but the functional form is different. These variables have curves with a gentle upward slope over the entire range. The slope is greater than that of performance below the aspiration level, but smaller than that of performance above the aspiration level. The model estimates differ from the prediction only in the absence of a downward sloping relation from performance to investment below the aspiration level. Performance relative to the aspiration level affects asset growth as expected, and its effect size is as large as that of the other variables in the specification.

Figure 4.3 shows the determinants of machinery growth, and is very similar to figure 4.2. Note the difference in the scale of the vertical axis, however, which shows that the annual production of the shipyard in the previous year has a rather strong effect on the machinery growth. This is the only control variable with a significant effect on machinery growth. Performance relative to the aspiration level has a horizontal relation below the aspiration level, indicating no effect, and a declining relation above it. The range is lower than in the case of total assets, showing that performance affects machinery less than total assets.

The growth rates of production assets and machinery behave as predicted by performance feedback theory. Search and risk taking declines when the firm performance is above the aspiration level, reducing the growth rate. The findings also differ from the theory in one respect. There was no relation from the level of performance to the growth rate when the performance was below the aspiration level, suggesting high inertia. That these firms should be inert is not surprising, however, since they are very large, and organizational inertia is argued to be greater in large firms (Hannan and Freeman 1984). Again we see that success reduces search and risk taking more than failure increases it.

This section and the preceding ones have shown that performance feedback affects a variety of consequential organizational behaviors. Risk taking, research and development, innovations, and asset investment are all behaviors that can be viewed as strategic actions for the firm. They are organizational changes managers resort to when seeking to solve performance problems, and often have strong effects on organizational performance. The effects are not always benign, as should be clear when considering the potential for mistakes (in retrospect) in both innovations and asset investment, and of course in risk taking generally.

For many scholars, the strategic changes that matter most are changes in the market niches of firms. Market niche changes involve one of two risky alternatives. One is that the firm enters a new and untried niche, which involves great uncertainty about how the potential customers will react. The other is to enter a niche occupied by other firms, which involves great uncertainty about the ensuing competitive battle. Market niche changes are choices that require both search for solutions and tolerance of risk, and are a good way to end this review of evidence on performance feedback theory.

4.5   Strategic change

One of the most important decisions a manager can make is to change the product-market strategy of the organization. The product-market strategy orients the organization towards the environment and chooses its intended sources of support. It specifies the products or services to make and the customers to target. It is one of the first strategic decisions an organizational founder will make, as business plans typically take the product and market as the starting point and work out the implications for other decisions such as structure, staff, and financing. The product-market strategy is not easily changed – new firms often need top management turnover or an economic crisis to do so (Boeker 1989), and older firms have been seen to pursue their original markets or products long after these have lost the potential to support the organization economically (Christensen and Bower 1996; Starbuck and Hedberg 1977).

Product-market strategy has an important role in the theory of organizational ecology, as it is one of the four core features of the organizations that are claimed to be structurally inert (Hannan and Freeman 1984).[3] Organizational ecology theorists view product-market strategy as particularly inert because of organizational interdependence and strategic maintenance of external relations (Barnett and Freeman 2001). Because the product-market strategy is linked with decisions in production, marketing, sales, and procurement, changing it requires substantial coordination of functions, and thus has high organizational risk. Resistance, uncooperativeness, or simple inability to work together can cause the

---

[3] The others are the organizational mission, the authority system, and the production technology. Production technology is of course closely related to the investment behavior studied in the previous section, but the analyses shown there are not direct tests of inertia theory since they show the change in the value of the production technology, whereas the inertia hypothesis concerns change in the *functions* of the production technology.

intra-organizational coordination to go awry, spoiling an otherwise sound attempt to change the product-market strategy. In addition to this, there is the environmental risk. Changing the product-market strategy requires changing either the customers or the product sold to the customers, and often also involves replacing suppliers and other exchange partners. The organization thus breaks off its relations with some of the exchange partners that have supported it and searches for new ones to replace them, and runs the risk of having its new strategy rejected by environmental actors that it needs to obtain resources. These considerations suggest that changing the product-market strategy has high financial and organizational risk. As a decision with high potential for changing the organization's performance, positively or negatively, it is a good test of the theory of performance feedback.

Performance feedback theory predicts that performance below the aspiration level increases the likelihood that an organization will change its product-market niche. Pioneering work on this prediction compared the rates of curriculum change in departments of a university during periods of financial security and adversity (Manns and March 1978). The availability of students is an important driver of financial performance of any university, and it is particularly important for a private school such as Stanford University, where the research was conducted. Curriculum change affects the attractiveness of the university to current and prospective students through its effect on course content and on the diversity, marketing, and accessability of courses. Curriculum change is a core change for a university. It offers the prospect of improving the attractiveness of the school, but also implies costly change of production routines and the risk that the changes will be viewed as unattractive by students or educators (Kraatz and Zajac 1996). It may face internal resistance, especially in departments that have high research reputations and thus a lower need to appeal to students. Manns and March (1978) found that the rate of curriculum change was increased during adversity, and that this increase was greater in departments with low research reputations, thus supporting both the main proposal of change in response to low performance and the secondary proposal of more change in weaker parts of the organization. The greater change in low-reputation departments gives direct support to the rule of searching in vulnerable areas of the organization in response to performance below the aspiration level (Cyert and March 1963).

A series of studies on a major curriculum change in liberal arts colleges in the USA has provided additional support for this prediction (Kraatz 1998; Kraatz and Zajac 1996; Zajac and Kraatz 1993). These studies examined the adoption of professional programs such as business or computer science in liberal arts colleges, which clearly is a major change of product-market niche for an educational institution that derived part of its rationale from opposition to occupation-specific training (Brint and Karabel 1991). The studies showed that colleges adopted professional programs in response to low performance and despite substantial opposition to such adoption among their faculty and alumni. Of particular interest is the finding that the adoption process combined imitation of other colleges (especially successful ones) with performance feedback (Kraatz 1998). This suggests that problemistic search can also result in finding solutions in the organizational environment by observing what similar organizations do.

Research on the effect of performance feedback on organizational change in a set of United Kingdom firms recovering from decline showed that internal or external indicators of organizational decline triggered search behaviors by the management or external intervention threats (Grinyer and McKiernan 1990). Such problemistic search was followed by a diverse set of changes ranging from apparent low-risk changes such as improvement of production efficiency to strategic changes such as entry or exit of markets. Low-risk operational changes were more frequent than the high-risk strategic changes. This could reflect a process of local search leading to operational changes first and strategic changes only when the operational changes failed, but it could also reflect a preference for changes with low organizational risks. Even the high-risk changes were to some extent conservative, as they often involved exiting businesses outside the core strategic interests of the firm. As I argued in section 3.2, exiting noncore businesses has low organizational risk because such businesses rarely have powerful managers, and the need for coordination and adjustment with other units is likely to be low.

A later study sought to decompose the effect of performance on change into direct effects and effects mediated by top management team composition and change or by top management perceptions of the environment (Lant, Milliken, and Batra 1992). This study used a composite measure of strategic change derived from thirteen different product-market strategies (such as low price, high quality, service), the organizational structure, and the control system. The performance was measured as the difference between the firm's ROA and the median ROA of the industry, giving a social aspiration level. The results showed that changes were more likely to occur in firms with low performance, and also showed that management turnover and environmental awareness led to change. Management change and greater awareness of the competitive environment can be caused by low performance, so the study showed both an unmediated and a mediated effect of performance on change. A study on the same industries and with similar methods but data from a later time period failed, however, to find an effect of performance (Gordon et al. 2000). This inconsistency is puzzling, but may have been caused by a redefinition of the change variable to include changes in corporate control, which is a change that would usually be imposed on the firm by its owners rather than autonomously decided by its managers.

Several recent studies have confirmed these findings. Greater strategic change in organizations performing below their aspiration level has been found in studies of the airline industry (Audia, Locke, and Smith 2000; Miller and Chen 1994), semiconductor industry (Boeker 1997), hospital industry (Audia and Boeker 2000), and trucking industry (Audia, Locke, and Smith 2000). Audia and associates investigated whether firms made strategic changes after industry deregulation. It seems obvious that deregulation changes the rules of competition by removing constraints on firm behaviors and increasing competitive interdependence, and thus should lead to adjustments in market strategy. In the airline industry, the old strategy of premium service was the only way of increasing profits as long as the route structure was fixed and monopolistic, but the flexible route structure allowed by deregulation made new strategies possible: costs could be cut and planeloads balanced by rearranging the routes to form a hub-and-spoke network; low-price strategies became powerful weapons in defending territory or winning head-to-head competition; quality management became a meaningful activity because travelers had a choice of carriers on many routes. The seemingly obvious opportunity to adjust strategies was lost on the carriers that were successful before deregulation, however, as they showed a much greater persistence with the old strategy than unsuccessful carriers. Because many of the new strategies were superior in the new environment, the carriers that changed the least had the lowest performance. Audia, Locke, and Smith (2000) obtained the same results in the trucking industry, and Audia and Boeker (2000) obtained the same results in the hospital industry, showing that this pattern was not unique to airlines. Audia and Boeker (2000) also found that hospitals with more heterogeneous boards of directors were more likely to make strategic changes, suggesting that group processes can compensate for some of the effect of high performance on risk tolerance.

Audia, Locke, and Smith (2000) were also interested in organizational mediators of the performance effect. They showed experimentally that decision makers with past successes displayed less strategic change both due to motivational factors, such as satisfaction with their current performance and confidence in their problem-solving ability, and cognitive factors, such as decreased search for information. Although the experimental subjects were undergraduate students working on a business simulation, the effect of prior performance was exactly the same as that of the managers: success before deregulation led to rigid strategies after deregulation. A second business simulation explored whether subjects could be trained to make greater adjustments of their strategies after deregulation (Audia and Boeker 2000). This study gave subjects different forms of decision-making training, including scenario generation, search for dissenting information, and search for environmental threats. The first two helped decision makers adjust their strategies, suggesting that training in collecting and interpreting information can make the strategies of successful firms more responsive to environmental change.

These studies examined a straight-line relation from performance to change, so they looked for curve 3.2(c) in chapter 3. Work on format change in radio stations provided the first test of the kinked-curve relation in figure 3.2(b) (Greve 1998). This curve reflects the predictions that firms are less likely to change when the performance is high relative to the aspiration level and that organizational inertia weakens the effect of performance feedback below the aspiration level. Format changes in radio stations are product-market changes with consequences for the strategic position and internal organization. The format of a radio station is the type of programming it delivers. Formats are categorized by different types of spoken content, such as news, talk, or sports, and by different kinds of music, such as country and western, jazz, or modern rock. Music formats are usually designed to appeal to a specific demographic segment, as defined by age and gender composition. Many formats are highly specific in choosing artists with strong appeal in their target demographic group and weak appeal elsewhere, such as the formats adult contemporary or oldies. Formats are market-niche strategies that determine what kind of listener is targeted with what kind of programming. They are also connected with a set of staffing, programming selection, and evaluation routines designed to maximize the appeal of the station to its target market.

I analyzed the following format changes. *All changes* includes all changes to the format or of the station, and the others are subsets of these changes. *Format change* includes all changes to the main format, and excludes changes in the form of programming (live, satellite, or prerecorded). *Satellite entry* includes entries to satellite format, a novel form of low-cost programming during the study period. *Innovative change* includes only changes to a set of four new formats that diffused during the study period. The purpose of analyzing subgroups of changes was to examine whether the risk of different format changes modified the effect of performance feedback. Among the subsets, innovative change had highly uncertain consequences and a likely need to replace current staff with staff members more knowledgeable in the new format. Satellite entry had more certain consequences because it reduced costs greatly, but would lead to the firing of most announcers. Both changes were thus organizationally risky, but innovative change was also financially risky. In interviews, radio station managers and staff indicated that wholesale replacement of announcers as a result of format changes was rather common in the industry, so it was a type of risk that managers were familiar with.

Table 4.7 shows the estimates of models of the four different change events. Since the probability of changes is expected to decrease as the performance increases both above and below the aspiration level, the market share relative to the aspiration level should be negatively related to format change both above and below the aspiration level, but should be closer to zero below the aspiration level. This should hold for both the historical and social aspiration level. For all changes, the reaction to both social and historical aspiration levels is as predicted: higher performance reduces the probability of change, and the reduction is greater above the aspiration level. Success reduces change more rapidly than failure encourages change, showing greater risk aversion when performance increased, modified by organizational inertia below the aspiration level.

For new formats the reaction to historical aspiration levels is also as predicted. For social aspiration levels there is lower probability of change as the performance increases above the aspiration level, but there is no relation between the performance and the probability of change below the aspiration level. This suggests that inertial forces are very strong below the aspiration level, making the reaction to very low performance nearly the same as the reaction to performance just below the performance level. Inertia below the aspiration level is seen also for historical aspiration levels for innovative formats and both aspiration levels for other production changes. In sections 4.3 and 4.4, the same relation was found for the product innovations and asset growth of shipbuilders, so strong inertia below the aspiration level is not unique to radio broadcasters. For satellite entry, there is no kink in the curve either for social or historical aspiration level, so for this outcome the aspiration level does not appear to change the behavior. It is the only outcome where the performance response curve has no kink, so most of the evidence supports the relation between performance feedback and organizational change depicted in figure 3.2(c).

Figures 4.4 and 4.5 show the estimated response curves for all changes and for innovative, satellite entry, and production changes, respectively. For all changes, the effect of historical and social aspiration levels are nearly identical – greater performance reduces the probability of making a change, and the reduction is greater above the aspiration level than

Table 4.7 Logit models of format changes in response to performance feedback[a]

	All changes	New format	Innovative format	Enter satellite	Other production change
Share – social aspiration (above zero)	-0.187**	-0.219**	-0.039	-0.194**	-0.210**
	(0.023)	(0.030)	(0.049)	(0.058)	(0.069)
Share – social aspiration (below zero)	-0.048**	-0.008	0.015	-0.114**	-0.046
	(0.016)	(0.019)	(0.050)	(0.031)	(0.042)
Share – historical aspiration (above zero)	-0.168**	-0.136**	-0.249**	-0.080	-0.264*
	(0.037)	(0.040)	(0.092)	(0.073)	(0.102)
Share – historical aspiration (below zero)	-0.054**	-0.053**	0.041	-0.072**	0.003
	(0.011)	(0.014)	(0.041)	(0.020)	(0.032)
Inconsistent aspiration levels	0.020	0.004	-0.052	0.049	0.103
	(0.020)	(0.023)	(0.054)	(0.043)	(0.063)
Change below zero:					
Share – social aspiration	0.139**	0.210**	0.054	0.080	0.164†
	(0.031)	(0.039)	(0.079)	(0.072)	(0.089)
Share – historical aspiration	0.113**	0.084†	0.290**	0.008	0.267*
	(0.037)	(0.046)	(0.092)	(0.081)	(0.114)
Number of changes:	2140	1296	206	417	251
Log likelihood	-5832.65	-4231.81	-107.08	-1784.00	-1226.18
Log likelihood test	987.28**	567.14**	46.43**	295.89**	14.26**

†p<.10; *p<.05; **p<.01; two-sided significance tests.

[a]Logit models with standard errors of estimates given in parentheses. Control variables for number of stations in market, multiunit corporation, size of corporation, share by market size, format changes in local market, recent change by radio station, recent changes in markets of corporation, and recent changes by stations in corporation are not shown. Standard errors of the coefficient estimates are shown in round brackets.

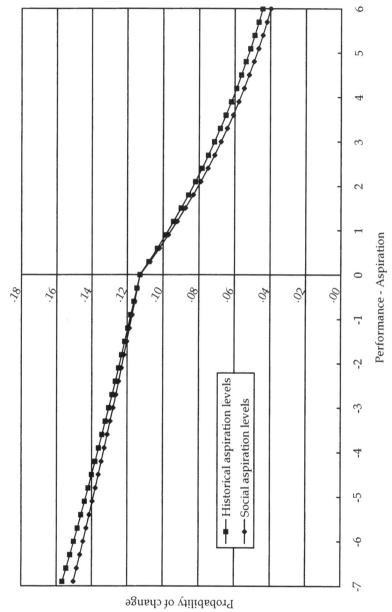

Figure 4.4 Format change in response to performance feedback

119

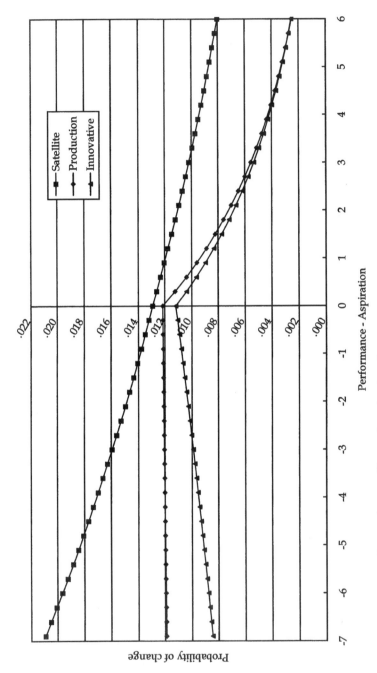

Figure 4.5 Innovative, satellite, and production change
Source: Greve (1998b). Copyright © 1998 by Cornell University.

120

below it. For satellite, production, and innovative changes, the graphs suggest that the risk level of an outcome determines the strength of the kinked-curve effect. Satellite entry was the behavior with the lowest risk and the only behavior where the relation from performance to the probability of change approximated a straight line with no kink at the aspiration level. Innovative entry was the behavior with the greatest risk, and also had the strongest kink in the curve – like shipbuilding investments and innovations, which also are very risky, the relation was horizontal below the aspiration level and sharply declining above it. As suggested in chapter 3, considerations of organizational risk clearly affect the shape of the curve linking performance feedback to organizational change.

4.6   Summary of evidence

The evidence on product-market change clearly shows that performance feedback determines the probability of major organizational changes and that aspiration levels affect the reaction to performance feedback. This evidence does not stand alone, however, but rather caps evidence on a sequence of organizational outcomes: risk taking, research and development expenditures, innovations, investment, and, finally, change of product-market niches. There are some differences in how organizations react to performance feedback for these different behaviors, and these differences are consistent with what we would expect from the different risk levels of the behaviors. Thus, the main story told by this evidence clearly supports the behavioral theory of the firm and the integration with risk theory. The variations in results seem consistent with explanations for the kinked curve that involve risk, and thus offer additional support for the theory.

The evidence is clear and strong, and most of it is very recent. As the graphs of the model predictions showed, performance feedback has very substantial effects on the rate of organizational change. If strength of results is a good criterion for guiding researcher attention, these findings suggest that performance feedback effects should be studied more intensively than they have been so far. Performance feedback predicts many different forms of organizational change. The findings are consistent across a range of dependent variables that have earlier been addressed by different theories or, in the case of investment, rarely been studied. If the range of behaviors that can be explained by a single theory is a good criterion for guiding researcher attention, then performance feedback effects should be studied more intensively than before. Finally, all behaviors studied in this chapter are risky and strategically important for the firm. If the importance of behaviors that can be explained by a theory is a criterion for guiding researcher attention, then performance feedback effects should be studied more intensively. It is hard to escape the conclusion that the earlier neglect of performance relative to aspiration levels in empirical research urgently needs to be amended by more research.

The usefulness of performance feedback theory is not limited to its ability to predict a variety of strategically important organizational changes. Performance feedback theory can help managers design performance feedback systems in ways that enhance organizational adaptation to the environment. It can also help researchers in related fields of management improve their theory. In chapter 6, I outline implications of this research in detail. The behavioral theory of performance feedback has important implications for strategic management and organizational design, which are covered in section 6.1. It also has strong links with other research traditions and important remaining questions that should be explored, and these are discussed in sections 6.2 and 6.3, respectively. Before turning to these implications, a tour of some statistical methods useful for advancing this research is made in chapter 5.

5   Advanced topics

Chapter 4 reviewed the main findings of several studies of performance feedback on organizations. It aimed to give enough detail for readers interested in applying the insights of performance feedback research to theory or practice of management, but stopped short of a full description of how the research was done. For researchers interested in doing research on performance feedback processes, additional details on how the studies were done would be helpful. This chapter aims to give an overview of research methods used in performance feedback studies and more detailed descriptions of the radio and shipbuilding data used in chapter 4. The descriptions are meant to supplement the general knowledge of research methods one gets from methodology courses and textbooks, so I will point to methods rather than describe them in detail.

5.1   Basic methods

Performance feedback affects many organizational behaviors, and research on performance feedback requires that each behavior be analyzed with a suitable method. These methods also need to be sufficiently standardized to allow comparison of findings across studies of different outcomes. The preceding chapters have shown studies on decision-making processes that triggered behaviors such as strategic change, innovations, investment, and R&D expenditures. These behaviors differ in many respects, including the decision makers responsible for outlining plans and making the final decision, the extent and type of uncertainty involved, the degree to which the decisions can be reversed if they prove to be mistakes, and other organizational and environmental characteristics. Such considerations enter the modeling stage when variables are selected. Before doing so, an even more basic concern is to choose the statistical model linking the explanatory variables (independent variables) to the outcome (dependent variable).

The type of behavior largely drives this choice. For example, strategic change either occurs during a given period or not, giving a binary (no change or change; zero or one) outcome. Counting the number of innovations in a given year is an outcome that takes the values zero or a positive integer. New investment is a continuous variable that takes only positive values, but we can also consider net investment, which takes positive or negative values, or growth in investment. Such differences result in different estimation frameworks, such as choice analysis, count analysis, or continuous-variable analysis. For all of these outcomes it makes sense to consider whether past behaviors affect the present, and this is usually captured by including measures of past behaviors or commitment in the model.

Thus, the general approach is to let the outcome measure determine the statistical model linking the independent variables to the dependent variable and a list of candidate control variables that include effects of past behaviors. Other control variables are measures of environmental opportunities, threats, and social models. Measures of organizational capabilities and constraints can also be included. The model and the control variables become a framework for studying the effect of performance feedback, and the researcher can rely on earlier studies of the same outcome to make a realistic and complete model. The modeling framework can thus be made without referring to performance feedback theory. With the framework in place, the performance variables should be defined so that they closely follow aspiration level theory.

Here I first outline the basic methods in general form, and then give examples of specific models that can be used in performance feedback research. The following notation is needed:

Y is the outcome to explain. This variable can be an event, such as making an innovation, a binary variable, such as whether strategic change occurred in a given year, a count of events, such as the number of innovations an organization made in a year, or a continuous dependent variable, such as the research and development budget of an organization. Although the type of variable obviously affects what kind of statistical model will be estimated, it is unimportant for the conceptual model of the learning process.

$F(\beta, X)$ is the stochastic function that converts a set of covariate values X and covariate coefficients β into the outcome variable Y. Thus, $Y = F(\beta, X)$. This function varies depending on the form of the response variable and the assumptions made on how the covariates affect the response variable. The usual assumption is a linear regression, so for simplicity I will use the form $Y = F(\beta X)$ throughout this discussion. The function is always stochastic, that is, F has an error term that inserts noise between the prediction and the outcome.

P is the performance variable, as in chapter 3. It is assumed to be a continuous-valued numeric variable, which means that it can be summed, averaged, and multiplied with other numbers.

L is the aspiration level, again as in chapter 3.

t is a time subscript, which in this chapter refers to discrete periods (in other methods, t can be continuous time).

I is an indicator variable that takes the value 1 if the expression in its subscript is true, 0 if the expression on its subscript it false. Thus $I_{P>L}$ has the value 1 when P (performance) is greater than L (aspiration level), and 0 otherwise.

Hypothesis testing

With this notation in hand, we can discuss the basic method. The goal is to investigate whether the difference between performance and aspiration level affects Y, and whether the effect is stronger above the aspiration level than below it. All my analyses in the preceding chapters have estimated equations of the following form:

$$Y_{t+1} = F[\beta_1 (P_t - L_t) I_{Pt>Lt} + \beta_2 (P_t - L_t) I_{Pt\leq Lt} + \boldsymbol{\beta} \mathbf{X}_t] \qquad (5.1)$$

Here, β_1 is the slope of the performance effect when the performance is above the aspiration level, β_2 is the slope of the performance effect when the performance is below the aspiration level, and $\boldsymbol{\beta}$ is a vector of slopes for the control variables in the specification ($\mathbf{X}$). The control variables often reflect other theories and may be associated with separate hypotheses. All independent variables are measured one period before the dependent variable Y. For simplicity, assume that higher values of the dependent variable mean greater change or risk taking, so β_1 and β_2 are hypothesized to be negative. Also, since inertia counteracts the effect of performance below the aspiration level, the slope of β_1 is steeper than the slope of β_2. Both slopes are negative, so this implies that $\beta_2 > \beta_1$.

The expression above (5.1) is called a spline specification, which means it contains a variable ($P_t - L_t$) that can have different slopes above and below a given point, but the effect of this variable is continuous everywhere (it does not jump). Tests of whether low performance increases the probability of change can be taken directly from the significance tests of the coefficient estimates of β_1 and β_2. Evidence of whether the "kink" in the curve is statistically significant can be found by testing whether β_2 equals β_1. Such tests are built into many statistics packages (such as the *test* statement in stata), but can also be done by hand. The trick is to manipulate equation 5.1 as follows:

$$Y_{t+1} = F[\beta_1(P_t - L_t)I_{Pt>Lt} + \beta_2(P_t - L_t)I_{Pt\leq Lt} + \beta X_t] \qquad (5.1)$$

$$Y_{t+1} = F[\beta_1(P_t - L_t)I_{Pt>Lt} + \beta_1(P_t - L_t)I_{Pt\leq Lt}$$
$$- \beta_1(P_t - L_t)I_{Pt\leq Lt} + \beta_2(P_t - L_t)I_{Pt\leq Lt} + \beta X_t]$$

$$Y_{t+1} = F[\beta_1(P_t - L_t) + (\beta_2 - \beta_1)(P_t - L_t)I_{Pt\leq Lt} + \beta X_t] \qquad (5.2)$$

Equation 5.2 is a regression that enters $(P_t - L_t)$ alone and with an interaction with an indicator variable of whether it is negative. It is exactly the same model as equation 5.1. The manipulation has isolated the difference of the slopes as the coefficient estimate of $(P_t - L_t)I_{Pt\leq Lt}$, so now the significance test of that variable is a test of whether the slopes β_1 and β_2 are significantly different. The technical expression for what the test of whether β_2 equals β_1 does is "testing a constraint". It means that the researcher estimates a model where β_1 and β_2 are allowed to be different, but then asks whether they can be given the same value without making the model significantly worse.

5.2   Estimation of aspiration levels

Because aspiration levels are so important for the theory, good estimates of the aspiration levels are important for the empirical research. In principle this is easy to do, because the theory contains careful specification of how aspiration levels are set, as discussed in chapter 3. The formulae given there introduce some subtle estimation issues that need to be addressed in order to make good empirical studies, however, and they are discussed here.

Social aspiration level

As described in chapter 3, a social aspiration level is made by observing the performance of a reference group of other organizations that are salient and similar to the focal organization. This process of social comparison results in an aspiration level that can be computed as a weighted mean of the performance levels of organizations in the reference group, as follows:

$$L_t = \sum_{a\in R} \omega_a P_{at} \bigg/ \sum_{a\in R} \omega_a \qquad (5.3)$$

Here, R is the reference group. The weights ω_a indicate the degree of closeness or relevance of each other organization a to the focal organization, and can be computed from differences in salient organizational characteristics such as size or from proximity, centrality, or structural equivalence in social networks, as in many studies of diffusion through social networks (Davis and Greve 1997; Soule 1997; Strang and Tuma 1993). The analyses presented earlier assumed homogeneous influence, so the weights were all set to one. Thus, the social aspiration level was the arithmetic average of the performance of all other organizations in the focal market.

$$L_t = \sum_{a \in R} P_{at}/N \tag{5.4}$$

Here, N is just the number of organizations in the reference group R.

There are good reasons to suspect that studies will show that social aspiration levels are made with heterogeneous weights. Research on the cognitive structures of managers has found that managers distinguish firms based on rather detailed information on their market and production processes (Peteraf and Shanley 1997; Porac and Rosa 1996; Porac and Thomas 1990; Porac, Thomas, and Baden-Fuller 1989). They are more aware of spatially proximate firms (Gripsrud and Grønhaug 1985; Lant and Baum 1995) and seem to prefer information on market similarities to information on production-process similarities (Clark and Montgomery 1999). Such cognitions have a wide range of behavioral consequences, such as imitation of specific competitive behaviors or the overall strategy of firms judged to be similar (Fiegenbaum and Thomas 1995; Osborne, Stubbart, and Ramaprasad 2001; Reger and Huff 1993) and selective response to competitive attacks based on the similarity of the attacking organization and the focal organization (Chen and Hambrick 1995; Clark and Montgomery 1998; Porac et al. 1995).

Competitor cognition may also affect the formation of aspiration levels. Firms that are viewed as similar are not only targets of imitation and more threatening competitors; they are also highly relevant targets for social comparison. Firms that have similar markets and production processes fulfill the classical relevance criterion of social comparison processes by being similar on dimensions predictive of performance (Festinger 1954; Kruglanski and Mayseless 1990; Lewin et al. 1944). They should thus be more influential in creating the social aspiration level than other firms, including firms in the same industry but with different market niches or technologies.

Finding out which firms are most influential in the creation of an aspiration level is an important empirical challenge for aspiration-level research. A multi-method approach for creating social aspiration levels with heterogeneous influence would be to use interview methods to discover which other organizations managers pay attention to, and then to use the resulting cognitive maps (Porac and Thomas 1990) to construct weights. One might first elicit important dimensions on which organizations differ through procedures such as the repertory grid technique, then use cluster analysis of the organizations with the chosen dimensions as criteria for identifying clusters (Ketchen and Palmer 1999). Once the clusters are identified, the mean performance of each cluster can be used as the aspiration level (Ketchen and Palmer 1999). Ideally the fit of a model using such a differentiated aspiration level should be compared with that of a model using an undifferentiated aspiration level and with models using alternate definitions of clusters. Such testing would provide evidence on the extent to which differentiated managerial cognition influences social aspiration levels.

Analysis of cognitive groupings is a promising but costly method of making the weights. Researchers may also try to discover the weights directly from data on strategic changes. This can be done, but the precision of the direct approach relies heavily on having sufficient data and a model that is otherwise correctly specified. The method is similar to the grid search method for finding historical aspiration levels described below and the methods used to find discount factors in studies of organizational experience curves (Audia and Sorenson 2001; Greve 1999a; Ingram and Baum 1997, 2001).

To estimate weights from the data, assume that a variable w is the dimension along which the weighting changes (e.g., w might be firm size or geographical proximity) and a functional form for how the weight depends on w. Then compute social aspiration levels where this function has different slopes, estimate equation 5.1 with each candidate slope, and select the one with the best fit to the data. Thus, if the weight is an inverse function of the difference between the values of w for the focal organization (w_f) and the other organization (w_a), then the following formula is used to compute social aspiration levels:

$$\omega_a = (|w_f - w_a|)^{-s} \tag{5.5}$$

Here, s is a positive number that can be varied to find a good estimate of how quickly the relevance decreases as the difference in w increases. For example, an s of two means that a doubling of the difference makes the other organization one-fourth as important. Side-by-side comparison of alternative specifications is then used to choose the best, and the confidence in the choice of specification can be assessed by Bayesian methods for selection of non-nested models (Raftery 1995). Formula 5.5 needs to be modified if some organizations are identical on the focal variable, however, as it will attempt to divide by zero in that case. A simple rescaling procedure would be to add one to the difference.

Historical aspiration level

The historical aspiration level is made by recalling the past performance of the focal organization. More recent performance feedback has greater weight because it is easier to recall and more relevant to the current state of the organization. A common method for assigning weights is the exponential weighted-average historical aspiration level (Herriott, Levinthal, and March 1985; Lant 1992; Mezias and Murphy 1998), which can be expressed either in recursive form (5.6 below) or as a total summation (5.7) below,

$$L_t = AL_{t-1} + (1 - A)P_{t-1} \tag{5.6}$$
$$L_t = (1 - A) \sum_{s=1,\infty} A^{s-1}P_{t-s} \tag{5.7}$$

In these expressions, A is a number between zero and one expressing how much weight is put on the previous aspiration level in determining the new aspiration level. A high A means slow adjustment of the aspiration level. Since the speed of adjusting the aspiration level is not known, it needs to be estimated when analyzing the effect of historical aspiration levels. The simplest way is by a grid search, which is a technique that relies on estimating equation 5.1 many times with varying levels of A (say, 0.1, 0.2, ..., 0.9), and then choosing the one that gives the best overall model fit. Below I give a more advanced method of estimating A.

An obvious problem with a historical aspiration level is that the equation sums backwards indefinitely, or at least until the organization is founded. This is not a practical assumption, but data-collection and computation can be simplified by noting that the product $A^{s-1}P_{t-s}$ becomes very small when A is below one and s is high. Thus, little precision is lost if the historical aspiration level is computed from performance data that start just a few years before the measurement of the behaviors. When aspiration levels on accounting measures of profit are used, it is often easy to get long time series on the performance, so the practical problems caused by this summation are minor. When using performance measures that are costly to collect, it may be necessary to consider the costs and benefits of collecting data further back in time.

Many variations on the basic aspiration level equations can be made, as discussed in section 3.1. Biases such as optimism can be built in; multiple sources can be integrated into a single aspiration level; the median performance level can be substituted for the mean in social aspiration levels. Some of these variations may turn out to be difficult to estimate or to explain no more than simpler measures, but they are worthwhile trying once the basic model has been tested and proven robust.

Estimation of aspiration level adjustment speed

Estimating the aspiration level adjustment speed from data on performance and strategy changes is a methodological challenge, since regular regression methods assume that the function to be estimated is a linear combination of covariates, while aspiration-level updating leads to covariates that are nonlinearly dependent on the values of previous observations. Recall that the basic model of change as a function of historical aspiration levels is a spline function, like this:

$$Y = F[\beta_1(P_t - L_t)I_{Pt>Lt} + \beta_2(P_t - L_t)I_{Pt\leq Lt} + \boldsymbol{\beta X}] \qquad (5.1)$$

Here, P_t is the (observed) performance and L_t is the (unobserved) aspiration level which is an exponential weighted average, like this:

$$L_t = (1 - A) \sum_{s=1,\infty} A^{s-1}P_{t-s} \qquad (5.7)$$

The combination of these two equations is the source of difficulties, since either splines or exponential averages of lagged variables can be used as regressors without particular difficulties. Regression with exponential averages of lagged variables is known as the geometric lag model in econometrics, which is usually estimated through nonlinear least squares (e.g., Greene 2000: 720–723). To do so, the analyst needs to find the adjustment parameter A by the same grid search procedure that was described earlier. Equation 5.1 is estimated using a variety of candidate A values within the possible range of zero to one, and the A that gives the regression with the lowest sum of squares is chosen. Once the best A is found, the regression coefficients are given by that regression and the standard errors can be calculated from it.

The combination of a spline and an exponential average can also be estimated by nonlinear least squares if the response variable Y is continuous, but other models call for direct estimation of the log likelihood function implied by expressions 5.1 and 5.6. The log likelihood function will differ depending on the statistical model assumed, but as an example we can use the logit function (Greve 2002b). This example is of special interest to research on organizational change, where the response variable is often an indicator variable of whether change has occurred during a given time interval, which can be analyzed with the logit model. In that case, the log likelihood is given by (Amemiya 1985: 271):

$$\text{Log } L = \sum YF(x) + \sum(1 - Y)(1 - F(x)) \qquad (5.8)$$

Here, $F(x)$ is the cumulative density function for the logit ($e^x/[1 + e^x]$) and the summations are over all observations.

As noted earlier, the data on past performance used to generate L may be truncated at some point due to unavailable data or costly data collection. In that case the following approximation of computing the aspiration level based on the n previous performance measures is used:

$$L \approx \left[\sum_{t=1,n} A^t P_{-t}\right] \bigg/ \sum_{s=1,n} A^s \qquad (5.9)$$

The denominator of this expression is a scaling factor to ensure that the weights sum to one. The formula for the sum of a series can be used to simplify the denominator, yielding the following expression, which is computationally easier:

$$L \approx \left[\sum_{t=1,n} A^{t-1} P_{-t}\right] (1 - A)/(1 - A^n) \qquad (5.10)$$

The spline function is also a source of a minor technical problem. The change in coefficient when the performance equals the aspiration level makes the likelihood function non-differentiable at that point. It is still possible to find the maximum likelihood by conventional methods, but since estimation programs differ somewhat in their handling of non-differentiability it is worthwhile experimenting with the estimation method. When I used the TSP estimation software (Hall 1993) on the radio data, the solutions reached by analytic and numeric methods for maximum likelihood estimation were similar. In that software, a robust analytic-numeric method (the Broyden-Fletcher-Goldfarb-Shannon algorithm) is available and recommended for difficult estimation problems, but the more standard modified-Newton method also worked well (Greve 2002b).

To examine whether this estimation process could recover the parameters of a sample of organizations, I analyzed data from simulated populations of organizations with different aspiration level updating speeds (Greve 2002b). I found a tendency for this method to underestimate the effect of performance above the aspiration level (β_1) when few periods of performance were used to estimate the aspiration level. This bias was reduced when more periods contribute information, and was minor for eleven periods. Other coefficients were close to the real value even when few periods are used. The results suggest that an estimator based on many periods of performance level is precise, and the main imprecision introduced by having fewer periods is that the estimate of the performance feedback effect is smaller than the actual effect.

5.3   General concerns in study design

The choice of statistical method is the culmination of the methodological work, but several decisions taken earlier are more important. These are decisions on the outcome variable, the sample, and the data collection procedures. Researchers have considerable leeway in deciding the general study design, but the credibility of the results will depend on these decisions. Next I describe some of the ideas that underpin my study designs, and suggest which of these would be valuable to retain in future studies of performance feedback and which can be changed.

The first idea is that the theory is applied to study firm behaviors rather than individual attitudes or even firm plans or intentions for behaviors. This is done as a way of dividing labor between work that develops theory and experimental evidence on human reactions to performance feedback and work on the organizational consequences of performance feedback. The basic results from the individual-level literatures are well known both from attitude and behavior measures, but moving to the organizational level introduces unique issues such as organizational inertia, competing claims for the attention of decision makers, and negotiations and coalition-forming behavior. These issues may introduce systematic differences in how organizations change their behaviors in response to performance feedback. In particular, the kinked-response curve in figure 3.2(c) is probably an organizational phenomenon without an individual-level counterpart. The emphasis on studying organizational behaviors is a feature of performance feedback research that should be retained, but researchers should also be open to using findings from individual-level research to inform the organization-level theory.

The second idea is the type of firm behavior that can be studied through the lens of performance feedback theory. I emphasize strategic decisions in this book, and have two reasons for doing so. The first is that the considerations of risk and inertia that play a role in determining the shape of the response curve (see chapter 3) are very important for strategic changes, so this outcome fits the theory well. The second is that the study of strategic change is a very active research area, with participation from researchers of both strategic management and organization theory. Both of these intellectual traditions have been influenced by the behavioral theory of the firm, so they are fertile ground for spreading these ideas. Thus, studying strategic decisions is a good starting point for testing and promoting this theory, but it is not a limitation of focus that should be kept.

These concerns suggest that changes in research focus should be expected as performance feedback research gains strength. It seems very useful to investigate the effects of performance feedback on decisions that are less important strategically, including decisions taken below the top management level of the organization. Studying other outcomes would help establish just how deep into the organization inertia and risk concerns reach, and could be used as a vehicle for examining the effect of subunit goals on the behavior of subunit managers and employees. Researchers have already started exploring these questions (Audia and Sorenson 2001; Mezias and Murphy 1998), and more studies are likely to follow. While the interest of strategy researchers may fade as performance feedback research moves into lower levels of the organization, this move will allow performance feedback researchers to establish contact with the tradition on goal-seeking behavior in organizations reviewed in chapter 2 (Locke and Latham 1990).

The third idea is that that performance feedback research analyzes performance measures that organizations generate and report to their members (and often also to outsiders) as part of their operations. Because of the importance of profit measures to organizations, they are central to this research tradition. This reflects the idea that organizations respond to goals that managers pay attention to, and does not constitute a claim on the primacy of profit variables over other goal variables on normative grounds. Indeed, which goal variables are best and whether multiple goal variables are better than a single one are important debates for both researchers and practitioners (Kaplan and Norton 1996; M. W. Meyer 1994). What should be preserved here is not a focus on return on assets or even profit measures in general, but a focus on the goal variables that the focal organizational form is known to use. This could mean different variables for certain kinds of organizations (such as nonprofit organizations) and multiple variables for organizational forms pursuing multiple goals. One could even use the methods of performance feedback research as a technical device for exploring which goals are important in a given organizational form. A kinked-curve response function between a given goal variable and a strategically important outcome variable would strongly suggest that decision makers care about that goal variable.

The fourth idea is that performance feedback research follows organizations over time. Studies that follow a group of organizations over time are called longitudinal in organizational theory and panels in econometrics, and have a number of advantages over cross-sectional study designs. Full discussions of these advantages are given in methodological treatments (Blossfeld and Rohwer 1995; Davies 1987; Tuma and Hannan 1984) and will not be repeated here, but the most important advantages for performance feedback research deserve to be mentioned. Studies over time have greater ability to show the direction of causality, stronger controls for organizational differences, and better estimates of historical aspiration levels. The first two advantages are quite general and are the reason for the substantial shift from cross-sectional to longitudinal research designs in management research over the last couple of decades. The third reason is specific to performance feedback research, and suggests that performance feedback researchers should be at least as interested in studies over time as researchers in other parts of management research.

Causality means that we can say not only that two variables, X and Y, are related, but also that variable X is the cause of Y. Informally stated, X causes Y means that changes in X will lead to changes in Y that would not have occurred without the change in X (Pearl 2000 provides a rigorous treatment). The direction of causality problem is that a statistical association of X and Y could mean that X causes Y, Y causes X, a third variable Z causes X and Y, or some mix of these three mechanisms. This leads to two kinds of erroneous inference. One is erroneous causal direction, as when X does not cause Y but is statistically associated with it because Y causes X or Z causes X and Y. The other is incorrectly estimated strength of the effect of X on Y, as when X causes Y but also Y causes X or Z causes X and Y.

Both kinds of errors are a clear possibility in research on organizations, because organizational behaviors often affect each other mutually or are jointly affected by third causes such as events in the organizational environment. The direction of causality problem is especially prominent when performance and strategic behaviors are studied, as the relation between these variables clearly can be causal in both directions. After all, managers change strategic behaviors in response to low performance because they believe that strategic behaviors affect performance. The traditional response to such bi-directional relationships has been cross-sectional designs where the variable claimed to be causal is lagged one period. Having X happen before Y is a necessary but not sufficient condition of X causing Y. It fails to provide strong evidence on causality because the reverse-cause or third-cause problems can cause statistical associations to differ strongly from causal ones when either X, Y, or a third cause, Z, changes slowly. Causal inference from cross-sectional data thus requires some "action" in X and sufficiently rapid response of Y – assumptions that cannot be tested in a cross-sectional design.

With a longitudinal design, it is possible to sort out both directions of a bi-directional causal relation and control for third causes if the correct variables have been collected. In performance feedback research, the main difficulty is that the relation from strategic change to performance differs for high- and low-performing organizations, so it is somewhat harder to study the effects of strategy on performance than the other way around. A pair of studies I did on performance as a cause and an effect of strategic change in radio stations illustrates the difficulties caused by the bi-directional relation and how they can be solved (Greve 1998b, 1999b). It turned out that the effect of change on performance could not be accurately estimated without also estimating the effect of performance on change and incorporating this estimate into the model. Such endogenous-variable models are complex, but the complexity of the models is a result of the complexity in nature. Performance feedback researchers frequently use longitudinal research designs that should give secure attribution of the direction and strength of causality, and this is a feature of the research that should be retained.

Controls for organizational differences are a second strength of longitudinal research designs. Organizational differences are a form of "third cause" that lead to problems of inference, but deserve special attention because they are such a frequent issue in organizational research. Organizations differ in many respects related to the propensity to make changes, either because of systematic differences such as the age effect on inertia or idiosyncratic differences such as organizational culture. The effect of these differences on causal attributions can be traced back to the definition of causality – X causes Y if a change in X causes a change in Y that would not otherwise have happened. If some organizations are prone to make changes regardless of their performance, the "would not otherwise have happened" part of this definition complicates the task of showing how performance feedback affects organizational change. The cure is to estimate the amount of change that each organization is prone to make and factor it out when estimating how performance feedback affects change. This requires following the organizations over time. Organizational differences are not always great – recall that it was hard to find any organizational effect on innovation rates in section 4.3 – but it is important to test for them.

Finally, historical aspiration levels are made by examining the past performance of the organization, which requires the researcher to collect data on the performance at least as far back as the managers consider the past to be important. This does not compel the researcher to have longitudinal data on the outcome variable also, since one could collect many years of performance data and one year of outcome data. The potential for all organizations in a given year to be affected by third causes such as a common social aspiration level or events in the environment makes it unlikely that good estimates of the historical aspiration level updating parameter A can be formed based on one year of outcome variables, however, since idiosyncratic events in the focal year could easily throw the estimates off. Only longitudinal data on the dependent variable give confidence in the estimate of the historical aspiration level.

Longitudinal study design is thus a feature of the research design that should be preserved in future studies. It provides causal inference and strong controls for organizational differences. A focus on firm behaviors rather than decision-maker attitudes or intentions is a second feature that should be retained, as it helps keep organizational performance feedback research distinct from individual performance feedback research. A focus on *strategic* behaviors has helped introduce performance feedback research to the field of strategic management, but performance feedback processes may well affect other organizational behaviors as well. A focus on organizational measures that managers pay attention to is necessary because only they are covered by the theory, but researchers could consider more measures than have been analyzed so far.

5.4   Radio broadcasting

Chapter 4 presents evidence on how performance feedback affects a variety of strategically important behaviors from my studies of the US radio broadcasting industry and Japanese shipbuilding industry. In order to get to the results quickly, the descriptions of these industries and the data collection from them were omitted from that chapter. Full descriptions are available in the papers from these studies, but for ease of reference I give an outline in this and the next section.

My first study of performance feedback was the radio format study reported in section 4.5. Radio broadcasting is a fruitful setting for testing effects of performance feedback because audience estimates are a shared and very important performance measure for radio stations. Audience estimates are scrutinized by a station's top manager, programming manager, and salespeople and are used to guide decisions on programming, advertising rates, targeted advertisers, and format changes. Because radio broadcasting has many local markets, there is cross-sectional variation in social aspiration levels. Because data are available over time, it is possible to get good estimates of historical aspiration levels. Audience share estimates are a goal variable viewed as important by all radio station managers and sufficiently public that data are easy to compare across time and stations for the managers and easy to collect and analyze for the researcher.

The strategic behavior studied for the radio stations was change in the format, which is a niche product-market strategy. Radio stations target specific groups of listeners by selecting a format, which is a combination of program content, announcer style, timing of program and commercial material, and methods for listener feedback and quality control. There are about thirty main formats (M Street Corp. 1992), and even more when variations on the main formats are counted. Experienced broadcasters can recognize 100 format variations. The composition of the audience differs depending on the format. Demographic profiles of some well-known formats include audiences concentrated in the teen demographic (Contemporary Hit Radio), an 18–34 mostly male audience (Modern Rock), and an even 35–54 distribution with mostly women (Adult Contemporary) (Arbitron 1991b). The size of the audience of a station depends on its choice of format and the formats of competing stations. A good choice of format can locate the station in a munificent niche with little competition, giving a large audience and high advertising revenue, but it is difficult to find an unused format that is attractive to a large audience.

Regulatory limits on transmission power mean that the competition in radio broadcasting takes place in the local city market. US broadcasting consists of about 450 different radio markets, ranging in size from New York and Long Island (population 16,321,400) to Juneau, Alaska (population 26,200) (M Street Corp. 1992), plus many locations too small to be classified as markets. The Arbitron Company, which is the dominant audience measurement firm, had 261 markets scheduled for measurement in 1991 and 1992 (Arbitron 1991a), but the set of measured markets changes occasionally as Arbitron adds or drops markets.

The audience estimates are published in market reports that list all stations with measurable influence in the market, regardless of whether they subscribe to the service or not, so they give a comprehensive view of the listening patterns in the market. Although the audience measures are estimates, and hence have some standard error and possible bias (Apel 1992), the consequences are just as serious as if they had been entirely accurate. They are presented to advertisers to justify advertising rates and sell advertising spots, in effect becoming real sources of revenue for the station. In an interview, a program director referred to the audience measures (informally called ratings) as a "report card" and then noted their significance for station revenue: "Nine times out of ten, if you have good ratings, you can charge good rates for your commercials, sell lots of commercials, and bring in as much revenue as possible. And the only source of revenue that radio stations have is advertising."

In addition to showing the effect of performance relative to historical and social aspiration levels on product-market change, radio broadcasting offered an opportunity to examine how alternatives with different risk levels have different relations with performance. This is because the format changes could be roughly divided into different risk levels. The alternative with highest risk consists of entries into one of the formats Soft Adult Contemporary, New Age, Urban Contemporary, and Soft

Urban Contemporary. These formats were recently developed and had few adopter stations throughout the study period. They were especially risky choices, as there was less knowledge available on the market potential and programming practices of these formats than on the better-known formats. This event is called *innovative format*. A low-risk event is entry into a *satellite format*. Satellite formats are provided by programming services that sell, for money or a portion of the advertising time, ready-made programming in a number of different formats. Buying a satellite feed reduces operating costs by eliminating announcers and programming staff, and it offers a retreat option, as many satellite services offer a range of formats, allowing the station to change easily if the format fails in the market. This makes entry into satellite format a low-risk alternative. Another low-risk event is *production change*, which consists of all changes among the production modes, live, simulcast, or satellite, that do not also change the format. Finally, *new format* consists of all format changes except entry into innovative or satellite formats and should have a risk level between innovative and satellite entry.

The specific performance measure used here was the 12 + Metro audience share (Monday–Sunday, 6 am–midnight). It shows the average proportion of all listeners over 12 years old tuned in to the focal station during the broadcast week. It is a gross market share that does not take into account which age segment the station targets, and is convenient for comparing the audiences of stations with different formats. Many other measures exist in the Arbitron audience reports, showing audience in specific demographic and time segments (Arbitron 1992). These detailed measures are useful for programming management and sales, but since their interpretation depends on the format of the station, they are less useful for cross-station comparison of performance, and they are not given in the usual industry data books, such as Duncan or M Street Corp.'s publications.

For evaluating how broadcasting managers use audience estimates to form social and historical aspiration levels it is useful to know the layout of the Arbitron market reports. The reports have a preamble about market characteristics and station broadcast facilities, and then present the audience estimates (Arbitron 1992). The first table is called "Metro Audience Trends" and shows for each station the most recent and the four preceding audience estimates. This is shown for a number of day parts and demographics, but the first displayed is the 12+ Mon.–Sun. 6 am–mid used in this study. Each station's history is displayed along the row, and all the stations in the market are shown alphabetically down the column. This creates a clear opportunity for both historical and social comparisons of the audience and appears to encourage social comparison with the entire market as a comparison group. This presentation of audience measures is important because it reflects the rating agency's judgment of what measures broadcasters are interested in, and it directs the attention of managers towards these measures, thus enacting them as important performance measures in this industry.

Data on the format changes were obtained from the M Street Journal, which reports on format changes in radio stations nation-wide in addition to giving other news of interest to radio managers. M Street Journal classifies formats into thirty categories, but uses sub-categories and remarks to give additional details on the changes if the formats are unusual or of special interest. Data on the audience share of the stations were obtained from Duncan's American Radio, which lists shares in 160 markets since 1975 or their inclusion in the Arbitron reports (if later than 1975). Some stations with low audience shares throughout the time period are omitted from Duncan's reports.

In addition to the variables describing performance feedback, I included measures to capture the effect of competition in the market, format changes by other stations in the market, corporate size, station income, and station and corporation experience with change. The latter two variables are relevant to the discussion of search processes since a history of reacting to adversity by changing the format will make format change an easily accessible solution, making it more likely that the organization will change its format. Including both performance feedback and the recent experience with change should separate out this momentum effect so that the net effect of performance feedback is estimated.

Radio broadcasting provided several advantages as a setting for performance feedback research. It had many organizations in many different markets with a high level of competition, giving a lot of "action" on the independent variables and good data for estimating the aspiration levels. It was easy to identify the important strategic variable for radio broadcasters, because the format is so central for their success. Although format changes are highly consequential for the station and thus risky, they can be implemented so quickly that it is realistic to model the managerial response as occurring within a year of the performance feedback, which simplified the modeling. These features made radio broadcasting useful for investigating the effect of performance on strategic change in organizations. As the findings in section 4.5 showed, performance feedback had strong effects on the format-change decisions of radio station managers, and the effects followed the kinked-curve prediction. The first test of performance feedback theory was thus a success.

5.5   Shipbuilding

I chose shipbuilding as the second industry to investigate performance feedback effects because it is in many ways the opposite of radio broadcasting. The product is not pleasant sounds broadcast through the air; it is a ship – the largest transportation vehicle in existence today. The production plant is immensely larger and more expensive, with single pieces of machinery (such as numerically controlled cutting machines) worth more than all the equipment in a radio studio and cranes capable of lifting the weight of the building housing a radio station. These differences should not matter for a truly generalizable theory. Performance feedback theory does not say anything about small organizations broadcasting music and large organizations cutting and welding steel; it is a theory of how managers change strategic behaviors in response to feedback on a goal variable they care about. The difference between a shipbuilder and a radio station, if there is any, should be in the goal variables managers pay attention to and the behaviors they view as strategic.

Shipbuilders are indeed somewhat different along those dimensions. Although there is some evidence that they care about sales, the costs of operations are so large and so variable across products that it seemed more reasonable to study profit measures than sales measures. Thus, the shipbuilding study examined the effect of profit goals on their strategic behaviors. Shipbuilders also have resources that give them more strategic leeway than radio stations. Whereas radio stations usually do only incremental in-house product development and rely instead on scanning of the industry to discover major format innovations, product development is done in-house by shipbuilders and used both for incremental upgrades and major innovations. This allowed me to analyze the resources allocated to research and development and the innovations launched by the shipbuilders. Also, shipbuilders have expensive and technologically complex production plants, and derive competitive advantages from having plants that are superior to those of their competitors, so I could study the asset growth of their factories.

There are multiple measures of profits that can be used as goal variables. The most commonly used are accounting measures that scale the profits by measures of organizational size for comparability across organizations. Of these, return on assets (ROA), return on sales (ROS), and return on equity (ROE) are popular among managers and researchers on strategic management. Consistent with the recommendations in section 5.3, the studies used the measure that managers viewed as most important for the focal decision. ROE has both an organizational component (the profitability from the current assets) and a financial (the mix of equity and debt used to finance the assets), and is often inferior for organizational dependent variables. ROS is preferable when studying the market behaviors of firms, such as the entry into new market niches. ROA is preferable for studying asset- and production-related behaviors since it is a measure of how well the firm converts its assets into profits. Thus, I used ROA for the analyses reported here. ROA had some volatility in these data, but was also autocorrelated within firms with a coefficient of 0.60. This means that the previous-year ROA explains 36% (0.6^2) of the variation in ROA. This autocorrelation fell only slightly, to 0.55, when adjusted by the social aspiration level, so firms experienced multi-year runs of low (or high) performance relative to their peers. When adjusted by the historical aspiration level, the autocorrelation fell to 0.06, so the performance adjusted by historical aspiration level was not affected by the earlier value.

Adjustment of the historical and social aspiration level was done according to the procedures described earlier in the chapter. For shipbuilding, the social aspiration level was set to the average performance of the other firms in the Japanese shipbuilding industry in the preceding years. There were few large Japanese firms in operation, between seven and eleven depending on the year, and it is quite reasonable to assume that managers of these firms would view the other firms as a social reference group indicating what the performance could and should be like. The historical aspiration level was made by the grid-search method described in section 5.2, and had a rather fast updating with high weight on the most recent period. To test for a different effect of performance on innovations above and below the aspiration level, the effect of performance was specified as a spline function, as described in section 5.1.

There are multiple strategic changes that a shipbuilder can implement in response to low performance, and a subset of these was studied. The R&D intensity was studied as an indicator of search behaviors. The growth of production assets was studied as a form of risky strategic search. The production assets of shipbuilders are very expensive, and are strategically important because their size and quality can determine which kinds of ships can be built and at what cost. As perhaps the riskiest behavior, the launching of technological innovations as new products was studied. Innovations are difficult to develop in a technologically mature industry such as shipbuilding, and even when the development is done their market prospects are unclear. Like all innovators, the shipbuilder has to make guesses about the market interest of a new technology (Burgelman and Sayles 1986), and there is high uncertainty about whether these guesses will be correct.

The history of the Japanese shipbuilding industry gives clues to the importance of assets and innovations in the strategies of the firms. The

Japanese shipbuilding industry was unusually young and underdeveloped for an island nation, as the Tokugawa government that controlled Japan until 1868 pursued an isolationist policy that included banning the construction of ocean-going ships. When Japan was opened to the outside world, shipbuilding was pursued as an economic opportunity for entrepreneurs and a strategic activity for the nation. The resulting industry included both members of the familiar list of enterprise groups (e.g., Mitsubishi, Hitachi, Mitsui) and firms concentrating on shipbuilding but linked with a main bank and a web of suppliers (e.g., Ishikawajima-Harima, Sasebo). The industry experienced the variable economic conditions that are usual for shipbuilders everywhere, and had its heyday during the 1960s when a prolonged boom in shipbuilding coincided with Japanese technological supremacy in important market niches. The technological supremacy came as a result of more than a decade of developing the product technology and production routines, as well as expanding the capacity of the shipyards to take on the production of the largest ships in the world. When the world demand for large and technologically advanced oil tankers expanded, the Japanese shipbuilders benefited from their technological prowess and investment in very large docks.

The study followed the shipbuilding industry through a period of challenging economic conditions. The 1973 oil shock caused great losses of sales, followed by a period of reorganization and recovery. The market for ships was still worse than in the 1960s, which saw so much expansion of capacity that the firms were saddled with high fixed costs. After the oil shock, many firms made their yards more flexible to take on other production tasks. In addition to general engineering, Japanese shipbuilders have manufactured products such as nuclear reactors (Mitsubishi), missiles (Kawasaki), and amusement park rides (Sanoyasu Meisho). Thus, the shipbuilders faced a choice of pushing for technological advances and investment in shipbuilding or developing their other markets. Many of them followed a strategy of pursuing both of these options at once.

R&D intensity. To test how performance relative to aspirations affects the R&D intensity of firms, I analyzed the R&D intensity (R&D expenditures divided by sales) of the Japanese shipbuilding firms from 1970 to 1995. The shipbuilding industry has an advanced technological base and substantial – but discretionary – research and development. The Japanese firms had a high rate of launching innovations, so their R&D appears to have been effective. Hundley et al. (1995) used a multi-industry sample to show that Japanese firms increased their R&D when the performance was low, suggesting that R&D is a behavior that Japanese firms adjust in response to performance feedback. Studying this issue in shipbuilding can show whether this result holds up when a single industry is studied over time and strong controls for environmental conditions, firm differences, and autocorrelation of R&D intensity over time are applied. These statistical controls should factor out many of the external influences on R&D so that any effects that remain can safely be attributed to the performance feedback.

The research and development intensity can be modeled by linear regression, but it is necessary to control for inertia in the budget allocation process and firm differences. To some extent these two concerns have overlapping effects. Inertia in the budget allocation process will cause the next-year R&D budget to depend on the current-year R&D budget, thus creating autocorrelation in the error term. Similarly, firm differences not controlled for in other ways will lead to autocorrelation in the error term. The models thus clearly need to specify autocorrelation, and may also need to contain variable- or fixed-effects controls for firm differences. Preliminary analyses showed that variable effects were significant but fixed effects were not, so the analyses apply variable effects.[1]

Innovations. To test how performance relative to aspirations affected the rate of launching innovations, I analyzed the innovations of the large Japanese shipbuilding firms from 1970 to 1995. These firms had an advanced technological base and the ability to make innovations, but were not required to do so. Although the cost of labor was higher in Japan than in most competing nations, it constituted such a low proportion of the total cost that these firms could compete with existing technology and an emphasis on price and quality. Long experience in reducing the labor input made Japanese shipbuilders remarkably productive (Chida and Davies 1990), and large portions of the shipbuilding market did not require the latest technology. Innovations were deliberate choices to enter risky – high-profit potential, high-loss potential – markets in addition to the current markets with more predictable incomes. Although the firms faced comparable competitive conditions and incentives to innovate, the data showed great variation in the rate of launching innovations. The firms launched between zero and eight innovations per year (zero in most years), and even the firms with the highest rate of launching innovations had several years with none. Performance feedback theory suggests that performance differences of these firms explain the variation in innovation rates.

To find the innovations of these firms, the monthly journals Techno Japan and New Technology Japan were read, and all innovations in the shipbuilding industry were coded. These two journals were regarded as

---

[1] Textbooks in econometrics such as Greene (2000) describe these methods and discuss the issues involved in choosing between them.

complementary sources, since New Technology Japan is published by the Japan Export and Trade Research Organization and oriented towards innovations with ready market applications, while Techno Japan is published by Fuji Research and oriented towards innovations that represent significant engineering progress. Some innovations were not attributable to any of the firms in the data, as they were made by other firms, usually suppliers. The data include 246 innovations made by firms in the data, 35 made by smaller shipbuilders, 84 made by firms that were not shipbuilders (most by suppliers), 10 made by research centers (most by the shipbuilders' association), and two made by individuals. The innovations made by firms outside the study population did not enter the dependent variable, but were counted in the control variable for innovations in the industry during the previous year.

The data were analyzed in two steps. The first step took as its dependent variable whether or not a firm made any innovations in a given year, and was done as a logit (binary choice) model. The second took as its dependent variable the number of innovations made by a firm in a given year, which can be zero, and was done as a Poisson (count) model. This was done because a problem in analyzing count data is that the results can depend on the statistical distribution, and it is difficult to ensure that the correct distribution is chosen unless the data set is large. Analyzing the binary choice of whether one or more innovations happened or not is more robust, so a comparison of the results from these two approaches should reveal which results are very secure and which may depend on the method of analysis.

Investment. Greater availability of data allowed a longer study period for investment than for innovations, and the study period from 1964 to 1995 encompasses a wide range of economic conditions including a period of sustained growth from 1964 to the 1973 oil shock. During that period, firms invested heavily in their facilities in response to the good economic conditions and to fortify their position in the profitable markets for very large and special-purpose ships. The 1973 recession caused by higher oil prices diminished demand for shipping services in general and oil shipping in particular, and shippers reacted by halting new orders and canceling ships on order or under construction. The shipbuilders reduced the ship-production capacity under a program where the government helped negotiate joint cuts in many firms. Some firms continued to invest in their facilities even as they reduced the capacity for making ships, as they made their yards more flexible to take on other production tasks. Although the firms acted jointly when the oil crisis started, they were generally competitive and displayed a wide range of reactions to the variations in economic conditions. To show how the variation in firm investment behavior could be explained by performance feedback theory, I collected data on the value of the total production facility and the machinery for each shipyard of the firms in the data.

The value of a firm's production facility in a given year obviously depends on the size it had in the previous year: machines depreciate gradually and are replaced or added as needed. This can be modeled as a growth process, where the value of the production facility in one year is a function of the previous-year value and a growth rate determined by a set of covariates. Performance feedback, slack, and other variables affect the value of production facilities by determining the growth rate. The growth rate was also allowed to depend on the current size, as earlier work on organizational growth has shown that large firms grow more slowly than small firms (Barnett 1994; Barron, West, and Hannan 1995; Hart and Oulton 1996).

Control variables. The behavioral theory of the firm also predicts that organizational slack should affect search activities such as R&D and decisions to change the organization, such as by investing and making innovations. Hence, the studies of shipbuilding also used measures of absorbed slack, which is slack absorbed as excessive costs, and unabsorbed slack, which consists of easily marketable assets such as cash and securities. Absorbed slack in operations was measured as the ratio of selling, general, and administrative expenses (SGAE) to sales. Unabsorbed slack was measured as the ratio of quick assets (cash and marketable securities) to liabilities. Finally, the ability to borrow constitutes potential slack and was measured through the ratio of debt to equity (Bromiley 1991). Because greater debt gives lower borrowing ability, potential slack has a negative effect if greater slack increases innovations. The slack measures require that the organizations be involved in similar forms of business, since they include both normal and excessive costs and resources, and thus are only meaningful when comparing organizations with similar types of operation. Since these organizations are all in the same industry, the measures should be comparable.

To take into account the general economic conditions of shipbuilding, the following industry variables were coded from various volumes of the Ministry of Transportation's annual Statistical Abstract of Shipbuilding (Zousen Toukei Youran): annual production is the annual finished tonnage (scale: million G/T) completed by the Japanese shipbuilders. The worldwide growth in shipping income is the total income of the shipping industry divided by its previous-year value. The annual high and low rates for shipping oil between key markets were also coded, and from these data the oil freight rate was computed as the annual midpoint rate from Hampton to Japan (scale: $/ton). The latter two variables reflect the economic conditions of the shipping industry in general and the oil shipping industry in particular, and are viewed as leading indicators of construction activities. Oil shipping was particularly important for Japanese shipbuilders, who were pioneers in building cost-effective large oil tankers.

The shipbuilding industry was in many ways a tougher test case for performance feedback than radio broadcasting. It had fewer firms and only one market, making the time dimension more important for separating the effects of social and historical aspiration levels. Accordingly, this study uses more years of data than the radio station did. Shipbuilding had active competition and considerable volatility of performance, so there was sufficient change in the independent variable to observe how organizations behave under different levels of performance. The shipbuilding industry is a setting where there are multiple strategic behaviors, which allowed examination of more outcome variables than radio broadcasting did. On the other hand, many of the strategic changes require lengthy implementation, which calls for the use of statistical techniques to capture changes that occur over time periods longer than a year. The shipbuilding industry is a good example of the difficulties performance feedback researchers are likely to face when examining large manufacturing firms, and it helps instill confidence in the theory and methods to see that clear effects of performance feedback were found in spite of these difficulties.

6   Conclusion

In the previous chapters we have seen the theory and the findings – now it is time to take stock and ask what it all means. Managers seek to solve problems. Managers don't seem to pursue opportunities. Is this something that should affect the practice of management? Does it have important consequences for the economy? To answer these questions, we need to examine the practical implications of performance feedback theory for the competitiveness of firms and the evolution of industries. We have seen that organizations respond to performance feedback by changing a variety of strategic behaviors, and this new knowledge can be used to make management systems that give more competitive and durable organizations. It requires some consideration, however, because here we are playing with fire – performance feedback is so consequential for how organizations adapt to their environment that poorly designed systems can have dire consequences.

We can also ask what researchers should learn from these findings. "More research is needed" will be one recommendation – it always is – but this advice is only useful if we think carefully about what research would be most valuable at this point. First we should look around in the landscape of theory and research on organizations and ask whether there are major research traditions that could learn something from performance feedback theory. Often much of the payback from a new theory comes from incorporating its insights in work that has neglected the process it studies. We should also look forward, and ask what more we would like this theory to tell us. There are still areas where the evidence is thin, so "more of the same" research is valuable. There are also places where researchers have moved quickly past sticky theoretical problems deemed difficult to solve in the first set of studies. Now that a basic set of findings has been presented, we should be confident enough to return to these problems. The result might be a more elaborate theory, but the theory and findings are currently so simple and clear that a little elaboration will not do any harm.

6.1   Practical implications

Performance feedback processes give managers many levers for controlling the organization. Top managers can choose which goal variables to emphasize, including how many goal variables the organization and its units should have. They can design the reporting of performance in ways that influence how other managers set aspiration levels. They can design organizational structures and routines so that certain forms of search are favored over others. Finally, top managers can design reward systems that influence the risk-taking behavior of organizational members including lower-level managers.

Once these choices are made, top managers can almost take their hands off the wheel, because goals, aspiration levels, and decentralized decision making turn the organization into an adaptive system. The system takes advantage of detailed knowledge of the organizational operations available only at lower levels of management, and may be superior to direct intervention from the top – at least if the performance feedback system is designed well. In practice, organizational needs for coordination and consistency require that this bottom–up system be combined with some top–down decision making, but it is crucial for organizational adaptation that the bottom–up part works well. Knowledge on how to solve problems often resides near the bottom. Let us examine some of the design considerations to see whether performance feedback research can be used to answer the question of which performance feedback systems are better for the firm.

Choosing goals. Formal organizations and goals are inextricably linked in theory and practice. Most definitions of organizations in theoretical treatments use the goal-setting aspect of organizations to distinguish formal organizations from other kinds of social groups (Scott 1987). Setting goals and examining performance feedback is a taken-for-granted part of the practice of management. Indeed, one rarely asks whether goals actually affect behavior. According to the research reported here, goals certainly do affect behaviors ranging from individual effort and risk tolerance to organizational search and strategic change. Thus, there is no need to worry about whether goals are effective management tools, but there is reason to carefully examine whether the effects are benign. There can be functional or dysfunctional goals and performance feedback procedures, and performance feedback research can help us distinguish the two.

First, we might wonder whether managers independently choose organizational goals or whether they are led to examine goals that are presented to them by external mechanisms such as organizational budgeting routines, inter-organizational influence attempts, or media attention. The issue is an old one in organizational theory. The most common answer seems to be that multiple external and internal constituencies seek to impose goals on the organization that suit their interests, so the goal-selection process is highly contentious. Managers cannot choose organizational goals except by wresting control over the goal-setting process away from those other constituents or making side agreements with them (Pfeffer and Salancik 1978; Selznick 1957). Most often, they make side agreements.

The list of interested parties is daunting. Exchange partners, public policy makers, interest groups – small and large, mass media, and the general public all feel free to make demands on organizations. Although these differ in influence depending on their importance for the organizational resource acquisition (Pfeffer and Salancik 1978), suggestions have been made on general effects on the goal-setting process. Because capital is the most mobile resource critical to organizational operations, suppliers of capital and intermediaries such as financial analysts and fund managers have been argued to be the most influential constituency of large modern organizations (Useem 1996). Others also influence the organization. Because of its immediacy and large sphere of influence, the press has been shown to greatly affect organizational behavior (Dutton and Dukerich 1991). Even greater immediacy is afforded by a role in the decision-making process, resulting in great researcher attention to the one forum for strategic decision making where outsiders regularly participate: the board of directors (Hambrick, Nadler, and Tushman 1998).

Internal constituencies are also important in the goal-setting process. Managers of organizational subunits are clearly not naïve about how goals can affect decision making, and often seek to set goals for themselves and others that can be used to justify desired alternatives. Cyert and March (1963) described how multi-dimensional goals could be negotiated one at a time as decision-makers search for an alternative that is supported by a sufficiently large coalition. Similarly, negotiation of minimally acceptable performance levels and desired performance levels can be used to sift through different risky alternatives until a management team finds an alternative that satisfies a set of negotiated criteria (Shapira 1994; Shapira and Berndt 1997). Such pre-negotiation of performance criteria protects managers from adverse consequences of low performance by preparing their peers for disappointments.

In addition to the balancing of interests involved in setting organizational goals, there are also constraints arising from how managers cognitively process goals. By now the alert reader has noticed that all studies of performance feedback in this book concerned goals *quantified* through some formal procedure. That is not a coincidence. Numbers are easy to process: they can be compared and ranked, displayed visually as trends or charts, and have clear definitions that can be written down for future recall. This cognitive simplicity and perhaps also the fact that many managers have training in quantitative analysis give numeric goals a certain magical quality (March 1994): anything that can be boiled down to a number is more likely to get organizational attention than non-numeric goals. This cognitive preference shifts attention in systematic ways. For example, a non-numeric goal of high quality easily becomes a numeric goal of low error frequency. Some nuances are lost in the translation, so overly faithful fulfillment of a numeric goal measure might reduce fulfillment of the corresponding non-numeric goal (Kerr 1975).

The need to be responsive to different constituencies and the attraction towards numbers place strong constraints on the kinds of goals that firms pursue, but do not completely determine them. Managers pursuing profitability have variously attended to market share (thought to be a cause of profitability), return on assets (an accounting measure of profitability), and stock return (appreciation of equity value), and arguments could be invoked in favor of any of these measures. One argument is that the choice is essentially arbitrary, but since either of these measures captures only one aspect of profitability, regular shifting of measures is required to keep managers from adapting too much to one goal (M. W. Meyer 1994). Shifting of measures is a good response to the problem of over-adaptation to a given measure, but ignores that some goal measures really are better than others.

Considerations of how different goal variables fit organizational search and individual risk tolerance allow more specific conclusions. Recall that an important feature of problemistic search was its initial focus on organizational activities close to the symptom. This means that goals that cannot easily be assigned to given organizational activities can be ineffective, as the ill-defined location of the problem may prevent organizations from initiating search. Search is often not a desired activity in an organizational unit, because it draws resources away from everyday activities that contribute to goal fulfillment, and it may result in proposals to change the unit that will cause conflict. Uncertainty about where the search should occur can be used to duck responsibility. Stock returns clearly lack specificity, and so do accounting measures of overall performance such as return on assets. Goals close to specific organizational activities, such as product failure rates or proportion of revenue from recent products (a much-used performance measure in dynamic industries), are more effective in initiating organizational search.

Goals close to specific organizational activities sometimes indicate the incorrect problem area, as when manufacturing quality drops because of poor product redesign. In this case, the initial response of improving the manufacturing process is unlikely to help, and a correct solution to the problem has to wait until the search has expanded. While overly specific goals certainly can delay or prevent adaptation, it should be noted that the advice of choosing performance measures that will correctly indicate problem areas is not practical. It is unreasonable to expect decision makers to anticipate in which area problems will occur, and it may be good enough to have search start in the wrong area and later expand, as problemistic search tends to do when a problem persists. Better yet, multiple specific goals can be used instead of a single general goal (Kaplan and Norton 1996), but limitations on the attention spans of managers suggest that multiple goals cannot be assigned without some division of responsibility for each goal or rough ranking of their importance. A single manager will have difficulty keeping track of many goals.

It is also important that the performance feedback be paced in a way that matches the speed of search and decision making. Here performance feedback research has reached an important and counter-intuitive conclusion: shortening the period between reports of performance can make performance feedback dysfunctional. This advice goes against the instincts of managers who want frequent performance feedback, and it is also against rational notions that more information cannot possibly be bad for decision making. The rational argument in favor of more information is easy to dismiss. It assumes that a decision maker can choose to ignore information if it is known in advance that the information will lead to bad choices, but the assumptions that one can know in advance that information will be misleading and that information can be ignored are highly suspect. In contrast, bounded rationality allows for situations where less feedback is better.

The manager's intuition that frequent feedback from a process is helpful in managing it is worth taking seriously, however, since it is certainly true in many areas of life. We drive our cars looking ahead constantly rather than intermittently, and prefer that others do the same! The car-driving analogy has been much abused in management,[1] however, and this time is no different. Driving is a poor analogy of management because it draws attention away from the role of uncertainty, which is the key feature of managerial decisions. The usefulness of performance feedback is not primarily determined by its frequency but by its effectiveness

---

[1] One of the worst examples is dismissing learning from performance feedback by referring to it as "driving a car by looking through the rear-view mirror." Since the most recent performance of an organization is a good predictor of its future performance, performance feedback is more like the speedometer than the view through your rear-view mirror. Cars and organizations are better handled by keeping track of the speed *and* the view ahead.

in predicting future outcomes. Predictive power is negatively related to frequency because of uncertainty and trends. Uncertainty argues for intermittent feedback because short-term measures of performance are less precise than longer-term measures (Lounamaa and March 1987). A short-term measure is strongly influenced by unique events that may be poorly understood by the decision maker – the kind of events that we often refer to as random noise. For example, a customer who mistakenly orders too much can cause two ticks in the sales chart if the frequency of performance feedback is short enough: an uptick in the period of the large order and a downtick in the next period when the customer seeks to reduce stocks. The difference may be large enough to suggest a problem with sales and cause an unwary manager to go looking for solutions. But there are no solutions because there is no problem, only random noise. In the longer term, the effect of any one unique event will be watered out unless the event is big, like a recession. Big events have effects on performance that managers can understand and take into account when interpreting performance feedback, so they are less likely to mislead managers than small events.

Imprecision in performance measures is especially harmful if decision makers overlook it. Random noise and trends are easily overlooked sources of imprecision in performance measures. Random noise can cause apparent performance improvements that, if taken seriously, will lead managers to conclude that a problem has been fixed, thus interrupting search processes and preventing the organization from taking needed strategic action. This problem is known to some managers, as seen in this response from Amazon.com's Jeff Bezos to a journalist asking him to explain why his stock value fell 20 percent in one day: "We've all seen this movie before. Stocks that can be up 20 percent in a day can be down 20 percent in a day" (Stone 2000).

Trends in performance feedback can make the future performance either better or worse than the current performance, so some knowledge of the context is needed to determine how they affect performance feedback. One of the most general trends in organizational behavior is the efficiency gain of learning by doing (Argote 1999), however, and this trend will make recently initiated activities appear worse than activities that the organization has some experience with (Levitt and March 1988). This bias is greater the more frequent performance feedback is taken, and suggests that frequent performance feedback can prevent organizations from persisting with new strategic initiatives. Again, the problem is known to managers, as seen in the same interview when Jeff Bezos explained the losses on the first Christmas season of selling of toys and electronics: "We did a fantastic job for customers at great expense to ourselves because there was a lot we needed to learn."

While uncertainty and trends give reasons for skepticism when performance measures are taken too frequently, the simple response of dismissing performance feedback is also wrong. Instead, performance measures should be reported and discussed at intervals that are long enough to evaluate them precisely. Since improvements in data collection and processing allow many performance measures to be taken very frequently, this often means that they should be aggregated over longer periods than would be technically feasible. Information technology has not made quarterly and annual reports obsolete; rather, it has given organizations a choice of how frequently to process performance feedback. Wise managers tailor this frequency to match the speed of industrial and organizational change processes.

The discussion so far has assumed that managers try to improve the organization, so the task is to design a reporting system that gives information that helps boundedly rational managers discover organizational problems. This is different from the agency theory argument that the function of performance measures is to align the interests of the manager with those of the owners (Fama 1980). These theories address different problems. While performance feedback theory assumes that uncertainty and bounded rationality make it hard for managers to choose an optimal strategy, agency theory assumes that managers are capable of choosing an optimal strategy but may be unwilling to do so because they have other interests (Jensen and Meckling 1976; Lambert, Larcker, and Weigelt 1993). The task of agency theory is not to aid the manager in finding good strategies, but to link stockholder and manager wealth so that the manager is rewarded or punished depending on how well stockholder wealth is managed. Clearly agency theory has a somewhat bleaker view of managerial intentions and a somewhat brighter view of managerial abilities.[2]

This difference of perspective causes conflicts in the specific advice. For example, stock options are a favored agency-theoretic incentive device because they closely tie managerial wealth to stockholder value, but are problematic from the viewpoint of performance feedback theory. Stock-value measures are available frequently; indeed they can be obtained on a minute-by-minute basis.[3] This frequency of feedback is so great that the use of stock value or appreciation as a goal will run into the problems of random noise and trends, leading to temporal myopia and resulting

---

[2] The reader may wonder why researchers do not give advice about the remaining two cases: a manager who is fully rational and acting in the organization's interest, and a manager who is boundedly rational and selfish. The answer is that the former case seems unproblematic, and the latter seems difficult to predict. The combination of bounded rationality and selfishness is common enough to be worth more investigation.

[3] A manager with a PC connected to the Internet can have a running ticker of the company share price on the screen. A manager actually installing such a ticker could justifiably be accused of lacking a long-term time perspective.

strategic inertia (Levinthal and March 1993; Useem 1996). Stock options are suitable for governing a rational and selfish manager, but are far from ideal for guiding a boundedly rational and well-meaning manager.

Generating aspiration levels. The natural way of evaluating performance feedback is to compare the most recent performance level with an aspiration level. There is so much evidence for the use of aspiration levels in decision making that it is no use discussing whether aspiration levels are functional or not: there simply is no alternative. Aspiration levels can be generated by many different processes, however, and individuals seem to be able to use a variety of stimuli to make their aspiration levels. This flexibility suggests that it is worthwhile asking whether organizations should make information available to managers in ways that encourage certain forms of aspiration levels over others.

Control over how managers set aspiration levels can easily be accomplished by thoughtful design of the performance reporting system. If managers are presented with performance measures and information useful for forming aspiration levels on the same sheet of paper, they are unlikely to look much further. Many reporting systems have default presentation of information that leads managers to favor certain aspiration levels. Accounting reports show the previous-period and current-period performance next to each other, and thus encourage a historical aspiration level. The radio audience reports discussed earlier showed a matrix of historical performance horizontally and competitors' performance vertically, encouraging a dual focus on historical and social aspiration levels. Many reports generated in strategic planning and marketing do the same. Such reports can be designed so that they emphasize the aspiration level viewed as most helpful for organizational adaptation.

A quick review of section 3.3 should convince the reader that the form of aspiration level matters for organizational competitiveness. Aspiration levels guide the timing of strategic actions just as much as the actual performance does, and a key to a competitive organization is to know when to change and when not to. Although the specific findings vary somewhat depending on the assumptions, some patterns stand out. First, aspiration levels that adapt to experience outperform fixed aspiration levels. Simply put, there is no way of building a fixed aspiration level into the organizational routines that can anticipate the future well enough to outperform aspiration levels that adapt to circumstances. This includes the "natural" aspiration level zero (the status quo).

Second, historical and social aspiration levels have the advantage of adapting to experience, but they adapt in different ways and are appropriate for different environments. The idiosyncratic nature of a historical aspiration level can cause it to be a poor reflection of what the organization can achieve in a competitive market, and it is particularly likely to go astray when the competitive environment changes greatly. On the other hand, markets with imperfect competition can have structural bases for performance differences among organizations due to different resources or capabilities, and historical aspiration levels may help organizations in such markets time their strategic changes better than social aspiration levels can. Thus, the tradeoff of social versus historical aspiration levels is simple. Historical aspiration levels are better for highly unique organizations and the oligopolistic markets they give rise to; social aspiration levels are better for uniform organizations in highly competitive markets.

In principle it is easy to select the best form of aspiration level by evaluating the uniqueness of the focal organization. The main obstacle is that managers are apt to overestimate the uniqueness of their organization. For example, radio broadcasting is close to a classical competitive market with easy entry (during the Reagan-era soft enforcement of licensing rules) and efficient factor markets, yet many broadcasting managers felt that their station had unique capabilities and should not be compared to others. The analysis reported in section 4.5 showed that radio managers weighted social aspiration levels equally with historical ones, however, so their actual behavior was better adapted to the competitive environment than their descriptions of what they did.

When making social aspiration levels, the choice of reference group is important. Judgment of the similarity of the focal organization with other organizations can help managers make differentiated social aspiration levels where the most similar organizations have greater weight. Again, this differentiation is only helpful if managers are objective judges of organizational similarity. Many findings on "lazy cognition" show that similarity judgments are driven by the availability of information more than the usefulness, suggesting that managers need help to form good reference groups. Formal procedures such as benchmarking against competitors may improve similarity judgments if the choice of which competitors to benchmark against is driven by an analysis of both the markets and value chains of the focal and comparison organization. Intuitive judgments tend to favor market characteristics, which are easily available but may conceal differences in the underlying capabilities (Clark and Montgomery 1999). Intuitive judgments may also be too simple, as they generally rely on only a few of the many characteristics that distinguish organizations (Porac and Rosa 1996).

When making historical aspiration levels, the "stickiness" of the aspiration level is important. The decision maker updates the aspiration level by adjusting the past aspiration level towards the most recent performance, and this adjustment can be made with different speeds. Chapter 3 discussed evidence that quick adjustment of aspiration levels is often inferior to slow adjustment, but did not discuss how managers can be made to adjust the aspiration level slowly. The best way is to take advantage of the power of easily available information to frame decisions. Managers are much more likely to maintain sticky aspiration levels if they have information on past budgets or performance at hand, suggesting that "forgetful" performance reports that fail to present data more than a year old should be avoided. Long-trend charts should be encouraged. This advice sounds simplistic, but it is well adapted to the power of framing on human decision making: it is very easy to manipulate our decisions by changing the presentation of numbers. The authority to design how organizational activities are reported gives top managers a very strong lever for changing the organization.

Finding solutions. Problemistic search processes are focused on specific areas of the firm, which are determined by the performance measure that caused the initiation of search and by routine attention patterns in the organization (Ocasio 1997). Focused search clearly results from bounded rationality, and carries a risk of overlooking solutions that can be found outside the search area. Despite this risk, it may be unproductive to argue against focused search – wider search expends more organizational resources and does not necessarily give better decisions. A wide search process is less likely to overlook a problem area than a focused one, but there are two reasons to believe that this advantage is smaller than it appears. First, if an organization initiates a wide search for solutions, it is likely that each organizational unit involved in the search will feel less responsibility for solving the problem. As a result, solutions may fail to come forth or may be motivated by concerns other than the problem at hand, such as plays for power or resources.

Second, if a wide search brings out many possible solutions, the final decision is likely to be seen as a choice among the solutions. This has to do with an intuitive matching of one problem to one solution rather than any real substitution of solutions, as solutions generated by different organizational units are just as likely to be independent or complementary as they are likely to be substitutes. It is often worthwhile trying to prevent the competition among solutions caused by such one-to-one matching, but it is also useful to adapt the search procedures to this competition, since it cannot be completely eliminated. The best adaptation is to avoid overly wide search. Managers will choose among solutions based on the same intuitive mapping of problem symptom and organizational unit that would have been used to steer a local search process, wasting the non-local portion of the search. The result is high search cost and frustration in the organizational units that get their solutions rejected.

While the myopia of problemistic search thus seems to be an inevitable, and perhaps also efficient, result of bounded rationality, other aspects of search processes can be modified to increase their effectiveness. As noted earlier, multiple, specific performance measures better indicate where in the organization search should be localized than a single general measure. In addition to this, greater persistence in searching allows the search process to uncover other solutions than the most obvious ones. Indeed, an important issue in organizational search is how long to persist before implementing solutions. The persistence clearly is a manageable feature of search, since deadlines for working groups can be set to directly determine the duration of search (Gersick 1988) and minimal requirements for solutions can be set to indirectly determine the duration. Japanese firms frequently employ a device of forcing deeper search by giving product development teams goals that are impossible with the current technology. Such goal setting was involved in Canon's creation of the disposable copier cartridge (Nonaka and Takeuchi 1995) and Toyota's development of the hybrid engine (Murata 2000). Setting difficult goals does not guarantee that innovations will be made, but setting easy goals almost surely precludes innovations.

Long search processes tend to result in solutions that diverge more from the current activities, but this is only helpful if the organization is searching in the correct area. This leads to the counter-intuitive conclusion that long search processes are more productive when managers know cause–effect relations fairly well. In more uncertain environments, short search processes are better because quick implementation of a solution helps managers learn if they are searching in the correct problem area. One way of thinking about this is that highly uncertain environments reward incremental strategies of small steps (Lindblom 1959), but taking many small steps requires each step to be taken quickly. It should be noted that a process of taking many quick steps makes evaluation of the success of each step difficult because there is little information to learn from before the next step must be taken (March, Sproull, and Tamuz 1991), so a second tradeoff between speed and information quality also needs to be factored in.

Some of the local bias of problemistic search can be corrected by relying on slack and institutional search. These processes do not respond to performance feedback, so it is ineffective to adjust their intensity according to the organizational performance. Instead, they can be indirectly managed by setting the size of the organizational units devoted to institutional search and the level of slack in organizational units where slack search is likely to occur. These units produce a stream of solutions that are inspired by the ideas of organizational members rather than concrete performance problems. Although the solutions do not result from performance feedback, their implementation depends on the performance because high performance makes managers risk averse. As a result, institutional and slack processes often result in solutions that are ignored at the time that they are proposed, to the frustration of the innovator, but are likely to reappear when adverse performance feedback results in a problem-solving situation. Such stored solutions are often unrelated to the specific performance measure that initiated the problem solving, but have advantages over the solutions generated from problemistic search in being speedy and having strong advocates. In organizations facing highly uncertain technology or market environments, problemistic search is so slow and imprecise that other forms of search may be more productive.

Researchers have sometimes commented on the ability of large and seemingly inert corporations to suddenly renew themselves after crises (Kanter 1989). The puzzle of long-lasting inertia followed by a vigorous burst of change is best explained by the high levels of institutional and slack search and low risk propensity of these sleeping giants. They lead to a dammed-up supply of innovations that is released when a sudden onset of poor performance increases the managerial risk tolerance. For the employees and stockholders of large corporations, this is good news because it means that the inertia results from the good times rather than from the organizational structure, so there is no need to write off the organization. For managers of smaller organizations who wish to unseat the dominant firm of their industry, it suggests that a strategy of attacking slowly enough to prevent such awakenings should be given serious consideration (Chen and Hambrick 1995; Ferrier, Smith, and Grimm 1999). The benefits of slow attacks that start in peripheral markets have already been noted in technological competition (Christensen 2000), and extend to other kinds of competition as well.

Evaluating risk. Managerial tolerance for risk is greatly affected by performance feedback, with risk appearing much less attractive when the organization performs above the aspiration level. This also is an inevitable feature of organizational decision making, and there are strong indications that such adjustment of risk tolerances is helpful overall. Failure to adjust risk tolerances by performance feedback can result in decisions that undermine the competitive advantage of strong organizations and stall attempts to improve the competitiveness of weak organizations. Adjusting the risk tolerance of organization by performance feedback takes advantage of the regression to the mean (Greve 1999b). Because of the uncertain value of new strategies, strategic change is likely to be beneficial for a low-performing organization and harmful for a high-performing organization. This alters the payoffs from change so that a manager of a low-performing organization should take greater risks than the manager of a high-performing organization.

Although the overall pattern of risk tolerance adjustment is adaptive, some biases in risk evaluation suggest that organizational risk management can be improved. First, there are strong indications that managers believe that the status quo is a low-risk alternative. The best proof of this comes from the observation that organizations with past successes avoid making strategic changes even after major environmental events such as deregulation (Audia, Locke, and Smith 2000). This is a very surprising form of strategic inertia, as it seems obvious to most observers that major changes in the environment require strategic changes even in organizations with past success. Indeed, competition metes out swift and harsh punishment to organizations that fail to change under such circumstances (Audia, Locke, and Smith 2000).

Inertia in successful organizations is caused by the belief that the status quo has lower organizational risk because it does not cause the strains of asking managers to change the activities of their subunits. Indeed, even innocuous-looking proposals for change can meet opposition from managers who view them as threats to their careers, and perhaps managers of successful organizations can more easily argue that change is not needed even when events in the environment suggest otherwise. The concern with organizational risk is a symptom of a conflict of interest between the individual manager and the organization. Organizational risk is mainly a career risk for the manager proposing a change rather than a financial risk to the organization as a whole. For the organization, it is less important than the risk of being maladapted to the environment. While many strategic changes have both organizational and financial risk, there are clearly situations in which the status quo has greater financial risks than strategic change.

In addition to deregulation, discontinuous environmental changes such as new technologies, free trade agreements, and large shifts in consumer preferences create disjunctures in the competitive situation that make the organizational adaptation to the environment obsolete. The effects are often obvious in hindsight, but not at the time that strategic decisions have to be made. For example, smaller hard disk drives became valuable because they created new markets (Christensen and Bower 1996), aggressive territorial defense became valuable in the airline industry when prices were deregulated (Gimeno 1999), and the value of low fuel consumption in cars increased so much that the "minicars – miniprofits" maxim of US automakers became obsolete (Keller 1994). In all of these cases, long lead times from strategic choice to strategic implementation meant that the organization had to commit to a strategy before the environment had fully completed its change (disk drives, airlines) or before the effect of the environmental change was well known (automobiles).

The low risk of the status quo is caused by the mutual adaptation of the organization and its environment over time, and it vanishes when the environment undergoes radical change. The $5^1/_4$ inch hard disks really were better than $3^1/_2$ inch hard disks for the extant applications and stage of technological development. US auto customers really did prefer large cars, but were forced to rethink this preference when the cost of operating them escalated. Territorial accommodation really was better when public price controls made the number of airlines on a given route irrelevant to the airfare. As the environment changed, however, constraints on possible behaviors were removed, increasing the menu of alternative strategies. Risks and rewards to different behaviors changed, making prior knowledge obsolete. When the environment changes, boundedly rational managers judge risks not by complete analysis of alternatives, which is infeasible given the large number of alternatives, but through heuristics such as viewing the status quo as low risk or viewing strategic changes done by a plurality of its competitors as low risk. These heuristics could easily be wrong. A sufficiently radical environmental change has effects that make it difficult to predict the risk of any action or inaction, and imitation is useless if the imitated organization knows as little as the organization that imitates (Huff 1982; Rao, Greve, and Davis 2001).

While radical environmental changes are important because of their great consequences, smaller-scale changes seem to be more common. In those situations, the conventional ranking of the status quo as less risky is likely to be true, but only in the strict sense that it has lower variance. The strict definition of risk is not always useful to managers. The low risk of the status quo could include outcomes such as a steady but sure erosion of market share, which is often less attractive than the wide dispersion (negative and positive) of outcomes following from making strategic changes. It is still important to recognize that risk and expectation are different constructs that both need to be evaluated when choosing alternative strategies. A conscious choice of taking risk prepares the organizational members for poor outcomes, but choices based on too high expectations and unevaluated risk generate disappointments (Harrison and March 1984). There is a strong tendency towards underestimating the risk of a chosen alternative, as managers often overlook the effect of unexpected events or believe that they can negotiate or maneuver the organization away from their adverse effects (Shapira 1994).

The analysis preceding a given decision is unimportant as long as the decision leads to performance exceeding the aspiration level, but will matter if the resulting performance is lower than the aspiration level.

Low performance resulting from a change that was claimed to have low risk undermines managerial credibility, making further strategic changes under the same management difficult. The likely result is a regression to the status quo before the change, followed by conflict and eventual replacement of the management team. Repetition of this sequence of events leads to a downward spiral that may end in failure of the organization (Hambrick and D'Aveni 1988). Low performance resulting from a change that was known in advance to be risky can be reacted to more effectively because it is a smaller threat to managerial credibility. Regression to the earlier status quo is still possible, but so are additional large changes or smaller adjustments to the strategy. If the potential for better decisions is not sufficient to motivate a realistic assessment of risk, the circumscription of future strategic choices resulting from unrealistic pre-decision judgments should be.

Making decisions. The most conspicuous effect of performance feedback on organizational decision making is the tendency to drastically reduce the rate of making risky decisions when the performance is above the aspiration level, but to increase it only slowly when the performance is below the aspiration level. Success prevents strategic change more than failure promotes it. Organizational inertia and commitment to prior decisions are the prime causes of this behavioral pattern, which has been observed for many risky behaviors and organizational forms. The resulting kinked-curve relation from performance to strategic change is a stable feature of behavioral decision making that seems hard to escape, but we should still consider whether its effects are beneficial and whether organizational decision making can be adapted to it.

After several presentations of the kinked curve to various audiences, I have found that the reaction to it is nearly unanimous. The overall decline in risk taking as the organizational performance is increasing is viewed as laudable prudence; the flatter curve below the aspiration level is viewed as stick-in-the-mud inertia that ought to be prevented. It turns out that the instinctive reaction is only correct in some circumstances, as the optimal reaction to performance feedback differs depending on the environment. As in the discussion of aspiration level generation, the conclusion hinges on the competitiveness of the market.

Intense competition means that there are many firms with similar product offerings, leading to price pressure and squeezed profit margins. Among the conditions generating such competition, a lack of distinct organizational capabilities may be the most important. Distinct capabilities allow organizations with the most valuable capabilities to dominate the whole market or niches in the market, resulting in differentiation based on capabilities and less price competition within each market niche. The

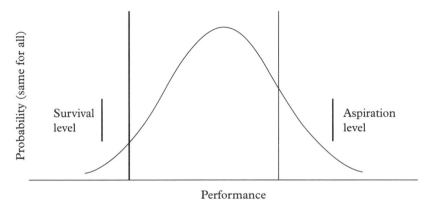

Figure 6.1 Strategic change with homogeneous capabilities

importance of capabilities for competition is well known, and sometimes leads to the recommendation that managers should focus all their attention on obtaining capabilities that give high performance. Since the performance hinges on good deployment of capabilities as well as on the capabilities themselves, this recommendation is wrong (Penrose 1959). With or without capability differences, managers need to use performance feedback to make strategies for how to use their organization's capabilities. It is still useful to know whether capabilities affect competition, because the heterogeneity of capabilities determines the optimal way of reacting to performance feedback.

Figure 6.1 illustrates the strategic choices of organizations in a market with homogenous capabilities. Since all organizations have the same capabilities but the performance consequences of different ways of deploying these capabilities are not known, all organizations face the same probability distribution over possible future performances. Let's assume that managers are concerned with an aspiration level of the performance they seek to achieve and a survival level of the minimal performance that will let the organization continue operating. A manager of an organization performing below its aspiration level will decide whether to change or not by balancing the hope of getting an outcome above the aspiration level against the fear of falling below the survival level. The way the curve is drawn in figure 6.1, the most likely outcome from a new strategy is that the organization will again be between the aspiration level and the survival level. The second-most likely is performance above the aspiration level, and the third-most likely is falling below the survival level (and thus, ruin). Because of the homogenous capabilities, the probabilities of these different outcomes are *independent of the current performance level*.

Under such conditions, it is not possible to justify the greater inertia below the aspiration level – on the contrary, organizations should be
increasingly willing to change as their current performance falls. Performance to the left of the peak in figure 6.1 implies that a change is likely
to improve the performance; any reduction in performance from a given
level will increase the probability of improvement without increasing the
probability of ruin. Reasoning outside the model for a moment, it seems
likely that members of a homogeneous population of organizations will
be able to use imitation and other devices to learn from each other how to
deploy their resources, leading to a gradual reduction of the uncertainty.
The probability distribution will become narrower and more peaked.
When this occurs, both gains and losses from changing will diminish.

Although this homogeneous world appears in many economic models, a different set of assumptions will seem more realistic to scholars of
strategy and organizations. Organizations have different sets of capabilities due to differences in resources, accumulated learning, and organizational structure and procedures. These capabilities are sticky – they
are difficult to appropriate for other organizations. An important component of this stickiness is the double uncertainty involved in competition
over capabilities, as managers are seeking to discover both how to deploy
capabilities most effectively and which capabilities are most valuable. Simultaneously solving these two tasks is not a reasonable task to ask of a
boundedly rational decision maker, so the likely result is that managers
know that organizational capabilities differ but not exactly how this can
be exploited.

Figure 6.2 illustrates the strategic choices of organizations in a market
with heterogeneous capabilities. In this figure, the capabilities of each
organization determine its probability distribution of possible performances, and the deployment of capabilities determines its current performance. For simplicity, I have drawn these probability distributions
as being equal except for a shift of the mean; the reader can experiment
with other ways of drawing them. Now consider an organization with performance between the aspiration level and the survival level. Note that
all points in that area could be a result of any of the capability curves, so
knowing the current performance does not tell which distribution belongs
to the focal organization. However, since the distributions have different
thickness (probability density) in the different points, an organization
with low performance is more likely to have low capabilities.

This difference in context drastically changes the strategic choice. Since
the current performance affects the judgment of capability, lower current performance leads to a higher estimated probability of ruin and a
lower estimated probability of exceeding the aspiration level. Under such

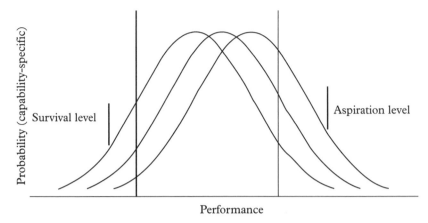

Figure 6.2 Strategic change with heterogeneous capabilities

conditions, inertia is not as unreasonable as intuition would have it. As long as survival is an organizational goal with similar importance to high performance, the kinked-curve decision rule is better than linear decision rules in environments with heterogeneous capabilities. It results in organizations that often fail to fulfill their aspiration levels, but have lower likelihood of outright failure than organizations following more responsive decision rules. The inertia of the kinked-curve decision rule means that it is not likely to win any beauty contests among management scholars, but its hardiness explains why it is so prevalent. Other rules simply don't survive as well as it does when organizational capabilities are heterogeneous.

For managers, there is no easy answer to the question of whether to accept some inertia when the organization falls below the aspiration level or whether to be quick to make changes. The tradeoff between survival and performance is a value judgment where decision analysis can only point out the tradeoff, not indicate the best solution. Current values suggest an emphasis on value creation for stockholders over the survival of the organization, but this judgment is based on assumptions of costless disposal of failed organizations and their workers. These conditions are highly dependent on the overall state of the economy. In good times, many failed firms are highly tradable assets, and many workers who do not wish to be traded with the firm can choose to go elsewhere instead. In less buoyant economic conditions, the tradability of firms and mobility of workers are both reduced. An economic downturn can make the consequences of risky choices much worse than they seemed at the time that they were made.

6.2   Related research

The theory of performance feedback and organizational change is a self-contained theory of how the organizational performance influences strategic decisions under uncertainty. The theory can be analyzed in isolation, but it is informative to study its links with other theories. Different research traditions of organizations and management overlap in the processes and outcomes studied, and comparing them in areas of overlap helps develop them further (Campbell 1969). When they study the same process, do they make the same prediction? When they study the same outcome, do they give the same results? When the research traditions are consistent, our confidence in their findings increase and we can move our attention to other research questions in order to avoid duplication of effort. When they are not consistent, we have a puzzle that can inspire more theoretical and empirical work and can ultimately advance the theories or replace them with better ones (Kuhn 1972; Lakatos 1978). Many theories have some sort of overlap with performance feedback theory, but here I emphasize five important theories that have strong links to it. They are learning theory, managerial cognition, institutional theory, organizational ecology, and agency theory.

Performance feedback theory belongs to a family of theories inspired by the behavioral theory of the firm and its concepts of experience, search, and routines. These theories are usually referred to as the Carnegie School (these days often a historical reference to a Golden Age) or learning theory (the more common but less well-defined term). Performance feedback theory shares assumptions with this group of theories, but has a unique domain and emphasis among the learning theories.

A recent and growing tradition in managerial cognition has drawn ideas from work on organizational enactment and individual cognition to explain how managers categorize other firms and differentially pay attention to them. This work is inspired by concerns of bounded rationality and cognition that also are prominent in performance feedback theory, and has given results on how organizational cognition and managers' mental maps moderate behaviors. It examines processes that are similar to those involved in aspiration-level updating, which makes it important to the development of performance feedback theory.

Institutional theory incorporates assumptions of boundedly rational and socially motivated behavior that are consistent with performance feedback theory, but it has a distinct emphasis on external agents of change. Performance feedback and institutional theory have a significant overlap of domain, since many outcomes studied as performance feedback outcomes here have been viewed as results of mimetic processes by institutional scholars. This overlap of outcomes makes a comparison of the results interesting.

Organizational ecology in its original form differed significantly in its basic assumptions of external agency and in its domain of organizational founding and failure, but has later moved towards a greater interest in adaptation processes and in organizational change as a dependent variable. There is particularly great overlap between the current version of inertia theory and performance feedback theory, so an analysis of the remaining differences is valuable.

Agency theory shares a concern with goals and performance measurement with performance feedback theory, but is based on a rational choice assumption. It has resulted in a significant amount of modeling work in economics and some efforts of integration with organization and management theory. Integration with the behavioral ideas of performance feedback theory is an important task for the progress of agency theory.

Learning theory. A discussion of learning theory needs to start with a definition of the subject. Here I adopt Levitt and March's (1988) definition, which states that learning theory views organizational behavior as being (1) based on routines, (2) adapted to experience, and (3) oriented to goals. Although it seems wide, this definition is sufficiently narrow to eliminate many other theories, including forward-looking theories like agency theory and some theories of strategic management, conflict-oriented theories such as resource dependence theory and various domination theories, theories lacking adaptation such as strict population ecology, and theories lacking a goal orientation such as institutional theory.

There are still many theories left under the learning theory category. They can be classified in several ways, and a popular classification is based on classifying the source of learning implicit in the theory. Organizations learn from direct experience, from interpretation of the experience, and from the experience of others, and retain this learning in an organizational memory (Huber 1991; Levitt and March 1988; Walsh and Ungson 1991). Another way of classifying learning theory is to note that it is difficult to put equal emphasis on routines, experience, and goals, so theories will tend to emphasize one of these over the others. Although no theory deals with one element of learning to the exclusion of others, the differences in emphasis allow us to distinguish theories of routines, of experience, and of goals.

Theories of routines include work on how organizational routines develop through the regular execution of work, such as in research examining learning curve effects on production costs (Argote 1999; Day and Montgomery 1983; Yelle 1979). This research has shown that organizations become more efficient as production experience accumulates, and some of this improvement in routines can be transferred across different organizational units. Organizations lose efficiency when their production system is idle (Argote, Beckman, and Epple 1990; Benkard 1999), so the efficiency gain must be maintained through continuous use of the routines. Also included in routine theory is work on organizational efforts to develop and utilize knowledge, often through a mix of regular production and special activities such as research and development (Leonard-Barton 1995; Nonaka and Takeuchi 1995; Starbuck 1992; Von Krogh, Roos, and Kleine 1998). Much of this work aims to discover which organizational structures and routines allow quick generation, absorption and application of new knowledge (Cohen and Levinthal 1990; Tsai 2001; Van den Bosch, Volberta, and de Boer 1999).

Work on routines also includes studies that examine specific types of organizational routines and the processes that modify them. Research on jobs and rules has been particularly important (March, Schultz, and Zhou 2000; Miner 1990, 1991; Schultz 1998; Zhou 1993). These streams of work show that routines are created and modified as a result of problem-solving activities in the organization, but suggest some differences in how the processes work. Jobs are born from opportunities given by the specific skills of individuals (Miner 1990), and rules are born from environmental turbulence (Zhou 1993). Both are modified by experiential learning within the organization (March, Schultz, and Zhou 2000; Miner 1991).

Theories emphasizing experience include work on organizational effects of salient environmental events, such as technological change, the diffusion of innovations, or firm failures (Cohen and Levinthal 1990; Henderson and Clark 1990; Miner et al. 1999; Strang and Soule 1998). Most of this work is on diffusion, and shows that a variety of innovative activities will be incorporated into organizations whose managers observe that other organizations have adopted them (Greve 2002a). Thus, innovations that are observed in the environment become potential solutions for organizational problems, making such observation a substitute for internal search. Research on experience also includes work on the interpretation of the organization's own experience. A good example is momentum theory, which uses interpretation arguments to suggest that organizations repeat and extend previous strategic commitments (Amburgey and Miner 1992; Kelly and Amburgey 1991). Researchers interested in the interpretation of experience have also shown that salient events in organizations are given interpretations that collapse the ambiguity of cause–effect relations in unique experiences into confidently held explanations and prescriptions for future action (March, Sproull, and Tamuz 1991; Schein 1992; Weick 1995).

Performance feedback theory emphasizes the goal orientation of organizations, and thus belongs to the third category of learning theory. It is the only well-developed theory of organizational goal orientation, which gives it a unique position within the field of organizational learning. Because it emphasizes an aspect of organizational learning that theories of routines and experience give little attention to, it is complementary to them. By suggesting a change in research emphasis, however, it is at least indirectly a competitor to these theories.

Let us start by discussing the complementarity. While it has so far not been used this way, performance feedback theory clearly has the potential to strengthen other theories of organizational learning. Learning curves have been studied extensively, and many variables are known to modify the speed of improvement in a production system (Argote 1999). From the viewpoint of performance feedback theory, the absence of performance and aspiration levels in learning-curve research is conspicuous and difficult to explain when considering how important these variables are for predicting rates of search and experimentation in other contexts. Learning curves are at least in part the result of search processes, which are known to be affected by performance feedback. Thus, it seems highly likely that learning curves are influenced by performance feedback from local goal variables such as unit costs, and possibly also from global goal variables such as firm profitability. It should be an important task for learning-curve research to look for such effects.

A similar attention to performance feedback would be natural in knowledge research if this research had the rate of search as its primary emphasis. Instead, knowledge researchers are more interested in qualitative studies of successful (and some unsuccessful) development processes to distinguish what organizational conditions lead to more successful knowledge development. Suggested variables are division of labor in the development process and routines for incorporating external knowledge, transmitting it internally in the organization, and allowing experimentation (Jelinek and Schoonhoven 1990; Leonard-Barton 1995). Performance feedback also affects product development, as I showed in chapter 4, and should be investigated further. Doing so requires a change in approach towards broader studies of many development projects, including projects that were stopped by management (Dougherty and Hardy 1996; Dougherty and Heller 1994).

Research on the diffusion of innovations among organizations has a long empirical record with remarkably little attention towards performance feedback. The studies reported here strongly suggest that innovations observed in an organization's environment will be imported when its performance is below the aspiration level, and some work has directly shown such effects (Greve 1998b). Studies of the diffusion of innovations that have performance variables are scarce, however, and when performance is included aspiration levels usually are not (Kraatz 1998). The reason seems to be two legacies from traditional diffusion research (Rogers 1995). First, diffusion studies have emphasized external pressure to adopt so much that organizational susceptibility to pressure has been neglected (Strang and Tuma 1993). Second, when susceptibility has been studied, the emphasis has been on stable characteristics of the adopter such as adopter categories (innovator, early adopter, early majority, and so on). Situational factors such as performance have been overlooked. The strong effects of performance feedback on organizational change suggests that diffusion researchers have overlooked an important variable.

We can turn the tables and ask how other theories of organizational learning can inform performance feedback theory. The potential seems great, especially in sharpening predictions on what kind of change the organization will do. It seems clear that search processes at least initially follow oft-traveled routes (Ocasio 1997), suggesting a momentum effect that would predict risky organizational changes of the same kind that the organization has done recently. There is an implicit recognition of this in many of the studies reported here. It is more or less an industry tradition for radio stations to turn to format change and for shipbuilders (in Japan, at least) to upgrade facilities and launch innovations, so it should be no surprise that these outcomes were effectively studied through performance feedback theory. One would expect less success in studying, say, radio station upgrades of production facilities[4] and shipbuilder size of sales force, as these are less frequently manipulated strategic variables. It would be valuable to make a more general integration of organizational momentum, industry recipe, and performance feedback theory.

Similarly, the assumption that the organization will find some solution when searching is an important part of performance feedback theory. Contrary to this assumption, many small organizations contain capabilities for the daily production and distribution task but lack slack resources to search effectively. Even in large organizations, many mass-production techniques keep workers busy with routine tasks at all times, leaving no time to search for improvements. The main contribution of quality management techniques to production efficiency may be in creating such slack time and allocating it to problem-finding and problem-solving activities. Organizations practicing lean management techniques may have so few resources that can be redirected to search activities that

---

[4] Or maybe not. I made four case studies of format changes, and two of those included changes in production assets.

their capability of generating solutions is severely limited. Instead, they can imitate solutions available in the environment, but in a solution-poor environment even this is difficult. Diffusion theory can be drawn on for predicting when environments are rich enough in solutions for resource-poor organizations to react to performance feedback, and when such organizations remain inert because solutions are hard to find.

Managerial cognition. A core assumption of organizational learning theory is that decisions are affected by how managers perceive and interpret their experience (Daft and Weick 1984). Managerial cognition is a research tradition that shares this view and has explored the details of how managers make mental maps of their competitive environment and use these maps to collect, interpret, and react to information (Porac and Rosa 1996). Managerial cognition is an applied branch of social cognition theory (Fiske and Taylor 1991), and shares its focus on how human memory is structured, used to control behavior, and changed in response to experience.

Memory structures contain categories of external actors and events along with information on their attributes (Fiske and Taylor 1991). The attributes are used to assign experiences to categories. Once assignments have been made, category information can be used to fill in missing information and predict future events. For example, certain behaviors are thought of as indicating competitive rivalry, so organizations showing those behaviors are categorized as rivals and expected to display other rivalry behaviors in the future. This expectation is used when the manager makes decisions that may involve the organization categorized as a rival. Categorization affects future behaviors directly through its use in prediction and indirectly through its use in processing and remembering relevant information about the focal actor, as information received later is used to test the initial categorization rather than to re-categorize the other actor from scratch (Fiske and Taylor 1991).

Much research on managerial cognition so far has focused on what the cognitive structures of managers look like. As social cognition theory would predict, managers categorize their competitors into groups based on a few characteristics ordered by importance (Porac and Thomas 1990). The result is a tree-like structure, where the most important criterion is applied first for a rough categorization, then the next-most important criterion, and finally a third criterion is applied (the trees are often not deeper than three levels). The judgments of similarity and relevance of a given competitor to the focal firm drop off sharply if it is categorized in a different group than the focal firm, causing managers to consider a small subset of the industry to be worthy of close monitoring (Lant and Baum 1995; Porac, Thomas, and Baden-Fuller 1989; Porac et al. 1995).

This categorization of competitors is much narrower than the actual set of firms that could affect the organization through their pricing and marketing behavior, so managerial cognition leads to competitive myopia.

The similarity judgments resulting from managerial mental maps affect information collection, which again shapes the competitive behavior of firms. As in work on the diffusion of innovations, a major finding of managerial cognition research is that firms imitate the competitors they view as most similar to themselves (Abrahamson and Fombrun 1994). Because mental maps of the industry are similar across managers working in different firms (Porac and Rosa 1996), the result is groups of firms that imitate each other, leading to convergence of strategies within each group over time (Fiegenbaum and Thomas 1995; Huff and Huff 1995; McKendrick 2001; Osborne, Stubbart, and Ramaprasad 2001; Reger and Huff 1993). Groups converge internally and diverge from other groups (Cool and Dierickx 1993), making it difficult for firms to move from one group to another (Mascarenhas 1989). Still, clear differences in the performance of different groups can cause groups to merge over time (McKendrick 2001; McKendrick, Doner, and Haggard 2000), so managers do not completely ignore the world outside their strategic group.

Performance feedback theory can contribute to managerial cognition theory by offering ideas on how performance relative to aspiration levels moderates the link from mental maps to behaviors. The occasional jumps between strategic groups seen in strategic group research are clearly innovative, high-risk behaviors, and it seems likely that they are predicted by performance below the aspiration level. A study of location strategies in the hard-disk drive industry implicated low performance when explaining why the US and Japanese firms, which initially formed different strategic groups with an international and a domestic manufacturing strategy, respectively, eventually converged to a strategy of manufacturing in Southeast Asia (McKendrick, Doner, and Haggard 2000). Interestingly, the convergence was not complete – most Japanese firms moved to the Philippines instead of to the Singapore–Thailand locations favored by US firms. It might also be worth exploring whether the movements towards the center of the strategic group result from performance feedback. We would expect that successful firms keep their current strategy, while firms with performance below the aspiration level implement mimetic changes (Greve 1998b).

Managerial cognition theory can contribute to performance feedback theory by giving a more accurate model of how social aspiration levels are made. The similarity judgments underlying strategic groups are most likely also used in judging the relevance of other organizations for evaluating performance, and thus are involved when managers construct social aspiration levels. There is already some evidence that a combination of performance feedback and managerial cognition theory can give aspiration levels that predict strategic change in organizations. Performance relative to social aspiration levels within cognitive strategic groups in the hospital industry predicted change in organizational technologies and market niches (Ketchen and Palmer 1999). Research on heterogeneous social aspiration levels would fit well into a larger set of research findings on how social similarity judgments affect a wide range of organizational behaviors, and deserves more attention than it has received so far.

Institutional theory. Institutional theory seeks to explain how elements of organizations, such as structures, routines, and occupations, are created and spread in society (Meyer and Rowan 1977; Scott 1995). These elements are called institutions and "consist of cognitive, normative, and regulative structures that provide stability and meaning to social behavior" (Scott 1995: 33). As an example of an institution, consider personnel management, which is a meaningful category of organizational behavior, a concrete organizational structure, and a set of rules and norms on how organizations should treat their employees. A given organization may have many possible institutional configurations, and the benefits of any such configuration are very difficult to establish. As a result, the design and management of organizations is done under high uncertainty, and managers often decide by following the examples of others or conforming to demands by actors outside the organization (DiMaggio and Powell 1983). This lets institutions spread through diffusion or advocacy by occupations or powerful organizations such as the state.

Institutional theory shares important assumptions with performance feedback theory. Uncertainty about the consequences of managerial choices plays a role in both theories, as does observation of other organizations. There are also important differences. Performance feedback emphasizes risk, but institutional theory does not. In the strategic decision-making problems studied by performance feedback theory, a decision is uncertain and consequential – after making a change, the organization may experience significant changes of performance. In the decisions to adopt institutions examined by institutional theory, the value of the decision is often unclear after it has been made as well. Many institutions have small effects on the organizational performance measures that managers tend to emphasize. Their effects on the organization's conformity with values and assumptions of societal actors may be large, but are difficult to assess (Meyer and Rowan 1977).

Once the risk aspect is removed, the predictions are also different. Institutions such as personnel management are thought to be important to fulfill societal and legal requirements, and so they spread among organizations through imitation and influence from professionals (Edelman 1990; Sutton and Dobbin 1996; Sutton et al. 1994). The benefits of these practices are uncertain even after adoption, as some of the alleged effects are to protect the organization against future lawsuits from employees. As a result, personnel management practices are adopted once and for all, with little chance of being re-evaluated and dropped. By contrast, equally uncertain behaviors like the adoption of securities for coverage by investment analysts also spread by imitation, but these are re-evaluated based on their performance and quickly abandoned if the analyst is disappointed (Rao, Greve, and Davis 2001). Institutions have been argued to differ from the technical core of organizations (Scott and Meyer 1983), which is similar to saying that they are different from activities with consequences that are easily measured.

Low performance is not argued to be necessary for an organization to adopt a new institution. Since having certain institutions is a performance in and of itself (Berger and Luckmann 1967; Goffman 1990), the spread of new institutions creates a kind of performance shortfall in organizations that do not have them yet (Meyer and Rowan 1977). Performance feedback theory and institutional theory thus discuss different causal sequences. In performance feedback theory, the problem comes first, and then managers search for a solution. In institutional theory, the solution comes first, and its proponents search for problems that it may solve (DiMaggio 1988). These do not have to be specific or current problems, but can consist of claims that organizations without the focal institution will be deficient in some sense or will face problems in the future. New institutions are not solutions to problems, but solutions searching for problems.

Researchers taking the perspective of performance feedback theory are likely to believe that the reversed sequence of events will not eliminate the role of performance in the adoption of institutions. Even if the solution comes first, it is easier to argue that it should be adopted in organizations with performance below the aspiration level. From the viewpoint of performance feedback theory, proponents of institutions act as "solution entrepreneurs" who use a problem of low performance to argue for the adoption of their favorite institution. This would predict that organizations with performance below the aspiration level are most at risk of adopting a new institution, an insight that could be applied to studies of the spread of new institutions.

Performance feedback theory also offers a challenge to the suggestion that institutions are kept over time or succeeded by a "new and improved" institution thought to solve the same problem. Abandoning prevalent institutions is a risky behavior that could be triggered by low performance of the organization overall or of the institution in question (when its effects can be assessed) (Greenwood and Hinings 1996; Oliver 1992). It is thus not clear whether institutions will be kept over time. Indeed, researchers have noted that hallowed institutions such as liberal arts education have been violated by colleges seeking to improve their performance (Kraatz 1998; Kraatz and Zajac 1996).

Performance feedback theory suggests a resolution to this theoretical problem. To a given organization, a new institution is an innovation, but established institutions are taken for granted (Meyer, Boli, and Thomas 1987). *Deviating* from established institutions is an innovation that entails risk because other actors may fail to recognize or support the focal organization if it differs too much from the taken-for-granted form (Deephouse 1996; Oliver 1991). Thus, performance feedback theory predicts that organizations with low performance are quick to adopt new institutions and abandon established ones. This prediction clearly deserves to become a part of future research on institutions.

On the other hand, institutional theory brings a puzzle to research on aspiration level decision making. The prediction that organizations will do various contentious, strenuous, and risky strategic actions in response to low performance seems to ignore the easy way out offered by the diffusion of new institutionalized structures or faddish management practices (Abrahamson 1991; Staw and Epstein 2000; Zeitz, Mittal, and McAulay 1999). Surely managers suspect that some of these practices have benign but small effects on the organizational performance. They might use adoption of such practices to act as if they are solving problems without actually taking risks. A sufficiently cynical manager would be tempted to stem criticism through this device, especially one who suspects that the current performance shortfall is temporary. Perhaps managers do adopt more new institutions when the performance is low – performance relative to the aspiration level is rarely studied as a cause of adopting institutions, so we cannot be sure. As the research reviewed in chapter 4 suggests, however, they also engage in risky organizational changes. Managers seem to be making serious effort to recover from low performance, not just putting on a show.

A more fundamental challenge from institutional theory is the idea that organizational goals are institutions that may differ across societies and over time, so performance feedback theory is explaining organizational behavior by a variable that keeps changing. In the heyday of PIMS and conglomerates, sales was king, then return on assets took over, and now managers are accountable for the movement of stock prices (M. W. Meyer 1994). How should this affect performance feedback theory and research? It seems that the theory is not much affected, since it does not make claims on what kind of goal managers will have. Still, it derives much of its relevance for management practice from the fact that managers have been paying attention to performance measures that have some connection with organizational competitiveness. The conclusions on organizational adaptation reviewed in section 3.3 hinge on this connection, and performance feedback would be unimportant for competitive advantage if managers were picking measures willy-nilly without worrying about the relevance to organizational competitiveness. Though there is a lively debate on the quality of various performance measures, we have not yet seen measures that are so arbitrary that they suggest that managers are willing to ignore their role in measuring organizational competitiveness.

Shifting attention among performance measures is a problem for empirical research on performance because it complicates the task of finding the right independent variable. To take a concrete example, the analyses of Japanese shipbuilders reported in chapter 4 took return on assets as the goal variable, as studies of US firms tend to do. This seems to ignore that many practitioners and some researchers have argued that Japanese firms pay more attention to market share than to profits. I think that this specific argument is wrong, and chose ROA deliberately rather than by reflex. Still, the question of generality and stability of performance measures is worth asking. Two arguments have been made. One is that there has been an increasing homogenization of the world society and economy, especially for corporate actors such as business firms (Meyer, Boli, and Thomas 1987). This has partly been a process of cultural influence, but dependence of firms on an increasingly international capital market has also contributed (Useem 1996). This argument would predict uniformity across society, but not necessarily stability over time.

The other argument is that local cultural influences are very strong, and tend to modify the form and reduce the influence of imported institutions (Guillen 1994). This argument would predict differences across societies but stability over time. The introduction of these issues into the debate is too recent for us to have a good empirical answer to which conception is right. They suggest that researchers need to be sensitive to the institutional context in which organizations operate, as goals can be created and modified through the processes that institutional theory emphasizes.

Population ecology. A large body of theory and empirical research on organizations has developed in the field of population ecology (Hannan and Freeman 1977, 1989). Ecological research emphasizes organizational demography – how the birth rates and life spans of organizations are determined, and how this affects the diversity of organizational populations (Carroll and Hannan 2000). At least initially, the theory contained little managerial choice, as environmental forces such as competition and institutionalization were the most-examined causes (Carroll and Hannan 1995b). Emphasizing the founding and failures of organizations as outcomes and environmental forces as causes was controversial and led to debates about the realism and usefulness of such research (Donaldson 1995; Perrow 1979). This is not surprising, as organizational theory is periodically drawn into debates on the primacy of environmental or internal causes that resemble the philosophical debates on free will in individuals (Astley and Van de Ven 1983; Hambrick and Finkelstein 1987; Hrebiniak and Joyce 1985), but the debate had little impact on actual research.

An ecological theory of only founding and failure would be useful for predicting the evolution of populations of relatively inert organizations, which was its initial purpose, but would have had little relevance for performance feedback theory. Population ecology has expanded its scope to also involve organizational change (Barnett and Carroll 1995), however, which brings it into closer contact with the theory of this volume. The most important point of contact is the theory of organizational inertia, which is both a theory of when organizations change and a theory of the consequences of change (Hannan and Freeman 1984; Peli et al. 1994).

According to inertia theory, organizational change is usually detrimental. Changing core features of the organization such as its product-market strategy or production technology weakens the organization's internal cohesion and its adaptation to environmental actors. The internal argument applies the learning-theory finding that organizational routines improve through repeated change, and thus that organizational changes require using new routines that are executed less efficiently (Amburgey, Kelly, and Barnett 1993; Barnett and Freeman 2001). This loss of efficiency causes increased operational costs and may lead to quality problems and mis-steps in the organization's relation with its resource environment. The external argument notes that the market for resource exchange relations is not fully efficient. Thus, replacing the content of exchanges or exchange partners consumes time and resources. Old exchange partners may resist changes in the content of exchange, and potential new exchange partners do not immediately trust the organization enough to trade with it on good terms (Barnett and Freeman 2001). The internal and external weaknesses cause organizations that have just changed to be more likely to fail (Amburgey, Kelly, and Barnett 1993; Barnett and Carroll 1995). The argument on why inertia is a common feature of organizations is a simple extension of the argument on its effects. Since change weakens organizations, organizational structures and procedures that encourage change are "lethal genes" that will become scarce through selection processes (Hannan and Freeman 1984; Peli et al. 1994).

There is a clear conflict between inertia theory's contention that organizational change is rare and hazardous and performance feedback theory's contention that organizational change is a predictable and often beneficial consequence of low performance. There is also some common ground in these two theories. Performance feedback theory predicts that organizations make fewer adjustments in the rate of change in response to low performance than to high, and underpins this kinked curve with inertia theory's arguments for why routines that encourage change are scarce in organizations. Simulations and empirical research from performance feedback theory has suggested that the kinked-curve relation from performance to change is a highly survivable behavioral rule because it lowers the exposure to the hazards of change (Greve 2002b). Thus, both theories recognize that change is hazardous, but performance feedback theory qualifies this with the argument that not changing is sometimes worse, so correctly timed change can be adaptive. Similar arguments are also seen in inertia theory and empirical work, suggesting that these theories will converge in the future (Barnett and Carroll 1995; Haveman 1992).

What seems most important for population ecology to learn from performance feedback theory is the contingent relation from current performance to benefits of change. Organizations changing when performing poorly have little to lose and may benefit from regression towards the mean, so for them the temporary weakening due to change is less important than the long-term benefits. Already inertia studies have started examining performance or competitive relations as a modifier of the effect of change on performance or survival (Greve 1999b; Ruef 1997), and more such research should be expected. This suggests a modification of the theory of inertia. The prediction from a selection perspective is no longer that organizations will stay inert, but rather that the most survivable relation from performance to change will become more frequent in organizational populations. As always when selection arguments are applied to organizational populations, it is important to keep in mind that the selection advantage of good routines may be too small to allow the organizations with most survivable routines to become predominant (Carroll and Harrison 1994). Simulations have suggested that the most robust performance feedback routines can outcompete other routines when failure rates are high or organizations that are founded mimic the most successful firms in the population (Greve 2002b).

What seems most important for performance feedback theory to learn from ecological theory is that organizations may select which parts to change based on their centrality to organizational operations. According to inertia theory, organizations have a core consisting of their (1) mission, (2) forms of control, (3) core technology, and (4) product-market strategy

(Hannan and Freeman 1984). These core parts are particularly central to the organization's operations, and are inert because changes to them would greatly disrupt the organization. Other portions of the organization are peripheral and can be changed with fewer adverse consequences. As a result, managers are likely to change peripheral structures before attempting change in core structures. This theory offers yet another answer to the question of where organizations will make changes in times of adversity: peripheral structures such as support units (e.g., personnel department, staff) or parts of the value chain that are distant from the customer (e.g., inbound logistics) are the most likely locations of change.

Theorists have thus made the following suggestions for where organizations will change when performance feedback indicates a problem: (1) near the symptom (behavioral theory of the firm), (2) in organizationally vulnerable areas (behavioral theory of the firm), (3) in areas with low organizational risk (risk theory), (4) in areas where changes have recently been made (momentum theory), and (5) in peripheral areas (inertia theory). This long list of candidates can be reduced somewhat by noting that some of these suggestions overlap. Organizational risk is the likelihood and seriousness of resistance to the proposed change, which is largely a function of the power of the organizational unit to be changed. Since organizationally vulnerable areas are defined to be units with low power, they are the same as areas where changes lead to low organizational risk. Similarly, the proposition that centrality in an interdependence structure gives power (Thompson 1967) suggests that peripheral areas are the same as organizationally vulnerable areas. What remains, then, are the suggestions that changes will occur near the symptom, in units with low power, and in units that have recently changed. These are competing theories of where change will occur, and further research is needed to know which are true. They may all be true in the sense that these are the areas where an organization is most likely to make changes, but the specific area chosen will vary depending on circumstances. For the time being, we know too little to predict what circumstances will lead to what kind of change, but we may soon be able to answer this question.

Agency theory. Agency theory is an economic theory of how one actor, called the principal, can use rewards to control the behavior of another actor, called the agent (Grossman and Hart 1982; Holmstrom 1979; Milgrom and Roberts 1992; Mirrlees 1975). Applied to organizations, it is used to argue which reward systems are best for making top managers do the bidding of stockholders or making lower-level employees do the bidding of their managers. The proposed reward systems almost invariably involve rewards for high performance in order to spur maximum effort. As noted earlier, this means that agency theory uses performance feedback to discipline organizational members rather than to help them diagnose problems.

An important issue for future research is the extent to which agency theory is compatible with performance feedback theory. There are important differences between these theories, especially in the extent to which they assume rational actors, but they share a concern with investigating how goals can help managers make decisions that improve their organization. Regardless of whether performance feedback theorists like the assumptions of full rationality underlying agency theory, it remains true that managers are agents of the organization's stakeholders and thus may need some mechanism to align interests. Regardless of whether agency theorists like the satisficing behavior of performance feedback theory, it remains a superior model of decision-making behavior. Clearly these two traditions should have a conversation in order to integrate the ideas of the other.

Some advances have already been made. Organizations involve risk taking at all levels, from the financial risks of owners to the career risks of managers and non-managerial employees. In good governance structures, individuals are allowed to control their own risk taking or can trust others who control it to act in their interest (Garud and Shapira 1997). Difficulties in achieving such alignment of risk and control include asymmetric judgments of risk due to different proximity to the decision-making process and asymmetric preference for risk due to different aspiration levels (Garud and Shapira 1997). The result is that individuals may end up taking more risk than they believe they are doing because they are not fully informed, or may be forced to take more risk than they prefer because they do not control the risk taking. A good example is when employee pension plans managed by the firm purchase the focal firm's stock, which gives the employees more concentrated risk than they would voluntarily choose.

When designing compensation systems to align individual risk taking with that of the organizational owners, additional difficulties arise from the mental accounting processes that individuals use to set aspiration levels for their own wealth (Heath 1995; Thaler 1985; Thaler and Johnson 1990). Payments that are conditional on organizational performance can make individual decision makers cross their aspiration level for wealth, leading to abrupt changes between risk aversion and risk taking (Wiseman and Gomez-Mejia 1998). Managers seeking to avoid compensation below the aspiration level may thus change organizational risk-taking patterns more abruptly than the owners would like them to, in effect over-reacting to the contingency of their payment. This problem is amplified when compensation is tied to volatile performance measures such as those tracking stock or product-market performance. Investors often prefer such measures because they are harder to manipulate by managers than accounting measures (Wiseman and Gomez-Mejia 1998). Risk theory suggests that the gain of getting measures that are difficult to manipulate is purchased by more volatile risk preferences. Thus, the performance feedback used to discipline often works at cross-purposes with performance feedback used to diagnose and solve problems, suggesting that the two uses of performance feedback will often need to be balanced against each other. A new agency theory that takes into account bounded rationality and performance feedback effects on behavior may have to be developed.

6.3   Future research

The review of research done so far has indicated that we know a great deal about how performance feedback affects some organizational behaviors. For other behaviors, we know little. The theoretical predictions that have been studied so far have an impressive record, but empirical research has only tested a limited set of predictions on how performance feedback controls the rates of making various organizational changes. There are many possible routes of advance from here. The theory could be used to make additional predictions, either from the current set of propositions or by adding others. We can strengthen the empirical evidence within the current domain of the theory, extend the domain, delineate the scope more precisely, and add theoretical propositions.

Let us start by defining some important concepts. Researchers working on a specific problem leave behind a written record of theory and empirical research and carry along a set of implicit or stated assumptions. Both the written record and the implicit assumptions are elements of a research program (Lakatos 1978), and often research programs can be advanced significantly by questioning some of the implied assumptions rather than just tinkering with problems in the written record. There are several places where changes can be made.[5] First is the *theory*, which is a set of concepts linked by causal propositions. The theory is often the easiest part of a research program to work with, because it is recorded in papers and in theory chapters of books such as this (see March and Simon, 1958 or 1993, for a particularly elegant example). Because it is

---

[5] These three paragraphs borrow heavily from lecture notes of Morris Zeldich Jr.'s course Basic Problems in Sociological Theory, which is still the best analysis of theory that I have encountered.

hard to change the core propositions of a theory without making a different theory, much theoretical work consists of adding propositions that allow additional predictions or more precise predictions. Sometimes theoretical progress can be made by using formal logic to clarify ambiguities in theory that have been expressed verbally (Peli et al. 1994). The core of performance feedback theory was developed in *A Behavioral Theory of the Firm* (Cyert and March 1963), and recent additions include the integration with risk theory (Bromiley 1991b) and the kinked-curve prediction (Greve 1998b). It is a lean and effective theory, and propositions can be added without making it unwieldy.

The second place where change can be made is the *domain* of the theory, which is the set of outcomes that it seeks to explain. Domains are difficult to identify without careful attention to omissions in the theoretical and empirical record, because they are rarely made explicit. This is because empirical researchers' selections of outcomes to study determine the domain, and they are guided by interest in the outcomes as much as by a theoretical strategy. But a theory is not limited to affecting the outcomes that happen to the interest of an empirical researcher, so systematically testing theory calls for attention to which outcomes would be most diagnostic for examining the theoretical process in question (Berger, Zelditch, and Anderson 1966). I have been very explicit about the current domain of performance feedback theory as being strategically important organizational changes determined by managers. This acknowledges my bias and gives a clear target to researchers who are interested in extending the domain. Performance feedback theory has the potential for affecting other outcomes as well, giving plenty of opportunities for additional empirical work.

The third place where change can be made is in the *scope* of the theory. The scope is the conditions under which the theory holds. The difference of scope and domain is that the scope concerns societal conditions that allow the mechanism of the theory to function, while the domain is the behaviors affected by the mechanism. Scope conditions are often implicit, but in a different way than domain conditions. Whereas actual domain conditions are often wider than researchers believe, that is, the theory applies to more outcomes than expected; actual scope conditions are often narrower than researchers believe. There may be multiple conditions that prevent an organization from making changes when the performance is low or staying the same when the performance is high, starting with general issues such as the extent of managerial discretion (Hambrick and Finkelstein 1987). These are difficult to discover empirically because our empirical methods are very good at extracting semi-spurious findings from a population of actors where some display the predicted effect and others don't.[6] Careful theoretical analysis is needed for making sharper delineation of the scope, and this is an important task in making theory more precise.

The theory, domain, and scope of a research program are related to each other, so changes in one can lead to changes in the other two. Currently, performance feedback research has a fairly narrowly delineated domain, and it is likely that the theory will be applied to additional outcomes. In doing so, researchers may discover scope conditions that they have not previously encountered. For example, maybe changes conducted by organizational subunits are not fully responsive to either top management goals or subunit goals, but to some combination of these or to other variables (Audia and Sorenson 2001). Such scope conditions can be turned into theoretical propositions by, for example, adding theory on when subunit managers will be attentive to top management goals or subunit goals. Thus, the opportunities for additional empirical research that are discussed in this section should be seen as opportunities to develop the theory as well as to test it.

It follows that a good path of progress can be found by first reviewing where in the current domain the evidence is thin. This will suggest areas where additional research is needed to increase our confidence in the findings. It will also suggest possible extensions of the domain to new dependent variables, and analysis of these extensions requires considering whether additions to the theory or scope conditions are necessary.

Current evidence. We know a lot about the risk taking of individuals, and also some about the risk taking of organizations. The main gap in our knowledge of risk taking is whether organizational inertia gives the predicted kinked-curve relation from performance to organizational risk taking. A second area where we are beginning to know much is in strategy changes such as market-niche changes – many studies have found an effect of performance feedback, and some also have shown a counteracting effect of inertia. These are the outcomes that we know most about, but their great importance for organizations suggests that further research is needed to resolve the questions that remain. For example, the kinked-curve relation has only been examined in a few studies, and aspiration level updating is not well enough documented empirically to allow firm conclusions on whether historical or social aspiration levels are predominant in organizations.

---

[6] This is a semi-spurious finding because the method makes an unbiased estimate of the average effect on the study population. Such an estimate is useful for raw prediction in a population with a similar mix of actors, but theoretically it misses an important point. The theory applies only to some of the actors, and it is important to discover the scope condition that determines which actors the theory applies to.

Research and development expenditures have been studied a great deal, and researchers often find the predicted decrease of such search activities when the performance increases. This is one outcome where the theory does not predict an effect of inertia, but naturally the absence of a kinked curve is difficult to prove. So far there is no evidence suggesting that inertia affects the adjustment of R&D expenditures according to performance feedback.

Although we know a fair amount about R&D expenses, which are inputs to the innovation process, we have little systematic evidence on the rate of making innovations. The research from the shipbuilding industry reported in section 4.3 suggests that firms launch fewer innovations when the performance is high, and that the increase in innovation when performance falls below the aspiration level is counteracted by an inertia effect. The result is a kinked-curve relation, consistent with the theory, but more evidence on this issue is needed to be confident of this finding. Innovation rates are important for the focal firm and the evolution of the industry, so additional research would be extremely valuable. Similarly, evidence on asset growth is very thin, but so far it is completely consistent with the theory. Asset growth is an important part of firms' buildups of strategic capability, and it would be natural for researchers in strategic management to investigate it further.

Extensions of domain. Future work should not just fill in evidence in places where little has been done so far; it should also investigate additional outcome variables. This will help explore how wide a domain the theory has, and some outcome variables can help build the theory by providing better understanding of the decision-making process. Replacement of the firm's CEO, for example, is clearly a high-risk, strategically important change that performance feedback theory can help predict. It is important, however, to distinguish planned succession from involuntary replacement. Planned succession is frequent, and is often timed at the usual retirement age and combined with the promotion of an heir-apparent who has been chosen and groomed for the job by the CEO (Cannella and Shen 2001; Ocasio 1999; Vancil 1987). Involuntary CEO replacement is an unplanned event that involves performance feedback along with boardroom politics and rivalry among executives (Boeker 1992; Fredrickson, Hambrick, and Baumrin 1988; Ocasio 1994; Puffer and Weintrop 1991).

Involuntary CEO replacement differs from the outcomes discussed in chapter 4 by being decided by the board of directors. It is a group decision rather than an individual one, and the group is composed of individuals who have a part-time relation with the organization and a highly diverse set of other experiences. It is far from clear how uniform their goal variables and aspiration levels are, and thus the goal conflict issue raised by group decision research is important to board-level decisions. Research on CEO replacement can indicate how performance feedback affects group decisions, and is thus important for developing performance feedback theory. It is also important for corporate governance theory, which has examined performance feedback effects on CEO replacement, but has not given aspiration levels the attention they deserve (but see Puffer and Weintrop 1991).

Multiple goals are also important when examining decisions involving both the top management layer and lower-level functions and divisions. This issue becomes prominent when researchers examine organizational changes that fall under the purview of a given organizational function. Organizational subunits have different goals than the top management when their interests are different or the organization has a control system that assigns subunit goals to their managers. Regardless of the reason for having multiple goals, it is important to learn how organizations resolve conflicts among goals held by different subunits, that is, horizontal goal conflict, and among goals held by subunits and goals held by the top management, that is, vertical goal conflict. Horizontal and vertical goal conflicts result in influence and bargaining processes among managers, and top managers may be unable to resolve the conflicts according to their goal variables. This raises the question of how much other goals than those held by top managers influence the decision-making processes of organizations.

At the very least, the potential for goal conflict suggests that researchers on performance feedback need to be alert to the possibility of multiple goals and aspiration levels affecting the behaviors. It may be useful to examine various subunit goals in addition to the usual profit goals that top managers often face. In addition to this, performance feedback theory can become a tool for uncovering power relations inside organizations through analysis of which goal variables are most important in explaining organizational change. A classic definition of power states that "A has power over B to the extent that he can get B to do something that B would not otherwise do" (Dahl 1957: 202–203). Following this definition, powerful actors in organizations can be identified by whether they affect organizational changes that would not otherwise have happened. This idea has been viewed as empirically unproductive since it is difficult to tell in retrospect whether A wanted the outcome that happened and B did not want this outcome (March 1966), and thus power becomes unclear because motives are unclear.

If we make two fairly stringent assumptions, performance feedback theory offers a way out of this dilemma. If we assume that attempts to change organizations often meet resistance, and that we know which managers care most about which organizational goals (Bower 1970; Fligstein 1990), it follows that the power of functional managers can be measured by seeing whether performance on their favored goal variable affects organizational changes. This approach will still suffer from the unpredictability that happens to all power models if individual power is allowed to be affected by past power use (March 1966), but seems to be a promising way to discover power relations.

Researchers can examine subunit behaviors as well as subunit goals. Some lower-level decisions have already been investigated. The advertising behavior of a firm relates to overall product-market strategy, but is usually viewed as a smaller decision that can be left to specialists, perhaps in consultation with top management. The themes of advertising campaigns can be altered, which changes the way the organization presents itself to the outer world if not its internal behaviors. Advertising campaigns can also involve risky behaviors such as attacks on competitors' products. Analysis of advertising behavior has shown an effect of performance feedback (West and Berthon 1997). More analysis is clearly possible, including an examination of whether inertia has an effect on how advertising campaigns are changed in response to performance feedback. The theory seems to imply that there is no inertial effect, since changes of advertising campaigns carry financial risk but not organizational risk.

Performance feedback theory can be applied to the diffusion of nonstrategic behaviors among organizations. Many technologies, practices, and structures are used in peripheral units of the organization where changes can be done without great organizational risk. The organization may adopt new information technology (Sandberg 2001), select an auditing firm (Han 1994), or add an investor relations department (Rao and Sivakumar 1999). These are all fairly minor changes compared with the strategic changes that we have discussed earlier, but all have the potential for affecting the organizational performance or social standing. The studies I just cited emphasize imitation as a driver of adoption, as I have also done in earlier work (Greve 1996), but it may be useful to combine this explanation with performance feedback. It seems reasonable that managers who adopt an innovation learn it from other organizations *and* are trying to improve organizational performance.

An additional theme for future research would be to examine what performance feedback in the decision-making process looks like "on the ground." Qualitative work on organizational decision making has tended to emphasize different aspects of the process depending on the specific organizations studied and the theoretical frame of the researcher. Performance feedback and aspiration-level processes might be rather subtle, since they are revealed mainly through whether managers look at a given performance variable, and whether they view certain values of it as good or bad. They may be difficult to discover for a researcher who is not primed to look for behaviors predicted by performance feedback theory. Researchers interested in aspiration levels have found that they played a role in the Cuban missile crisis (Whyte and Levi 1994) and other policy decisions (Vertzberger 2000), and experimental researchers have found that subjects talk about aspiration levels when making decisions (Hennig-Schmidt 1999). There are good opportunities for investigating performance feedback effects through direct observation of decision-making processes.

Qualitative work on decision-making processes has shown that contacts across multiple levels of management are important for decisions involving risk such as investments (Maritan 2001) or innovations (Dougherty 1992; Dougherty and Hardy 1996). Lengthy search processes involving proposal development at lower level and approval at higher level is common, suggesting that sustained attention to a problem or opportunity is needed for organizational change to be implemented. The search processes cut across horizontal functions and vertical levels in the organizations, and thus activate multiple aspiration levels and goal variables. In addition to qualitative work interpreting search processes from the viewpoint of performance feedback theory, quantitative research measuring variables such as the duration of the search process and the number of actors involved would provide additional knowledge of how performance feedback affects search. This is particularly useful because search and risk taking often have joint effects in performance feedback predictions, making it hard to distinguish which has the greater effect on the outcome. More detailed work on the search process may help separate these effects.

Although it is conducted by scholars from multiple disciplines and appears in a diverse set of journals, research on performance feedback processes in organizations is currently sharply focused on proving a basic set of propositions concerning how low performance causes organizations to change their strategic behaviors. These are important propositions, because they have direct consequences for organizational adaptation to the environment. Still, researchers can branch into other areas of investigation once they are satisfied with the basic findings, and performance feedback research could potentially end up as a sprawling affair that seeks to inform a wide range of managerial activities. It has little to lose from such an expansion, and it could end up influencing many research programs on how organizations make changes.

References

Abrahamson, Eric. 1991. "Managerial fads and fashions: the diffusion and rejection of innovations." *Academy of Management Review*, 16(3): 586–612.

Abrahamson, Eric and Charles J. Fombrun. 1994. "Macrocultures: determinants and consequences." *Academy of Management Review*, 19(4): 728–755.

Albert, S. 1977. "Temporal comparison theory." *Psychological Review*, 84: 485–503.

Amburgey, Terry L. and Anne S. Miner. 1992. "Strategic Momentum: the effects of repetitive, positional and contextual momentum on merger activity." *Strategic Management Journal*, 13: 335–348.

Amburgey, Terry L., Dawn Kelly, and William P. Barnett. 1993. "Resetting the clock: the dynamics of organizational change and failure." *Administrative Science Quarterly*, 38: 51–73.

Anderson, Philip. 1995. "Microcomputer manufacturers." *Organizations in Industry: Strategy, Structure, and Selection*, eds. G. R. Carroll and M. T. Hannan. Oxford: Oxford University Press. 37–58.

Andrews, Kenneth Richmond. 1971. *The Concept of Corporate Strategy*. Homewood, IL: Dow Jones-Irwin.

Antonelli, Cristiano. 1989. "A failure-inducement model of research and development expenditure: Italian evidence from the early 1980s." *Journal of Economic Behavior and Organization*, 12: 159–180.

Apel, Steve. 1992. "Understanding radio ratings: Why they're called 'Estimates'." *M Street Radio Directory*, ed. M Street Corp. New York: M Street Corp. 15–17.

Arbitron. 1991a. *Market Survey Schedule and Population Rankings*. Washington, DC: The Arbitron Company.

Arbitron. 1991b. *Radio Today 1990*. Washington, DC: The Arbitron Company.

Arbitron. 1992. *Arbitron Radio Market Report Reference Guide: a Guide to Understanding and Using Radio Audience Estimates*. Washington, DC: The Arbitron Company.

Argote, Linda. 1999. *Organizational Learning: Creating, Retaining, and Transferring Knowledge*. Boston, MA: Kluwer Academic Publishers.

Argote, Linda, Sara L. Beckman, and Dennis Epple. 1990. "The persistence and transfer of learning in industrial settings." *Management Science*, 36: 140–154.

Arndt, M. (2001). "Eli Lilly: life after prozac." *BusinessWeek*, 53–54.

Ashford, Blake E. and Alan M. Saks. 1996. "Socialization tactics: longitudinal effects on newcomer adjustment." *Academy of Management Journal*, 39(1): 149–179.

Astley, W. Graham and Andrew H. Van de Ven. 1983. "Central perspectives and debates in organization theory." *Administrative Science Quarterly*, 28: 245–273.

Atkinson, John William. 1983. *Personality, Motivation, and Action: Selected Papers.* New York: Praeger.

Audia, Pino G. and Warren Boeker. 2000. "Success, persistence, and regression to the mean." Manuscript, University of California, Berkeley.

Audia, Pino G. and Olav Sorenson. 2001. "A multilevel analysis of organizational success and inertia." Manuscript, University of California, Berkeley.

Audia, Pino G., Edwin A. Locke, and Ken G. Smith. 2000. "The paradox of success: an archival and a laboratory study of strategic persistence following a radical environmental change." *Academy of Management Journal*, 43(5): 837–853.

Badaracco, Joseph L. 1988. "General Motors' Asian alliances." Case no. 9-388-094. Boston, MA: Harvard Business School.

Bandura, Albert and Forest J. Jourden. 1991. "Self-regulatory mechanisms governing the impact of social comparison on complex decision making." *Journal of Personality and Social Psychology*, 60(6): 941–951.

Barley, Stephen R. and Gideon Kunda. 1992. "Design and devotion: Surges of rational and normative ideologies of control in managerial discourse." *Administrative Science Quarterly*, 37: 363–399.

Barnett, William P. 1994. "The liability of collective action: growth and change among early telephone companies." *Evolutionary Dynamics of Organizations*, eds. J. A. C. Baum and J. V. Singh. New York: Oxford. 337–354.

Barnett, William P. and Glenn R. Carroll. 1995. "Modeling internal organizational change." *Annual Review of Sociology*, eds. J. Hagan and K. S. Cook. Greenwich, CT: JAI Press. 217–236.

Barnett, William P. and John Freeman. 2001. "Too much of a good thing? Product proliferation and organizational failure." *Organization Science*, 12(5): 539–558.

Barnett, William P., Henrich R. Greve, and Douglas Y. Park. 1994. "An evolutionary model of organizational performance." *Strategic Management Journal*, 15(S2): 11–28.

Barney, Jay B. 1991. "Firm resources and sustained competitive advantage." *Journal of Management*, 17(1): 99–120.

Barney, Jay B. 2001. "Is the resource-based 'view' a useful perspective for strategic management research? Yes." *Academy of Management Review*, 26(1): 41–56.

Barney, Jay B. and Asli M. Arikan. 2001. "The resource-based view: origins and implications." *The Blackwell Handbook of Strategic Management*, eds. M. A. Hitt, R. E. Freeman, and J. S. Harrison. Oxford: Blackwell. 124–188.

Barron, David N., Elizabeth West, and Michael T. Hannan. 1995. "A time to grow and a time to die: growth and mortality of credit unions in New York City, 1914–1990." *American Journal of Sociology*, 100(2): 381–421.

Bazerman, Max H. 1984. "The relevance of Kahneman and Tversky's concept of framing to organizational behavior." *Journal of Management*, 10: 333–343.

Bazerman, Max H., Tony Giuliano, and Alan Appelman. 1984. "Escalation of commitment in individual and group decision making." *Organizational Behavior and Human Decision Processes*, 33: 141–152.

Benartzi, Schlomo and Richard H. Thaler. 1999. "Risk aversion or myopia? Choices in repeated gambles and retirement investments." *Management Science*, 45(3): 364–381.

Benkard, C. Lanier. 1999. "Learning and forgetting: The dynamics of aircraft production." NBER Report No. 7127. Cambridge, MA: NBER.

Berger, Peter L. and Thomas Luckmann. 1967. *The Social Construction of Reality*. New York: Doubleday Anchor.

Berger, Joseph, Morris Zelditch, and Bo Anderson. 1966. "Introduction." *Sociological Theories in Progress*, eds. J. Berger, M. Zelditch, and B. Anderson. Boston: Houghton Mifflin. i–xii.

Berger, Joseph, Susan J. Rosenholtz, and Morris Zelditch, Jr. 1980. "Status organizing processes." *Annual Review of Sociology*, 6: 479–508.

Bernstein, A. 2001. Do-it-yourself labor standards. *BusinessWeek Asian Edition*, November 19: 71–72.

Bertalanffy, Ludwig von. 1956. "General system theory." *General Systems: Yearbook of the Society for the Advancement of General Systems Theory*, eds. L. von Bertalanffy and A. Rapoport. 1–10.

Bettman, James R., Eric J. Johnson, and John W. Payne. 1990. "A componential analysis of cognitive effort in choice." *Organizational Behavior and Human Decision Processes*, 45(1): 111–139.

Blossfeld, Hans-Peter and Götz Rohwer. 1995. *Techniques of Event History Modeling*. Mahwah, NJ: Lawrence Erlbaum.

Boeker, Warren. 1989a. "Strategic change: the effects of founding and history." *Academy of Management Journal*, 32: 489–515.

1989b. "The development and institutionalization of subunit power in organizations." *Administrative Science Quarterly*, 34: 388–410.

1992. "Power and managerial dismissal: scapegoating at the top." *Administrative Science Quarterly*, 37: 400–421.

1997. "Strategic change: the influence of managerial characteristics and organizational growth." *Academy of Management Journal*, 40(1): 152–170.

Boeker, Warren and Jerry Goodstein. 1991. "Organizational performance and adaptation: effects of environment and performance on changes in board composition." *Academy of Management Journal*, 34(4): 805–826.

Bolton, Michele Kremen. 1993. "Organizational innovation and substandard performance: when is necessity the mother of innovation?" *Organization Science*, 4(1): 57–75.

Bottom, William P. 1998. "Negotiator risk: sources of uncertainty and the impact of reference points on negotiated agreements." *Organizational Behavior and Human Decision Processes*, 76 (November): 89–112.

Boulding, Kenneth E. 1956. "General systems theory: the skeleton of science." *Management Science*, 2: 197–208.

Bower, Joseph L. 1970. *Managing the Resource Allocation Process*. Homewood, IL: Irwin.

Bowman, Edward H. 1980. "A risk-return paradox for strategic management." *Sloan Management Review*, 21: 17–31.

Bowman, Edward H. 1982. "Risk seeking by troubled firms." *Sloan Management Review*, 23 (Summer): 33–42.

1984. "Content analysis of annual reports for corporate strategy and risk." *Interfaces*, 14(1): 61–72.

Brint, Steven and Jerome Karabel. 1991. "Institutional origins and transformations: the case of American community colleges." *The New Institutionalism in Organizational Analysis*, eds. W. W. Powell and P. J. DiMaggio. Chicago, IL: University of Chicago Press. 337–360.

Bromiley, Philip. 1991a. "Paradox or at least variance found: a comment on 'Mean-variance approaches to risk-return relationships in strategy: Paradox lost.'" *Management Science*, 37: 1206–1210.

1991b. "Testing a causal model of corporate risk taking and performance." *Academy of Management Journal*, 34(1): 37–59.

Bromiley, Philip, Kent D. Miller, and Devaki Rau. 2001. "Risk in strategic management research." *The Blackwell Handbook of Strategic Management*, eds. M. A. Hitt, R. E. Freeman, and J. S. Harrison. Oxford: Blackwell. 259–288.

Brush, Thomas H. and Kendall W. Artz. 1999. "Toward a contingent resource-based theory: the impact of information assymetry on the value of capabilities in veterinary medicine." *Strategic Management Journal*, 20: 223–250.

Budros, Art. 1997. "The new capitalism and organizational rationality: the adoption of downsizing programs, 1979–1994." *Social Forces*, 76(1): 229–249.

Burgelman, Robert A. 1991. "Intraorganizational ecology of strategy making and organizational adaptation: theory and field research." *Organization Science*, 2: 239–262.

1994. "Fading memories: a process theory of strategic business exit in dynamic environments." *Administrative Science Quarterly*, 39(1): 24–56.

Burgelman, Robert A. and Leonard R. Sayles. 1986. *Inside Corporate Innovation: Strategy, Structure, and Managerial Skills.* New York: Free Press.

Cachon, Gerard P. and Colin F. Camerer. 2000. "Loss-avoidance and forward induction in experimental coordination games." *Quarterly Journal of Economics*, 111: 165–194.

Camerer, Colin and Teck Hua Ho. 1999. "Experience-weighted attraction learning in normal form games." *Econometrica*, 67(4): 827–874.

Camerer, Colin and Martin Weber. 1992. "Recent developments in modeling preferences: uncertainty and ambiguity." *Journal of Risk and Uncertainty*, 5: 325–370.

Camerer, Colin F. and Roberto A. Weber. 1999. "The econometrics and behavioral economics of escalation of commitment: a re-examination of Staw and Hoang's NBA data." *Journal of Economic Behavior and Organization*, 39(1): 59–82.

Campbell, Donald J. and Karl F. Gingrich. 1986. "The interactive effects of task complexity and participation on task performance: a field experiment." *Organizational Behavior and Human Decision Processes*, 38: 162–180.

Campbell, Donald T. 1969. "Ethnocentrism of disciplines and the fish-scale model of omniscience." *Interdisciplinary Relationships in the Social Sciences*, eds. M. Sherif and C. W. Sherif. Chicago, IL: Aldine. 328–348.

Cannella, Albert A. and Wei Shen. 2001. "So close and yet so far: promotion versus exit for CEO heirs apparent." *Academy of Management Journal*, 44(3): 252–270.

Carlton, Jim. 1997. *Apple: The Inside Story of Intrigue, Egomania, and Business Blunders*. New York: Times Books.

Carroll, Glenn R. and Michael T. Hannan. 1995a. "Automobile manufacturers." *Organizations in Industry: Strategy, Structure, and Selection*. Oxford: Oxford University Press. 195–214.

　1995b. *Organizations in Industry: Strategy, Structure, and Selection*. New York: Oxford University Press.

　2000. *The Demography of Corporations and Industries*. Princeton, NJ: Princeton University Press.

Carroll, Glenn R. and J. Richard Harrison. 1994. "On the historical efficiency of competition between organizational populations." *American Journal of Sociology*, 100(3): 720–749.

Carver, Charles S. and Michael F. Scheier. 1982. "Control theory: a useful conceptual framework for personality-social, clinical, and health psychology." *Psychological Bulletin*, 92(1): 111–135.

Caves, R. E. and Michal E. Porter. 1977. "From entry barriers to mobility barriers: conjectural decisions and contrived deterrence to new competition." *Quarterly Journal of Economics*, 91: 241–262.

Chatman, Jennifer A. 1991. "Matching people and organizations: selection and socialization in public accounting firms." *Administrative Science Quarterly*, 36 (September): 459–484.

Chen, Ming-Jer and Donald C. Hambrick. 1995. "Speed, stealth, and selective attack: how small firms differ from large firms in competitive behavior." *Academy of Management Journal*, 38 (April): 453–482.

Chesney, Amelia A. and Edwin A. Locke. 1991. "Relationships among goal difficulty, business strategies, and performance on a complex management simulation task." *Academy of Management Journal*, 34(2): 400–424.

Chida, Tomohei and Peter N. Davies. 1990. *The Japanese Shipping and Shipbuilding Industries: a History of Their Modern Growth*. London: Athlone Press.

Christensen, Clayton M. 2000. *The Innovator's Dilemma: when New Technologies Cause Great Firms to Fail*. (2nd edn) New York: HarperBusiness.

Christensen, Clayton M. and Joseph L. Bower. 1996. "Customer power, strategic investment, and the failure of leading firms." *Strategic Management Journal*, 17(3): 197–218.

Cialdini, Robert B. 1993. *Influence: Science and Practice*. New York: HarperCollins.

Clark, Bruce H. and David B. Montgomery. 1998. "Deterrence, reputations, and competitive cognition." *Management Science*, 44(1): 62–82.

　1999. "Managerial identification of competitors." *Journal of Marketing*, 63(3): 67–83.

Cohen, Michael D., James G. March, and Johan P. Olsen. 1972. "A garbage can model of organizational choice." *Administrative Science Quarterly*, 17 (March): 1–25.

Cohen, Wesley M. and Daniel A. Levinthal. 1990. "Absorptive capacity: a new perspective on learning and innovation." *Administrative Science Quarterly*, 35 (March): 128–152.

Collins, Rebecca L. 1996. "For better or for worse: the impact of upward social comparison on self-evaluations." *Psychological Bulletin*, 119(1): 51–69.

Collis, David J. 1991. "A resource-based analysis of global competition: the case of the bearings industry." *Strategic Management Journal*, 12: 49–68.

Cool, Karel O. and Ingemar Dierickx. 1993. "Rivalry, strategic groups and firm profitability." *Strategic Management Journal*, 14(1): 47–59.

Cooper, Arnold C. and Dan E. Schendel. 1976. "Strategic responses to technological threats." *Business Horizons*, 19(1): 61–69.

Costa-Gomes, Miguel, Vincent P. Crawford, and Bruno Broseta. 2000. "Cognition and behavior in normal-form games: an experimental study." Working Paper No. 2000–02. Department of Economics, University of California, San Diego.

Crawford, Vincent P. 1995. "Adaptive dynamics in coordination games." *Econometrica*, 63(1): 103–143.

1997. "Learning dynamics, lock-in, and equilibrium selection in experimental coordination games." Working Paper No. 97–19. Department of Economics, University of California, San Diego.

Crott, Helmut W., Johannes A. Zuber, and Thomas Schermer. 1986. "Social decision schemes and choice shift: an analysis of group decisions among bets." *Journal of Experimental Social Psychology*, 22: 1–21.

Cyert, Richard M. and James G. March. 1963. *A Behavioral Theory of the Firm.* Englewood Cliffs, NJ: Prentice-Hall.

1992. *A Behavioral Theory of the Firm, 2nd Edn.* (2nd edn) Cambridge, MA: Blackwell.

Daft, Richard L. and Karl E. Weick. 1984. "Toward a model of organizations as interpretation systems." *Academy of Management Review*, 9(2): 284–295.

Dahl, Robert. 1957. "The concept of power." *Behavioral Science*, 2: 201–215.

Darr, Eric D., Linda Argote, and Dennis Epple. 1995. "The acquisition, transfer, and depreciation of knowledge in service organizations: productivity in franchises." *Management Science*, 41(11): 1750–1762.

Davies, R. B. 1987. "The limitations of cross-sectional analysis." *Longitudinal Data Analysis*, ed. R. Crouchley. Aldershot: Avebury. 1–15.

Davis, Gerald F. and Henrich R. Greve. 1997. "Corporate elite networks and governance changes in the 1980s." *American Journal of Sociology*, 103 (July): 1–37.

Davis, Gerald F., Kristina A. Diekmann, and Catherine H. Tinsley. 1994. "The decline and fall of the conglomerate firm in the 1980s: the deinstitutionalization of an organizational form." *American Sociological Review*, 59 (August): 547–570.

Davis, James H. 1992. "Some compelling intuitions about group consensus decisions, theoretical and empirical research, and interpersonal aggregation phenomena: selected examples, 1950–1990." *Organizational Behavior and Human Decision Processes*, 52(1): 3–38.

Day, George S. and David B. Montgomery. 1983. "Diagnosing the Experience Curve." *Journal of Marketing*, 47(2): 44–58.

Deephouse, David L. 1996. "Does isomorphism legitimate?" *Academy of Management Journal*, 39(4): 1024–1039.

DiMaggio, Paul J. 1988. "Interest and agency in institutional theory." *Institutional Patterns and Organizations: Culture and Environment*, ed. L. G. Zucker. Cambridge, MA: Ballinger. 3–21.

DiMaggio, Paul J. and Walter W. Powell. 1983. "The iron cage revisited: institutional isomorphism and collective rationality in organizational fields." *American Sociological Review*, 48: 147–160.

Dobbin, Frank R., John R. Sutton, John W. Meyer, and W. Richard Scott. 1993. "Equal opportunity law and the construction of internal labor markets." *American Journal of Sociology*, 99 (September): 396–427.

Donaldson, Lex. 1995. *American Anti-Management Theories of Organization: a Critique of Paradigm Proliferation*. Cambridge: Cambridge University Press.

Dougherty, Deborah. 1992. "Interpretive barriers to successful product innovation in large firms." *Organization Science*, 3(2): 179–202.

Dougherty, Deborah and Cynthia Hardy. 1996. "Sustained product innovation in large, mature organizations: overcoming innovation-to-organization problems." *Academy of Management Journal*, 39(5): 1120–1153.

Dougherty, Deborah and Trudy Heller. 1994. "The illegitimacy of successful product innovation in established firms." *Organization Science*, 5(2): 200–218.

Drazin, Robert and Claudia Bird Schoonhoven. 1996. "Community, population, and organization effects on innovation: a multilevel perspective." *Academy of Management Journal*, 39(5): 1065–1083.

Dumaine, B. 1990. "The turnaround champs." *Fortune* (July 16): 36–44.

Dutton, Jane E. and Janet M. Dukerich. 1991. "Keeping an eye in the mirror: image and identity in organizational adaptation." *Academy of Management Journal*, 34(3): 517–554.

Earley, P. Christopher. 1986. "Supervisors and shop stewards as sources of contextual information in goal setting: a comparison of the United States with England." *Journal of Applied Psychology*, 71(1): 111–117.

1993. "East meets West meets Mideast: further explorations of collectivistic and individualistic work groups." *Academy of Management Journal*, 36 (2 April): 319–348.

Ebers, Mark. 1995. "The framing of organizational cultures." *Research in the Sociology of Organizations*, 17: 129–170.

Edelman, Lauren B. 1990. "Legal environments and organizational governance: the expansion of due process in the American workplace." *American Journal of Sociology*, 95 (May): 1401–1440.

Einhorn, Bruce. 2001. "Betting big on chips: why TSMC boss Morris Chang is spending billions despite the slump." *BusinessWeek Asian Edition* (April 30): 18–21.

Einhorn, Hillel J. and Robin M. Hogarth. 1978. "Confidence in judgment: persistence in the illusion of validity." *Psychological Review*, 85(5): 395–416.

Ellsberg, D. 1961. "Risk, ambiguity, and the Savage axioms." *Quarterly Journal of Economics*, 75: 643–699.

Elsbach, Kimberly D. and Roderick M. Kramer. 1996. "Members' responses to organizational identity threats: countering the Business Week rankings." *Administrative Science Quarterly*, 41 (September): 442–476.

Erez, Miriam, P. Christopher Earley, and Charles L. Hulin. 1985. "The impact of participation on goal acceptance and performance: a two-step model." *Academy of Management Journal*, 28(1): 50–66.

Erickson, Bonnie H. 1988. "The relational basis of attitudes." *Social structures: A network approach*, eds. B. Wellman and S. D. Berkowitz. New York: Cambridge University Press. 99–121.

Esser, James K. and Joanne S. Lindoerfer. 1989. "Groupthink and the space shuttle Challenger accident: toward a quantitative case analysis." *Journal of Behavioral Decision Making*, 2: 167–177.

Fama, Eugene F. 1980. "Agency problems and the theory of the firm." *Journal of Political Economy*, 88(2): 288–307.

Ferrier, Walter J., Ken G. Smith, and Curtis M. Grimm. 1999. "The role of competitive action in market share erosion and industry dethronement: a study of industry leaders and challengers." *Academy of Management Journal*, 42: 372–388.

Festinger, Leon. 1942. "A theoretical interpretation of shifts in level of aspiration." *Psychological Review*, 49: 235–250.

1954. "A theory of social comparison processes." *Human Relations*, 7: 117–140.

Fiegenbaum, Avi. 1990. "Prospect theory and the risk-return association." *Journal of Economic Behavior and Organization*, 14: 184–203.

Fiegenbaum, Avi and Howard Thomas. 1986. "Dynamic and risk measurement perspectives on Bowman's risk-return paradox for strategic management: an empirical study." *Strategic Management Journal*, 7: 395–407.

1988. "Attitudes towards risk and the risk-return paradox: prospect theory explanations." *Academy of Management Journal*, 31: 395–407.

1995. "Strategic groups as reference groups: theory, modeling and empirical examination of industry and competitive strategy." *Strategic Management Journal*, 16(6): 461–476.

Fiol, C. Marlene. 1996. "Squeezing harder doesn't always work: continuing the search for consistency in innovation research." *Academy of Management Review*, 21(4): 1012–1021.

Fiske, Susan T. and Shelley E. Taylor. 1991. *Social Cognition*. New York: McGraw-Hill.

Fligstein, Neil. 1990. *The Transformation of Corporate Control*. Cambridge, MA: Harvard University Press.

Foster, Richard N. 1986. *Innovation: the Attacker's Advantage*. London: Macmillan.

Frank, J. D. 1935. "Individual differences in certain aspects of the level of aspiration." *American Journal of Psychology*: 119–128.

Fredrickson, James, Donald C. Hambrick, and Sara Baumrin. 1988. "A model of CEO dismissal." *Academy of Management Journal*, 32: 718–744.

Freeman, R. Edward and John McVea. 2001. "A stakeholder approach to strategic management." *The Blackwell Handbook of Strategic Management*, eds. M. A. Hitt, R. E. Freeman, and J. S. Harrison. Oxford: Blackwell. 189–207.

Fudenberg, Drew and Jean Tirole. 1991. *Game Theory*. Cambridge, MA: MIT Press.

Galaskiewicz, Joseph and Ronald S. Burt. 1991. "Interorganization contagion in corporate philanthropy." *Administrative Science Quarterly*, 36: 88–105.

Garland, Howard. 1983. "Influence of ability, assigned goals, and normative information on personal goals and performance: a challenge to the goal attainability assumption." *Journal of Applied Psychology*, 68: 20–30.

Garud, Raghu and Zur Shapira. 1997. "Aligning the residuals: risk, return, responsibility, and authority." *Organizational Decision Making*, ed. Z. Shapira. Cambridge: Cambridge University Press. 238–256.

Gersick, Connie J. G. 1988. "Time and transition in work teams: toward a new model of group development." *Academy of Management Journal*, 31(1): 9–41.

Ghemawat, Pankaj. 1991. *Commitment: the Dynamic of Strategy*. New York: Free Press.

Gimeno, Javier. 1999. "Reciprocal threats in multimarket rivalry: staking out 'spheres of influence' in the US airline industry." *Strategic Management Journal*, 20(2): 101–128.

Goethals, G. R. 1986. "Fabricating and ignoring social reality: self-serving estimates of consensus." *Relative Deprivation and Social Comparison: the Ontario Symposium*, eds. J. M. Olson, C. P. Herman, and M. P. Zanna. Hillsdale, NJ: Erlbaum. 135–158.

Goffman, Erving. 1990. *The Presentation of Self in Everyday Life*. New York: Anchor Books/Doubleday.

Gooding, Richard Z., Sanjay Goel, and Robert M. Wiseman. 1996. "Fixed versus variable reference points in the risk-return relationship." *Journal of Economic Behavior and Organization*, 29(2): 331–350.

Gordon, Shelley S., Wayne H. Stewart, Robert Sweo, and William A. Luker. 2000. "Convergence versus strategic reorientation: the antecedents of fast-paced organizational change." *Journal of Management*, 26(5): 911–945.

Green, Sandy E., Jr. 1993. "General Motors: Smith's dilemma." Case No. 9-494-020. Boston, MA: Harvard Business School.

Greenwood, Royston and C. R. Hinings. 1996. "Understanding radical organizational change: bringing together the old and the new institutionalism." *Academy of Management Review*, 21(4): 1022–1054.

Greve, Henrich R. 1996. "Patterns of competition: the diffusion of a market position in radio broadcasting." *Administrative Science Quarterly*, 41 (March): 29–60.

1998a. "Managerial cognition and the mimetic adoption of market positions: what you see is what you do." *Strategic Management Journal*, 19 (October): 967–988.

1998b. "Performance, aspirations, and risky organizational change." *Administrative Science Quarterly*, 44 (March): 58–86.

1999a. "Branch systems and nonlocal learning in populations." *Advances in Strategic Management*, eds. A. Miner and P. Anderson. Greenwich, CT: JAI Press. 57–80.

1999b. "The effect of change on performance: inertia and regression toward the mean." *Administrative Science Quarterly*, 44 (September): 590–614.

2002a. "Interorganizational learning from innovations: framework, findings, and future research." Manuscript, Department of Strategy, Norwegian School of Management BI.

2002b. "Sticky aspirations: organizational time perspective and competitiveness." *Organization Science*, 13(1): 1–17.

Greve, Henrich R. and Alva Taylor. 2000. "Innovations as catalysts for organizational change: shifts in organizational cognition and search." *Administrative Science Quarterly*, 45 (March): 54–80.

Grinyer, Peter and Peter McKiernan. 1990. "Generating major change in stagnating companies." *Strategic Management Journal*, 11: 131–146.

Gripsrud, Geir and Kjell Grønhaug. 1985. "Structure and strategy in grocery retailing: a sociometric approach." *The Journal of Industrial Economics*, 33(3): 339–347.

Grossman, S. and O. Hart. 1982. "An analysis of the principal–agent problem." *Econometrica*, 51: 7–45.

Guillen, Mauro F. 1994. *Models of Management: Work, Authority, and Organization in a Comparative Perspective*. Chicago, IL: University of Chicago Press.

Hall, Bronwyn H. 1993. *Time Series Processor Version 4.2 User's Guide*. Palo Alto, CA: TSP International.

Hambrick, Donald C. and Richard A. D'Aveni. 1988. "Large corporate failures as downward spirals." *Administrative Science Quarterly*, 33 (March): 1–23.

Hambrick, Donald C. and Sydney Finkelstein. 1987. "Managerial discretion: a bridge between polar views of organizational outcomes." *Research in Organizational Behavior*, 9: 369–406.

Hambrick, Donald C., David A. Nadler, and Michael L. Tushman. 1998. *Navigating Change: How CEOs, Top Teams, and Boards Steer Transformation*. Boston, MA: Harvard Business School Press.

Hamel, Gary. 1991. "Competition for competence and inter-partner learning within international strategic alliances." *Strategic Management Journal*, 12: 83–103.

Han, Shin-Kap. 1994. "Mimetic isomorphism and its effect on the audit services market." *Social Forces*, 73(2): 637–663.

Hannan, Michael T. and John Freeman. 1977. "The population ecology of organizations." *American Journal of Sociology*, 82: 929–964.

1984. "Structural inertia and organizational change." *American Sociological Review*, 49: 149–164.

1989. *Organizational Ecology*. Cambridge, MA: Harvard University Press.

Hantula, Donald A. and Charles R. Crowell. 1994. "Intermittent reinforcement and escalation processes in sequential decision making: a replication and theoretical analysis." *Journal of Organizational Behavior Management*, 14(2): 7–36.

Harrison, J. Richard and James G. March. 1984. "Decision making and postdecision surprises." *Administrative Science Quarterly*, 29 (March): 26–42.

Hart, Peter E. and Nicholas Oulton. 1996. "Growth and size of firms." *Economic Journal*, 106 (September): 1242–1252.

Haveman, Heather A. 1992. "Between a rock and a hard place: organizational change and performance under conditions of fundamental environmental transformation." *Administrative Science Quarterly*, 37 (March): 48–75.

Heath, Chip. 1995. "Escalation and de-escalation of commitment in response to sunk costs: the role of budgeting in mental accounting." *Organizational Behavior and Human Decision Processes*, 62(1): 38–54.

Heath, Chip and Amos Tversky. 1991. "Preference and belief: ambiguity and competence in choice under uncertainty." *Journal of Risk and Uncertainty*, 4(1): 5–28.

Heath, Chip, Richard P. Larrick, and George Wu. 1999. "Goals as reference points." *Cognitive Psychology*, 38(1): 79–109.

Henderson, Rebecca M. and Kim B. Clark. 1990. "Architectural innovation: the reconfiguration of existing product technologies and the failure of established firms." *Administrative Science Quarterly*, 35: 9–30.

Hennig-Schmidt, Heike. 1999. *Bargaining in a Video Experiment: Determinants of Boundedly Rational Behavior*. Berlin: Springer.

Herriott, Scott R., Daniel Levinthal, and James G. March. 1985. "Learning from experience in organizations." *American Economic Review*, 75: 298–302.

Hitt, Michael A., Robert E. Hoskisson, and Hicheon Kim. 1997. "International diversification: effects on innovation and firm performance in product-diversified firms." *Academy of Management Journal*, 40(4): 767–798.

Hoffman, Andrew J. and William Ocasio. 2001. "Not all events are attended equally: toward a middle-range theory of industry attention to external events." *Organization Science*, 12(4): 414–434.

Hogarth, Robin M. and Hillel J. Einhorn. 1990. "Venture theory: a model of decision weights." *Management Science*, 36(7): 780–803.

Hogarth, Robin M., Brian J. Gibbs, Craig R. M. McKenzie, and Margaret A. Marquis. 1991. "Learning from feedback: exactingness and incentives." *Journal of Experimental Psychology: Learning, Memory, and Cognition*, 17(4): 734–752.

Hogg, Michael E., Deborah J. Terry, and Katherine M. White. 1995. "A tale of two theories: a critical comparison of identity theory with social identity theory." *Social Psychology Quarterly*, 58(4): 255–269.

Holmstrom, Bengt. 1979. "Moral hazard and unobservability." *Bell Journal of Economics*, 10: 74–91.

Hong, Harrison, Jeffrey Kubik, and Amit Solomon. 2000. "Securities analysts' career concerns and herding of earnings forecasts." *RAND Journal of Economics*, 31: 121–144.

Hooks, Gregory. 1990. "From an autonomous to a captured state agency: the decline of the new deal in agriculture." *American Sociological Review*, 55 (February): 29–43.

Howell, Jane M. and Christopher A. Higgins. 1990. "Champions of technological innovation." *Administrative Science Quarterly*, 35(2): 317–341.

Hrebiniak, Lawrence G. and William F. Joyce. 1985. "Organizational adaptation: strategic choice and environmental determinism." *Administrative Science Quarterly*, 30: 336–349.

Huber, George P. 1991. "Organizational learning: the contributing processes and the literatures." *Organization Science*, 2(1): 88–115.

Huff, Anne S. and James O. Huff. 1995. "Stress, inertia, opportunity, and competitive position: a SIOP model of strategic change in the pharmaceuticals industry." *Academy of Management Best Papers Proceedings 1995*. Vancouver: Academy of Management. 22–26.

Huff, Anne Sigismund. 1982. "Industry influences on strategy reformulation." *Strategic Management Journal*, 3: 119–131.

Hundley, Greg, Carol K. Jacobson, and Seung Ho Park. 1996. "Effects of profitability and liquidity on R&D intensity: Japanese and US companies compared." *Academy of Management Journal*, 39(6): 1659–1674.

Ingram, Paul and Joel A. C. Baum. 1997. "Opportunity and constraint: organizations' learning from the operating and competitive experience of industries." *Strategic Management Journal*, 18 (Summer): 75–98.

2001. "Interorganizational learning and the dynamics of chain relationships." *Multiunit Organization and Multimarket Strategy*, eds. J. A. C. Baum and H. R. Greve. Oxford: Elsevier. 109–139.

Isenberg, D. 1986. "Group polarization: a critical review and meta-analysis." *Journal of Personality and Social Psychology*, 50: 1141–1151.

Janis, Irving Lester. 1982. *Groupthink: Psychological Studies of Policy Decisions and Fiascoes.* (2nd edn) Boston, MA: Houghton Mifflin.

Jelinek, Mariann and Claudia Bird Schoonhoven. 1990. *The Innovation Marathon: Lessons from High Technology Firms.* Oxford: Basil Blackwell.

Jensen, Michael C. and William H. Meckling. 1976. "Theory of the firm: managerial behavior, agency cost, and ownership structure." *Journal of Financial Economics*, 3: 305–360.

Johnson, H. Thomas and Robert S. Kaplan. 1987. *Relevance Lost: the Rise and Fall of Management Accounting.* Boston, MA: Harvard Business School Press.

Johnstone, Bob. 1999. *We were Burning: Japanese Entrepreneurs and the Forging of the Electronic Age.* New York: Basic Books.

Kahneman, Daniel and Amos Tversky. 1979. "Prospect theory: an analysis of decision under risk." *Econometrica*, 47(2): 263–291.

Kameda, Tatsuya and James H. Davis. 1990. "The function of the reference point in individual and group risk decision making." *Organizational Behavior and Human Decision Processes*, 46(1): 55–76.

Kamien, M. I. and N. L. Schwartz. 1982. *Market Structure and Innovation.* Cambridge, MA: Cambridge University Press.

Kanter, Rosabeth Moss. 1989. *When Giants Learn to Dance: Mastering the Challenge of Strategy, Management, and Careers in the 1990s.* New York: Simon and Schuster.

Kaplan, Robert S. and David P. Norton. 1996. *The Balanced Scorecard: Translating Strategy into Action.* Boston, MA: Harvard Business School Press.

Keller, Greg. 1994. "Saturn: a different kind of car company." Case No. 9-795-010. Boston, MA: Harvard Business School.

Kelly, Dawn and Terry L. Amburgey. 1991. "Organizational inertia and momentum: a dynamic model of strategic change." *Academy of Management Journal*, 34: 591–612.

Kerr, Steven. 1975. "On the folly of rewarding A, while hoping for B." *Academy of Management Journal*, 18: 769–783.

Ketchen, David J., Jr. and Timothy B. Palmer. 1999. "Strategic responses to poor organizational performance: a test of competing perspectives." *Journal of Management*, 25(5): 683–706.

Kluger, Avraham N. and Angelo N. DeNisi. 1996. "The effect of feedback interventions on performance: a historical review, a meta-analysis, and a preliminary feedback intervention theory." *Psychological Bulletin*, 119(2): 254–284.

Kraatz, Matthew S. 1998. "Learning by association? Interorganizational networks and adaptation to environmental change." *Academy of Management Journal*, 41(6): 621–643.

Kraatz, Matthew S. and Edward J. Zajac. 1996. "Exploring the limits of the new institutionalism: the causes and consequences of illegitimate organizational change." *American Sociological Review*, 61 (October): 812–836.

Kramer, Roderick M. 1998. "Revisiting the Bay of Pigs and Vietnam decisions 25 years later: how well has the groupthink hypothesis stood the test of time?" *Organizational Behavior and Human Decision Processes*, 73(2): 236–271.

Kreps, David M. 1990. *A Course in Microeconomic Theory*. New York: Harvester Wheatsheaf.

Kruglanski, Arie W. and Ofra Mayseless. 1990. "Classic and current social comparison research: expanding the perspective." *Psychological Bulletin*, 108(2): 195–208.

Kuehberger, Anton. 1998. "The influence of framing on risky decisions: a meta-analysis." *Organizational Behavior and Human Decision Processes*, 75(1): 23–55.

Kuhn, Thomas S. 1972. *The Structure of Scientific Revolutions*. (2nd edn) Chicago, IL: Chicago University Press.

Kunda, Gideon. 1992. *Engineering Culture: Control and Commitment in a High-Tech Corporation*. Philadelphia, PA: Temple University Press.

Kuran, Timur. 1988. "The tenacious past: theories of personal and collective conservativism." *Journal of Economic Behavior and Organization*, 10: 143–171.

Lakatos, Imre. 1978. *The Methodology of Scientific Research Programmes*. Cambridge: Cambridge University Press.

Lambert, Richard A., David F. Larcker, and Keith Weigelt. 1993. "The structure of organizational incentives." *Administrative Science Quarterly*, 38 (September): 438–461.

Langer, Ellen J. 1975. "The illusion of control." *Journal of Personality and Social Psychology*, 32(2): 311–328.

Lant, Theresa K. 1992. "Aspiration level adaptation: an empirical exploration." *Management Science*, 38(5): 623–644.

Lant, Theresa K. and Joel A. C. Baum. 1995. "Cognitive sources of socially constructed competitive groups: examples from the Manhattan hotel industry." *The Institutional Construction of Organizations: International and Longitudinal Studies*, eds. W. R. Scott and S. Christensen. Thousand Oaks, CA: Sage. 15–38.

Lant, Theresa K. and Amy E. Hurley. 1999. "A contingency model of response to performance feedback: escalation of commitment and incremental adaptation in resource investment decisions." *Group and Organization Management*, 24(4): 421–437.

Lant, Theresa K. and David B. Montgomery. 1987. "Learning from strategic success and failure." *Journal of Business Research*, 15: 503–518.

Lant, Theresa K., Frances J. Milliken, and Bipin Batra. 1992. "The role of managerial learning and interpretation in strategic persistence and reorientation: an empirical exploration." *Strategic Management Journal*, 13: 585–608.

Latane, Bibb, Kipling Williams, and Stephen Harkins. 1979. "Many hands make light work: the causes and consequences of social loafing." *Journal of Personality and Social Psychology*, 37(6): 822–832.

Latham, Gary P. and Lise M. Saari. 1979. "The effect of holding goal difficulty constant on assigned and participatively set goals." *Academy of Management Journal*, 22: 163–168.

Ledford, Gerald E., Jr., Edward E. Lawler, III, and Susan Albers Mohrman. 1995. "Reward innovation in Fortune 1000 companies." *Compensation and Benefits Review*, 27: 76–80.

Lehner, Johannes M. 2000. "Shifts of reference points for framing of strategic decisions and changing risk-return associations." *Management Science*, 46: 63–76.

Leonard-Barton, Dorothy. 1995. *Wellsprings of Knowledge: Building and Sustaining the Sources of Innovation*. Boston, MA: Harvard Business School.

Levinthal, Daniel A. and James G. March. 1981. "A model of adaptive organizational search." *Journal of Economic Behavior and Organization*, 2: 307–333.
1993. "The myopia of learning." *Strategic Management Journal*, 14 (Winter): 95–112.

Levitt, Barbara and James G. March. 1988. "Organizational learning." *Annual Review of Sociology*, eds. W. R. Scott and J. Blake. Palo Alto, CA: Annual Reviews. 319–340.

Levitt, Barbara and Clifford Nass. 1989. "The lid on the garbage can: institutional constraints on decision making in the technical core of college-text publishers." *Administrative Science Quarterly*, 34 (March): 190–207.

Lewin, Kurt, T. Dembo, Leon Festinger, and Pauline Snedden Sears. 1944. "Level of aspiration." *Personality and the Behavior Disorders*, ed. J. M. Hunt. New York: Ronald. 333–378.

Lieberman, Marvin B. and David B. Montgomery. 1998. "First-mover (dis)advantages: retrospective and link with the resource-based view." *Strategic Management Journal*, 19(12): 1111–1125.

Lindblom, Charles E. 1959. "The science of muddling through." *Public Administration Review*, 39: 341–350.

Locke, Edwin A. 1978. "The ubiquity of the technique of goal setting in theories of and approaches to employee motivation." *Academy of Management Review*, 3(3): 594–601.

Locke, Edwin A. and Gary P. Latham. 1990. *A Theory of Goal Setting and Task Performance*. Englewood Cliffs, NJ: Prentice-Hall.

Locke, Edwin A., Gary P. Latham, and Miriam Erez. 1988. "The determinants of goal commitment." *Academy of Management Review*, 13(1): 23–39.

Locke, Edwin A., Elizabeth Frederick, Elizabeth Buckner, and Philip Bobko. 1984. "Effect of previously assigned goals on self-set goals and performance." *Journal of Applied Psychology*, 69(4): 694–699.

Lopes, Lola L. 1987. "Between hope and fear: the psychology of risk." *Advances in Experimental Social Psychology*, 20: 255–295.

Lorenz, Edward. 1994. "Organizational inertia and competitive decline: the British cotton, shipbuilding, and car industries, 1945–1975." *Industrial and Corporate Change*, 3(2): 379–403.

Lounamaa, P. H. and James G. March. 1987. "Adaptive coordination of a learning team." *Management Science*, 33: 107–123.

M Street Corp. 1992. *M Street Radio Directory*. New York: M Street Corp.

MacCrimmon, Kenneth R. 1986. "Descriptive and normative implications of the decision-theory postulates." *Risk and Uncertainty*, eds. K. Borch and J. Mossin. London: Macmillan. 3–23.

MacCrimmon, Kenneth R. and Donald A. Wehrung. 1986. *Taking Risks: the Management of Uncertainty*. New York: Free Press.

Makadok, Richard. 1998. "Can first-mover and early-mover advantages be sustained in an industry with low barriers to entry/imitation?" *Strategic Management Journal*, 19: 683–696.

————— 1999. "Interfirm differences in scale economics and the evolution of market shares." *Strategic Management Journal*, 20: 935–952.

Manns, Curtis L. and James G. March. 1978. "Financial adversity, internal competition, and curriculum change in a university." *Administrative Science Quarterly*, 23: 541–552.

March, James G. 1962. "The business firm as a political coalition." *Journal of Politics*, 24: 662–678.

————— 1966. "The power of power." *Varieties of Political Theory*, ed. D. Easton. New York: Prentice-Hall.

————— 1981. "Footnotes to organizational change." *Administrative Science Quarterly*, 26: 563–577.

————— 1988a. "Introduction: a chronicle of speculations about decision-making in organizations." *Decisions and Organizations*. Oxford: Blackwell. 1–21.

————— 1988b. "Variable risk preferences and adaptive aspirations." *Journal of Economic Behavior and Organization*, 9: 5–24.

————— 1994. *A Primer on Decision Making: How Decisions Happen*. New York: Free Press.

————— 1996. "Learning to be risk averse." *Psychological Review*, 103(2): 309–319.

March, James G. and Johan P. Olsen. 1976. *Ambiguity and Choice in Organizations*. Bergen, Norway: Universitetsforlaget.

March, James G. and Zur Shapira. 1987. "Managerial perspectives on risk and risk taking." *Management Science*, 33: 1404–1418.

————— 1992. "Variable risk preferences and the focus of attention." *Psychological Review*, 99(1): 172–183.

March, James G. and Herbert Simon. 1958. *Organizations*. New York: Wiley.

March, James G., Martin Schultz, and Xueguang Zhou. 2000. *The Dynamics of Rules: Change in Written Organizational Codes*. Stanford: Stanford University Press.

March, James G., Lee S. Sproull, and Michal Tamuz. 1991. "Learning from samples of one or fewer." *Organization Science*, 2: 1–13.

Maritan, Catherina A. 2001. "Capital investment as investing in organizational capabilities: an empirically-grounded process model." *Academy of Management Journal*, 44(3): 513–532.

Marsden, Peter V. and Noah E. Friedkin. 1993. "Network studies of social influence." *Sociological Methods and Research*, 22: 127–151.

Martin, Beth Ann and Donald J. Manning, Jr. 1995. "Combined effects of normative information and task difficulty on the goal commitment–performance relationship." *Journal of Management*, 21(1): 65–80.

Mascarenhas, Briance. 1989. "Strategic group dynamics." *Academy of Management Journal*, 32(2): 333–352.

McCauley, Clark. 1989. "The nature of social influence in groupthink: compliance and internalization." *Journal of Personality and Social Psychology*, 57: 250–260.

McClelland, D. 1961. *The Achieving Society*. New York: D. Van Nostrand.

McGrath, Rita Gunther, Ian C. MacMillan, and S. Venkataraman. 1995. "Defining and developing competence: a strategic process paradigm." *Strategic Management Journal*, 16(4): 251–275.

McKendrick, David G. 2001. "Global strategy and population-level learning: the case of hard disk drives." *Strategic Management Journal*, 22(4): 307–334.

McKendrick, David G., Richard F. Doner, and Stephan Haggard. 2000. *From Silicon Valley to Singapore: Location and Competitive Advantage in the Hard Disk Drive Industry*. Stanford, CA: Stanford University Press.

McNamara, Gerry and Philip Bromiley. 1997. "Decision making in an organizational setting: cognitive and organizational influences on risk assessment in commercial lending." *Academy of Management Journal*, 40(5): 1063–1088.

1999. "Risk and return in organizational decision making." *Academy of Management Journal*, 42(3): 330–339.

McNamara, Gerry, Henry Moon, and Philip Bromiley. 2002. "Banking on commitment: intended and unintended consequences of an organization's attempt to attenuate irrational commitment." *Academy of Management Journal*, 45(2): 443–452.

Meindl, James R. and Sanford B. Ehrlich. 1987. "The romance of leadership and the evaluation of organizational performance." *Academy of Management Journal*, 30(1): 91–109.

Mellers, B. A., A. Scwartz, and A. D. J. Cooke. 1999. "Judgment and decision making." *Annual Review of Psychology*, 49: 447–477.

Meyer, John P. and Ian R. Gellatly. 1988. "Perceived performance norm as a mediator in the effect of assigned goal on personal goal and task performance." *Journal of Applied Psychology*, 73(3): 410–420.

Meyer, John W. 1994. "Rationalized environments." *Institutional Environments and Organizations: Structural Complexity and Individualism*, eds. W. R. Scott, J. W. Meyer, and associates. Thousand Oaks, CA: Sage. 28–54.

Meyer, John W. and Brian Rowan. 1977. "Institutionalized organizations: formal structure as myth and ceremony." *American Journal of Sociology*, 83: 340–363.

Meyer, John W., John Boli, and George Thomas. 1987. "Ontology and rationalization in the Western cultural account." *Institutional Structure: Constituting State, Society and the Individual*, eds. G. Thomas, J. W. Meyer, F. Ramirez, and J. Boli. Newbury Park, CA: Sage. 12–37.

Meyer, Marshall W. 1994. "The performance paradox." *Research on Organizational Behavior*, eds. L. L. Cummings and B. M. Staw. Greenwich, CT: JAI Press.

Meyer, Marshall W. and Lynne G. Zucker. 1989. *Permanently Failing Organizations*. Newbury Park, CA: Sage Publications.

Meyerson, Deborah and Joanne Martin. 1987. "Cultural change: an integration of three different views." *Journal of Management Studies*, 24: 623–647.

Mezias, Stephen J. and Patrice R. Murphy. 1998. "Adaptive aspirations in an American financial services organization: a field study." *Academy of Management Best Paper Proceedings CD-ROM*.

Milgrom, Paul and John Roberts. 1992. *Economics, Organization and Management*. Englewood Cliffs, NJ: Prentice-Hall.

Miller, Carol T. 1982. "The role of performance-related similarity in social comparison of abilities: a test of the related attributes hypothesis." *Journal of Experimental Social Psychology*, 18: 513–523.

Miller, Dale T., William Turnbull, and Cathy McFarland. 1988. "Particularistic and universalistic evaluation in the social comparison process." *Journal of Personality and Social Psychology*, 55(6): 908–917.

Miller, Danny. 1991. "Stale in the saddle: CEO tenure and the match between organization and environment." *Management Science*, 37(1): 34–52.

Miller, Danny and Ming-Jer Chen. 1994. "Sources and consequences of competitive inertia: a study of the US airline industry." *Administrative Science Quarterly*, 39 (March): 1–23.

Miller, Danny and Peter H. Friesen. 1982. "Innovation in conservative and entrepreneurial firms: two models of strategic momentum." *Strategic Management Journal*, 3: 1–25.

Miller, Danny and Jamal Shamsie. 1999. "Strategic responses to three kinds of uncertainty: product line simplicity at the Hollywood film studios." *Journal of Management*, 25(1): 97–116.

2001. "The resource-based view of the firm in two environments: the Hollywood film studios from 1936–1965." *Academy of Management Journal*, 39: 519–543.

Miller, Kent D. and Philip Bromiley. 1990. "Strategic risk and corporate performance: an analysis of alternative risk measures." *Academy of Management Journal*, 39: 756–779.

Miller, Kent D. and Wei-Ru Chen. 2002. "Variable organizational risk preferences: tests of the March–Shapira model." Manuscript, Krannert Graduate School of Management, Purdue University, Lafayette, IN.

Miller, Kent D. and Michael J. Leiblein. 1996. "Corporate risk-return relations: returns variability versus downside risk." *Academy of Management Journal*, 39(1): 91–122.

Milliken, Frances J. 1987. "Three types of perceived uncertainty about the environment: state, effect, and response uncertainty." *Academy of Management Review*, 12(1): 133–143.

Milliken, Frances J. and Theresa K. Lant. 1991. "The effect of an organization's recent performance history on strategic persistence and change: the role of managerial interpretations." *Advances in Strategic Management*, eds. P. Shrivastava, A. Huff, and J. Dutton. Greenwich, CN: JAI Press. 129–156.

Miner, Anne S. 1990. "Structural evolution through idiosyncratic jobs: the potential for unplanned learning." *Organization Science*, 1: 195–250.

1991. "Organizational evolution and the social ecology of jobs." *American Sociological Review*, 56: 772–785.

Miner, Anne S., Ji-Yub Jay Kim, Ingo W. Holzinger, and Pamela Haunschild. 1999. "Fruits of failure: organizational failure and population-level learning." *Advances in Strategic Management*, eds. A. Miner and P. Anderson. Greenwich, CT: JAI Press. 187–220.

Mirrlees, J. 1975. "The theory of moral hazard and unobservable behaviors, part I." Mimeo, Nuffield College, Oxford.

Mullins, John W., David Forlani, and Orville C. Walker. 1999. "Effects of organizational and decision-maker factors on new product risk taking." *Journal of Product Innovation Management*, 16(3): 282–294.

Murata, Y. 2000. Hybrid dream fueled drive into the unknown. *Asahi Evening News* (December 29): 3.

Myers, Daniel J. and H. Lamm. 1976. "The group polarization phenomenon." *Psychological Bulletin*, 83: 602–627.

Nichols, Nancy A. 1994. "Scientific management at Merck: an interview with CFO Judy Lewent." *Harvard Business Review*, 72(1): 89–99.

Noda, Tomo and Joseph L. Bower. 1996. "Strategy making as iterated processes of resource allocation." *Strategic Management Journal*, 17 (Summer Special Issue): 159–192.

Nonaka, Ikujiro and Hirotaka Takeuchi. 1995. *The Knowledge-Creating Company: How Japanese Companies Create the Dynamics of Innovation*. New York: Oxford University Press.

Northcraft, Gregory B. and Margaret A. Neale. 1986. "Opportunity costs and the framing of resource allocation decisions." *Organizational Behavior and Human Decision Processes*, 37: 348–356.

O'Leary-Kelly, Anne M., Joseph J. Martocchio, and Dwight D. Frink. 1994. "A review of the influence of group goals on group performance." *Academy of Management Journal*, 37(5): 1285–1301.

O'Reilly, Charles A., III and Jennifer A. Chatman. 1986. "Organizational commitment and psychological attachment: the effects of compliance, identification, and internalization on prosocial behavior." *Journal of Applied Psychology*, 71: 492–499.

Ocasio, William. 1994. "The political dynamics of contestation and control: the circulation and institutionalization of chief executive officers in US industrial corporations, 1960–1990." *Administrative Science Quarterly*, 39 (June): 285–312.

   1995. "The enactment of economic adversity: a reconciliation of theories of failure-induced change and threat-rigidity." *Research in Organizational Behavior*, eds. L. L. Cummings and B. M. Staw. Greenwich, CT: JAI Press. 287–331.

   1997. "Towards an attention-based theory of the firm." *Strategic Management Journal*, 18 (Summer): 187–206.

   1999. "Institutionalized action and corporate governance: the reliance on rules of CEO succession." *Administrative Science Quarterly*, 44 (June): 384–416.

Ocasio, William and Hyosun Kim. 1999. "The circulation of corporate control: selection of functional backgrounds of new CEOs in large US manufacturing firms, 1981–1992." *Administrative Science Quarterly*, 1999 (September): 532–562.

Oliver, Christine. 1991. "Strategic responses to institutional processes." *Academy of Management Review*, 16: 145–179.

1992. "The antecendents of deinstitutionalization." *Organization Studies*, 13: 568–588.

Osborne, J. David, Charles I. Stubbart, and Arkalgud Ramaprasad. 2001. "Strategic groups and competitive enactment: a study of dynamic relationships between mental models and performance." *Strategic Management Journal*, 22(5): 435–454.

Ostmann, Axel. 1992. "The interaction of aspiration levels and the social field in experimental bargaining." *Journal of Economic Psychology*, 13(2): 233–261.

Pascale, Richard. 1985. "The paradox of 'corporate culture': reconciling ourselves to socialization." *California Management Review*, 27: 26–41.

Payne, John W., James R. Bettman, and Eric J. Johnson. 1988. "Adaptive strategy selection in decision making." *Journal of Experimental Psychology: Learning, Memory, and Cognition*, 14: 534–552.

Payne, John W., Dan J. Laughhunn, and Roy Crum. 1980. "Translation of gambles and aspiration level effects in risky choice behavior." *Management Science*, 26(10): 1039–1060.

1981. "Further tests of aspiration level effects in risky choice behavior." *Management Science*, 27(8): 953–958.

Pearl, Judea. 2000. *Causality: Models, Reasoning, and Inference*. Cambridge: Cambridge University Press.

Péli, Gábor, Jeroen Bruggeman, Michael Masuch, and Breanndán Ó Nualláin. 1994. "A logical approach to formalizing organizational ecology." *American Sociological Review*, 59 (August): 571–593.

Penrose, Edith Tilton. 1959. *The Theory of the Growth of the Firm*. New York: Wiley.

Perrow, Charles E. 1979. *Complex Organizations: a Critical Essay (3rd edn.)*. Glenview, IL: Scott, Foresman.

Peteraf, Margaret and Mark Shanley. 1997. "Getting to know you: a theory of strategic group identity." *Strategic Management Journal*, 18 (Summer): 165–186.

Pfeffer, Jeffrey. 1994. *Competitive Advantage through People: Unleashing the Power of the Work Force*. Boston, MA: Harvard Business School.

1997. *New Directions for Organization Theory*. New York: Oxford University Press.

Pfeffer, Jeffrey and Gerald R. Salancik. 1978. *The External Control of Organizations*. New York: Harper and Row.

Pingle, Mark and Richard H. Day. 1996. "Modes of economizing behavior: experimental evidence." *Journal of Economic Behavior and Organization*, 29: 191–209.

Podsakoff, Philip M., Scott B. MacKenzie, and Michael Ahearne. 1997. "Moderating effects of goal acceptance on the relationship between group cohesiveness and productivity." *Journal of Applied Psychology*, 82(6): 974–983.

Porac, Joseph F. and Howard Thomas. 1990. "Taxonomic mental models in competitor definition." *Academy of Management Review*, 15(2): 224–240.

Porac, Joseph F. and José Antonio Rosa. 1996. "Rivalry, industry models, and the cognitive embeddedness of the comparable firm." *Advances in Strategic Management*, 13: 363–388.

Porac, Joseph F., Howard Thomas, and Charles Baden-Fuller. 1989. "Competitive groups as cognitive communities: the case of Scottish knitwear manufacturers." *Journal of Management Studies*, 26: 397–416.

Porac, Joseph F., Howard Thomas, Fiona Wilson, Douglas Paton, and Alaina Kanfer. 1995. "Rivalry and the industry model of Scottish knitwear producers." *Administrative Science Quarterly*, 40 (June): 203–227.

Powers, W. T. 1973. *Behavior: the Control of Perception*. Chicago, IL: Aldine.

Priem, Richard L. and John E. Butler. 2001. "Is the resource-based 'view' a useful perspective for strategic management research?" *Academy of Management Review*, 26(1): 22–40.

Puffer, Sheila M. and Joseph B. Weintrop. 1991. "Corporate performance and CEO turnover: the role of performance expectations." *Administrative Science Quarterly*, 36(1): 1–19.

Radner, Roy. 1996. "Bounded rationality, indeterminacy, and the theory of the firm." *Economic Journal*, 106 (September): 1360–1373.

Raftery, Adrian E. 1995. "Bayesian model selection in social research." *Sociological Methodology*, ed. P. V. Marsden. Cambridge, MA: Blackwell. 111–163.

Rao, Hayagreeva. 1998. "Caveat emptor: the construction of nonprofit consumer watchdog organizations." *American Journal of Sociology*, 103(4): 912–961.

Rao, Hayagreeva and K. Sivakumar. 1999. "Institutional sources of boundary spanning structures: the establishment of investor relations departments in the Fortune 500 Industrials." *Organization Science*, 10(1): 27–42.

Rao, Hayagreeva, Henrich R. Greve, and Gerald F. Davis. 2001. "Fool's gold: social proof in the initiation and abandonment of coverage by Wall Street analysts." *Administrative Science Quarterly*, 46 (September): 502–526.

Reger, Rhonda K. and Anne Sigismund Huff. 1993. "Strategic groups: a cognitive perspective." *Strategic Management Journal*, 14(2): 103–124.

Reinhardt, Andy. 2002. "Telcos in hell." *BusinessWeek Asian Edition* (April 1): 66.

Ridgeway, Cecilia L., David Diekema, and Cathryn Johnson. 1995. "Legitimacy, compliance, and gender in peer groups." *Social Psychology Quarterly*, 58(4): 298–311.

Rogers, Everett M. 1995. *Diffusion of Innovations*. 4th edn. New York: Free Press.

Roth, Alvin E. and Ido Erev. 1995. "Learning in extensive-form games: experimental data and simple dynamic models in the intermediate term." *Games and Economic Behavior*, 8: 164–212.

Rothkopf, E. Z. and M. J. Billington. 1979. "Goal-guided learning from text: inferring a descriptive processing model from inspection times and eye movements." *Journal of Educational Psychology*, 71: 310–327.

Ruef, Martin. 1997. "Assessing organizational fit on a dynamic landscape: an empirical test of the relative inertia thesis." *Strategic Management Journal*, 18(11): 837–853.

Ruefli, Timothy W. 1990. "Mean-variance approaches to risk-return relationships in strategy: paradox lost." *Management Science*, 36: 368–380.

Ruefli, Timothy W. and R. R. Wiggins. 1994. "When mean square error becomes variance: a comment on 'Business risk and return: a test of simultaneous relationships.'" *Management Science*, 40: 750–759.

Ruefli, Timothy W., James M. Collins, and Joseph R. Lacugna. 1999. "Risk measures in strategic management research: auld lang syne?" *Strategic Management Journal*, 20(2): 167–194.

Salancik, Gerald R. and James R. Meindl. 1984. "Corporate attributions as strategic illusions of management control." *Administrative Science Quarterly*, 29: 238–254.

Salovey, P. and J. Rodin. 1984. "Some antecedents and consequences of social-comparison jealousy." *Journal of Personality and Social Psychology*, 47: 780–792.

Sandberg, M. 2001. "IT Diffusion in Swedish organisations from an institutional-evolutionary perspective: results from a web survey in 1999." *Ekonomiska Samfundets Tidskrift*, 54(1): 25ff.

Sandelands, Lloyd E., Joel Brockner, and Mary Ann Glynn. 1988. "If at first you don't succeed, try, try again: effects of persistence-performance contingencies, ego involvement, and self-esteem on task persistence." *Journal of Applied Psychology*, 73(2): 208–216.

Saporito, Bill. 1998. "The fly in Campbell's soup." *Fortune* (May 9): 67–70.

Sauermann, H. and Reinhard Selten. 1962. "Anspruchsanpassungsteorie der Unternehmung." *Zeitschrift für die gesamte Staatswissenschaft*, 118: 577–597.

Schaubroeck, John and Elaine Davis. 1994. "Prospect theory predictions when escalation is not the only chance to recover sunk costs." *Organizational Behavior and Human Decision Processes*, 57(1): 59–82.

Schein, Edgar H. 1992. *Organizational Culture and Leadership*. San Francisco, CA: Jossey-Bass.

Schneider, Sandra L. 1992. "Framing and conflict: aspiration level contingency, the status quo, and current theories of risky choice." *Journal of Experimental Psychology: Learning, Memory, and Cognition*, 18(5): 1040–1057.

Schneider, Sandra L. and Lola L. Lopes. 1986. "Reflection in preferences under risk: who and when may suggest why." *Journal of Experimental Psychology: Human Perception and Performance*, 12(4): 535–548.

Schoemaker, Paul J. H. 1990. "Are risk-attitudes related across domains and response modes?" *Management Science*, 36(12): 1451–1463.

Schultz, Martin. 1998. "Limits to bureaucratic growth: the density dependence of organizational rule births." *Administrative Science Quarterly*, 43 (December): 845–876.

  2001. "Organizational learning." *Companion to Organizations*, ed. J. A. C. Baum. Blackwell. 415–441.

Schumpeter, Joseph A. 1976. *Capitalism, Socialism, and Democracy*. (3rd edn) New York: Harper and Row.

Schurr, Paul H. 1987. "Effects of gain and loss decision frames on risky purchase negotiations." *Journal of Applied Psychology*, 72(3): 351–358.

Scott, W. Richard. 1987. *Organizations: Rational, Natural and Open Systems*, 2nd edn. Englewood Cliffs, NJ: Prentice-Hall.

  1995. *Institutions and Organizations*. Thousand Oaks, CA: Sage.

Scott, W. Richard and John W. Meyer. 1983. "The organization of societal sectors." *Organizational Environments: Ritual and Rationality*, eds. J. W. Meyer and W. R. Scott. Beverly Hills, CA: Sage. 129–153.

Selten, Reinhard. 1998a. "Aspiration adaptation theory." *Journal of Mathematical Psychology*, 42: 191–214.

1998b. "Features of experimentally observed bounded rationality." *European Economic Review*, 42: 413–436.

Selznick, Philip. 1948. *TVA and the Grass Roots*. Berkeley, CA: University of California Press.

1957. *Leadership in Administration*. New York: Harper and Row.

Shalley, Christina E. 1995. "Effects of coaction, expected evaluation, and goal setting on creativity and productivity." *Academy of Management Journal*, 38(2): 483–503.

Shapira, Zur. 1994. *Risk Taking*. New York: Russel Sage.

2000. "Aspiration levels and risk taking by government bond traders." Manuscript, Stern School of Business, New York University.

Shapira, Zur and Donald J. Berndt. 1997. "Managing grand-scale construction projects: a risk-taking perspective." *Research in Organizational Behavior*, vol. 19, eds. B. M. Staw and R. I. Sutton. Greenwich, CT: JAI Press. 303–360.

Silverman, Brian S. 1999. "Technological resources and the direction of corporate diversification: toward an integration of the resource-based view and transaction cost economics." *Management Science*, 45(8): 1109–1124.

Simon, Herbert A. 1957. *Administrative Behavior*, 2nd edn. New York: Macmillan.

Singer, R. N., G. Korienek, D. Jarvis, D. McColskey, and G. Candeletti. 1981. "Goal-setting and task persistence." *Perceptual and Motor Skills*, 53: 881–882.

Singh, Jitendra V. 1986. "Performance, slack, and risk taking in organizational decision making." *Academy of Management Journal*, 29(3): 562–585.

Slater, Robert and Jack Welch. 1993. *The New GE: How Jack Welch Revived an American Institution*. Homewood, IL: Business One Irwin.

Soule, Sarah A. 1997. "The student divestment movement in the United States and tactical diffusion: the shantytown protest." *Social Forces*, 75(3): 855–883.

Spender, J. C. 1989. *Industry Recipes: an Enquiry into the Nature and Sources of Managerial Judgement*. Oxford: Blackwell.

Starbuck, William H. 1992. "Learning by knowledge-intensive firms." *Journal of Management Studies*, 29(6): 713–740.

Starbuck, William H. and Bo L. T. Hedberg. 1977. "Saving an organization from a stagnating environment." *Strategy + Structure = Performance*, ed. H. B. Thorelli. Bloomington, Ind: Indiana University Press. 249–258.

Staw, Barry M. 1976. "Knee-deep in the big muddy: a study of escalating commitment to a chosen course of action." *Organizational Behavior and Human Performance*, 16: 27–44.

1981. "The escalation of commitment to a course of action." *Academy of Management Review*, 6(4): 577–587.

Staw, Barry M. and Lisa D. Epstein. 2000. "What bandwagons bring: effects of popular management techniques on corporate performance, reputation, and CEO pay." *Administrative Science Quarterly*, 45(3): 523–556.

Staw, Barry M. and Ha Hoang. 1995. "Sunk costs in the NBA: why draft order affects playing time and survival in professional basketball." *Administrative Science Quarterly*, 40 (September): 474–494.

Staw, Barry M. and J. Ross. 1987. "Understanding escalation situations: antecedents, prototypes, and solutions." *Research in Organizational Behavior*, 9: 39–78.

Staw, Barry M., Lance E. Sandelands, and Jane E. Dutton. 1981. "Threat-rigidity effects in organizational behavior: a multi-level analysis." *Administrative Science Quarterly*, 26: 501–524.

Stinchcombe, Arthur L. 1965. "Social structure and organizations." *Handbook of organizations*, ed. J. G. March. Chicago, IL: Rand McNally. 142–193.

Stone, Brad. 2000. "Amazon.com talks back." *Newsweek Asian Edition* (July 10): 40.

Strang, David and Sarah A. Soule. 1998. "Diffusion in organizations and social movements: from hybrid corn to poison pills." *Annual Review of Sociology*, 24: 265–290.

Strang, David and Nancy Brandon Tuma. 1993. "Spatial and temporal heterogeneity in diffusion." *American Journal of Sociology*, 99: 614–639.

Sutton, John R. and Frank R. Dobbin. 1996. "The two faces of governance: responses to legal uncertainty in US firms, 1955 to 1985." *American Sociological Review*, 61 (October): 794–811.

Sutton, John R., Frank R. Dobbin, John W. Meyer, and W. Richard Scott. 1994. "The legalization of the workplace." *American Journal of Sociology*, 99 (January): 944–971.

Swinth, Robert L. 1974. *Organizational Systems for Management: Designing, Planning and Implementation*. Columbus, OH: Grid.

Taylor, Alva. 1998. "Layered selection environments: drivers for internal strategic change in high technology firms." Manuscript, Tuck School of Management, Dartmouth University.

Taylor, Alva and Michael Clement. 2000. "Cognitive rationing: informational influences on accuracy and risk taking by financial analysts." Manuscript, Tuck School of Management, Dartmouth University.

Tesser, Abraham. 1986. "Some effects of self-evaluation maintenance on cognition and action." *Handbook on Motivation and Cognition: Foundations of Social Behavior*, eds. R. M. Sorrentino and E. T. Higgins. New York: Guilford. 435–464.

Thaler, Richard. 1985. "Mental accounting and consumer choice." *Marketing Science*, 4(3): 199–214.

Thaler, Richard M. and Eric J. Johnson. 1990. "Gambling with house money and trying to break even: the effects of prior outcomes on risky choice." *Management Science*, 36(6): 643–660.

Thompson, James D. 1967. *Organizations in Action*. New York: McGraw-Hill.

Tindale, R. Scott, Susal Sheffey, and Leslie A. Scott. 1993. "Framing and group decision-making: do cognitive changes parallel preference changes?" *Organizational Behavior and Human Decision Processes*, 55(3): 470–485.

Tosi, Henry L. Jr. and Luis R. Gomez-Mejia. 1989. "The decoupling of CEO pay and performance: an agency theory perspective." *Administrative Science Quarterly*, 34 (March): 169–189.

Tristram, C. 1998. "Seagate shifts into R&D overdrive." *Electronic Business*, 24: 52–55.

210 References

Tsai, Wenpin. 2001. "Knowledge transfer in intraorganizational networks: effects of network position and absorptive capacity on business unit innovation and performance." *Academy of Management Journal*, 44(5): 996–1004.

Tuma, Nancy Brandon and Michael T. Hannan. 1984. *Social Dynamics: Models and Methods*. Orlando, FL: Academic Press.

Tushman, Michael L. and Philip Anderson. 1986. "Technological discontinuities and organizational environments." *Administrative Science Quarterly*, 31: 439–465.

Tversky, Amos. 1977. "Features of similarity." *Psychological Review*, 84: 327–352.

Tversky, Amos and Daniel Kahneman. 1974. "Judgment under uncertainty: heuristics and biases." *Science*, 185: 1124–1131.

Useem, Michael. 1996. *Investor Capitalism: how Money Managers are Changing the Face of Corporate America*. New York: Basic Books.

Van den Bosch, Frans A. J., Henk W. Volberta, and Michiel de Boer. 1999. "Coevolution of firm absorptive capacity and knowledge environment: organizational forms and combinative capabilities." *Organization Science*, 10(5): 551–568.

Van Huyck, John B., Raymond C. Battalio, and Frederick W. Rankin. 1997. "On the origin of convention: evidence from coordination games." *Economic Journal*, 107(442): 576–596.

Vance, Robert J. and Adrienne Colella. 1990. "Effects of two types of feedback on goal acceptance and personal goals." *Journal of Applied Psychology*, 75(1): 68–76.

Vancil, Richard F. 1987. *Passing the Baton: Managing the Process of CEO Succession*. Boston, MA: Harvard Business School.

Vertzberger, Yaacov Y. I. 2000. *Risk Taking and Decision Making*. Stanford, CA: Stanford University Press.

Von Krogh, Georg, Johan Roos, and Dirk Kleine. 1998. *Knowing in Firms: Understanding, Measuring, and Managing Knowledge*. London: Sage.

Walsh, James P. and Gerardo Rivera Ungson. 1991. "Organizational memory." *Academy of Management Review*, 16(1): 57–91.

Weber, Elke U. and Richard A. Milliman. 1997. "Perceived risk attitudes: relating risk perception to risky choice." *Management Science*, 43(2): 123–144.

Weber, Elke U., Christopher K. Hsee, and Joanna Sokolowska. 1998. "What folklore tells us about risk and risk taking: cross-cultural comparisons of American, German, and Chinese proverbs." *Organizational Behavior and Human Decision Processes*, 75(2): 170–186.

Wehrung, Donald A. 1989. "Risk taking over gains and losses: a study of oil executives." *Annals of Operations Research*, 19: 115–139.

Weick, Karl E. 1995. *Sensemaking in Organizations*. Thousand Oaks, CA: Sage.

Weiss, H. M., K. Suchow, and T. L. Rakestraw. 1999. "Influence of modeling on self-set goals: direct and mediated effects." *Human Performance*, 12(2): 89–114.

Welch, David. 2000. "Born to be a little too wild: How 'concept drift' changed GM's radical Aztek into an odd duck." *BusinessWeek Asian Edition* (December 18): 89–91.

Wernerfeldt, B. 1984. "A resource based view of the firm." *Strategic Management Journal*, 5: 171–180.

West, D. and P. Berthon. 1997. "Antecedents of risk-taking behavior by advertisers: empirical evidence and management implications." *Journal of Advertising Research*, 37(5): 27–40.

Wheeler, Ladd and Richard Koestner. 1984. "Performance evaluation: on choosing to know the related attributes of others when we know their performance." *Journal of Experimental Social Psychology*, 20: 263–271.

Wheeler, Ladd, K. G. Shaver, Robert A. Jones, G. R. Goethals, J. Cooper, J. E. Robinson, C. L. Gruder, and K. W. Butzine. 1969. "Factors determining the choice of a comparison other." *Journal of Experimental Social Psychology*, 5: 219–232.

Whyte, Glen. 1986. "Escalating commitment to a course of action: a reinterpretation." *Academy of Management Review*, 6: 311–321.

1993. "Escalating commitment in individual and group decision making: a prospect theory approach." *Organizational Behavior and Human Decision Processes*, 54(3): 430–455.

Whyte, Glen and Ariel S. Levi. 1994. "The origins and functions of the reference point in risky group decision making: the case of the Cuban missile crisis." *Journal of Behavioral Decision Making*, 7: 243–260.

Whyte, Glen, Alan M. Saks, and Sterling Hook. 1997. "When success breeds failure: The role of self-efficacy in escalating commitment to a losing course of action." *Journal of Organizational Behavior*, 18(5): 415–432.

Wilson, Anne E. and Michael Ross. 2000. "The frequency of temporal-self and social comparisons in people's personal appraisals." *Journal of Personality and Social Psychology*, 78(5): 928–942.

Wiseman, Robert M. and Philip Bromiley. 1991. "Risk-return associations: paradox or artifact? An empirically tested explanation." *Strategic Management Journal*, 12: 231–241.

1996. "Toward a model of risk in declining organizations: an empirical examination of risk, performance and decline." *Organization Science*, 7(5): 524–543.

Wiseman, Robert M. and Luis R. Gomez-Mejia. 1998. "A behavioral agency model of managerial risk taking." *Academy of Management Review*, 23(1): 133–153.

Womack, James P., Daniel T. Jones, and Daniel Roos. 1990. *The Machine that Changed the World: Based on the Massachusetts Institute of Technology 5-Million Dollar 5-Year Study on the Future of the Automobile*. New York: Rawson Associates.

Wood, Joanne V. 1989. "Theory and research concerning social comparisons of personal attributes." *Psychological Bulletin*, 106(2): 213–248.

Wood, Robert A. and Albert Bandura. 1989. "Impact of conceptions of ability on self-regulatory mechanisms and complex decision making." *Journal of Personality and Social Psychology*, 56: 407–415.

Wood, Robert E., Anthony J. Mento, and Edwin A. Locke. 1987. "Task complexity as a moderator of goal effects: a meta-analysis." *Journal of Applied Psychology*, 72(3): 416–425.

Yelle, L. E. 1979. "The learning curve: historical review and comprehensive survey." *Decision Science*, 10: 302–328.

Young, Greg, Ken G. Smith, and Curtis M. Grimm. 1997. "'Austrian' and industrial organization perspectives on firm-level competitive activity and performance." *Organization Science*, 7: 243–254.

Zajac, Edward J. and Matthew S. Kraatz. 1993. "A diametric forces model of strategic change: assessing the antecedents and consequences of restructuring in the higher education industry." *Strategic Management Journal*, 14 (Summer): 83–102.

Zeitz, G., V. Mittal, and B. McAulay. 1999. "Distinguishing adoption and entrenchment of management practices: a framework for analysis." *Organization Studies*, 20(5): 741–776.

Zhou, Xueguang. 1993. "The dynamics of organizational rules." *American Journal of Sociology*, 98(5): 1134–1166.

Zuckerman, Ezra W. 2000. "Focusing the corporate product: Securities analysts and de-diversification." *Administrative Science Quarterly*, 45(3): 591–619.

Index